Times Past

Reflections from Arizona History

Compiled by the **ARIZONA CAPITOL TIMES**

ARIZONA CAPITOL TIMES

We're your Capitol connection.

The *Arizona Capitol Times* is a publication of Arizona News Service, L.L.C., a subsidiary of

This book has been accepted as an Arizona Centennial 2012 Legacy Project by the Arizona Historical Advisory Commission.

Cover photo credits. Above the title, from left: Mariner's Juvenile Band, Arizona Heritage Center; drawing of Gila River Valley by Wm. H. Emory from his *Notes of a Military Reconnaissance*; local league baseball, Bisbee Mining and Historical Museum.

Below the title: clockwise from top left: John Clum with Indian scouts, Arizona Historical Society; Emil Marks, Bisbee Mining and Historical Museum; Roosevelt Dam, Salt River Project; Frank Luke, Jr., Arizona Historical Society; Grand Canyon Railroad inaugural run, W. Lane Rogers; Powderface — the diving horse, *Arizona Capitol Times* archives; Gov. George W.P. Hunt and Jesse Udall, University of Arizona Library; Sedona and T.C. Schnebly, Sedona Historical Society.

Center photo: Selim Franklin, Arizona Department of Library, Archives and Public Records.

Inside front jacket: a train used in a 1901 jail break, Arizona Historical Society, Tucson
Inside back jacket: Loyalty Sunday in Bisbee, Bisbee Mining and Historical Museum

Times Past

Reflections from Arizona History

Edited by Barry Gartell

ARIZONA CAPITOL TIMES
Phoenix, Arizona

ARIZONA CAPITOL TIMES
Ginger Lamb, Vice President & Publisher

Administration
Bobby Blatchley, Business Manager

Circulation and Marketing
Tyler Butler, Circulation, Marketing & Events Manager

Editorial
Matt Bunk, Managing Editor
Don Harris, Copy Editor
Jim Small, Staff Writer
Christian Palmer, Staff Writer
Bill Coates, Photographer and Staff Writer
Luige del Puerto, Staff Writer
Jeremy Duda, Staff Writer
Anjanette Riley, Staff Writer
Josh Coddington, Special Publications Coordinator
Aaron Stratton, Intern

Public Notices
Laura Kaminski, Manager
Laurene Pitzer, Typesetting
Maria Engelmann, Client Services
Linda McCurdy, Assistant
Laurinda Cook, Assistant

Arizona Capitol Reports
Vince Carbajal, Capitol Reports Manager
Phil Riske, Yellow Sheet Report Editor
Barry Gartell, Legislative Report Editor
Tasya Grabenstein, Capitol Reports Researcher
Tracy Keller, Capitol Reports Coordinator
Scott Newell, Capitol Reports Assistant
Burke Milnes, Capitol Reports Assistant

Display Advertising
Nadia Cerini, Representative
Juliana Norvell, Representative

Production
Julie Lanley, Manager
Gabe Turner, Artist

Publishers Emeritus
Ned & Diana Creighton

"Times Past" Authors/Researchers:

Burnice Armstrong
Joan Brundige-Baker
Ed Edwards
Jane Eppinga
Howard Fischer

Bonnie Greer
John Bret Harte
Tracy Keller
Stan Matthews
Joan Metzger

Mike Miller
W. Lane Rogers
Mark Santiago
Melanie Sturgeon
Dave Tackenberg

Jim Turner
Tom Vaughan
Reba Wells
Loren Wilson

Times Past: Reflections from Arizona History

Published by the **ARIZONA CAPITOL TIMES**
1835 West Adams Street
Phoenix, Arizona 85007
(602) 258-7026

Library of Congress Control Number: 2008909583
ISBN Number: 978-0-615-25117-2

Printed in the United States of America by O'Neil Printing, Phoenix, AZ
Bound by Roswell Bookbinding, Phoenix, AZ

Contents

Contents

Publisher's Foreward

When Dolan Media Company acquired Arizona News Service, L.L.C., publishers of the *Arizona Capitol Times*, in May 2005, I was aware of the company's rich history — that it had started in 1906 and had been in the Creighton family for three generations. After meeting with the political and business leaders of the state, it became quite clear how much a part of Arizona history were the *Arizona Capitol Times* and the Creightons. Ned and Diana Creighton not only reported — comprehensively and without bias — the news of Arizona government and politics, they celebrated Arizona's rich history within the newspaper with wit, sensitivity and an institutional memory that spanned decades.

I quickly discovered one of the most popular features in the newspaper was "Times Past," a column that pairs a photo from Arizona's history with an original essay, researched and written by a respected historian. The essay helped make the photo come alive, and the photo gave real substance and context to the essay. The first historical photo ran in a predecessor publication to the *Arizona Capitol Times* called *The Messenger*. On January 6, 1993, the "Times Past" name was added to the column. Almost 1,500 historical photographs and accompanying stories have appeared.

Through the years, subscribers urged the Creightons to publish a compilation of "Times Past" articles, and doing so was always on Ned and Diana's wish list. But covering the Legislature, the Governor's Office, elections and the occasional scandal or impeachment was always more important, and the "Times Past" book kept getting pushed down the priority list. On behalf of Dolan Media and the staff of the *Arizona Capitol Times*, I am proud to help fulfill this dream, not just as a token of gratitude to Ned and Diana for their years of service to Arizona but also — and more importantly — as a tribute to the state, its peoples and its rich history. We are all thrilled to be a contributing part of that history.

Ginger Lamb
Vice President & Publisher, *Arizona Capitol Times*/Arizona News Service, L.L.C.

....

Editor's Preface

The stories collected in this book represent a small fraction of the total that have appeared in the *Arizona Capitol Times* since 1980. We have tried to select those that illuminate something about the spirit of Arizona and its residents: their diversity of heritages, their inventiveness, their willingness to push the envelope, and perhaps above all, the state's incredible transition from a dusty and rugged frontier to an economic and political leader among the states.

Some of the stories in this book have been edited to reflect recent research or to correct errors in the original. Several have been merged with similar stories published at different times. Each story carries the name of the original researcher/author as well as the date on which the article was first published in the *Arizona Capitol Times*. Because of copyright restrictions, not all of the photos in this book are the same ones that ran with the original article. We have also supplemented original photos with others that add depth and context to the story.

I would like to express my gratitude to various staff members of the *Arizona Capitol Times* who assisted in the preparation of this book, notably Julie Lanley and Gabe Turner for design and layout, Burke Milnes who helped in the research and participated in the selection process, and Anjanette Riley, who prepared the index and assisted in numerous phases of the project. Tracy Keller deserves special mention: she steered me clear of many mistakes and guided me out of many a quandary. Because Tracy was editor of the newspaper version of "Times Past" for three years, she brought a keen understanding and clarity of purpose to the preparation of this book. She also did yeoman's work as principal proofreader.

I would like to thank all the original contributors to "Times Past" articles and everyone who helped in the selection and editing process for this book. Any errors that remain are solely my responsibility.

Barry Gartell
Editor

Introduction

Our family's involvement in news publishing began in 1899, when James Edwin Creighton, called "Ned," joined two early-day papers, the *Phoenix Herald* and the *Arizona Graphic*. By 1902 he felt sufficiently established to buy a newspaper for himself and purchased the *Arizona Gazette*, but he was under-financed and sold it after only two years. In 1906 he founded the Arizona News Service, reporting actions of the territorial Legislature to mining and railroad interests. In the beginning, he sent his dispatches about the legislature via telegraph from a corner of the lobby of the Adams Hotel, where J.C. Adams made space for him to run a small news-desk.

To keep money coming in between the then very short legislative sessions, he invented a newsletter and had it typed, four carbons at a time, on onionskin paper (which, being so thin, allowed more carbons per typing). The paper was yellow, and thus the *Yellow Sheet Report* was born.

In 1946, Ned's son Robert purchased a weekly newspaper called *The Messenger*. He decided to put a personal stamp on the publication by printing early-day photos of Phoenix citizens and landmarks. Being a Phoenix native and having grown up during the time that the little town of 15,000 souls became a small city and then a big one, he determined to record the town's early history in photos — some unique to the family and others generally available from historical organizations. For the first few years after he bought *The Messenger*, he published his photos on the front page together with notes about the people and places in them.

In the early 1950s the management of the Adams Hotel, then the downtown watering hole for politicians and lobbyists, asked him to loan part of his collection to decorate the famous Adams Bar. He assembled a framed collection of perhaps 100 photos, and they became part of the background at the bar.

In 1985, his son and daughter-in-law, Ned and Diana Creighton, decided to revive the tradition of publishing historic photos in what had become the *Arizona Capitol Times* and to expand their subject area to the entire state. Diana contacted individuals and state historical groups for regular contributions to "Times Past." It quickly became one of the paper's most popular features and remains so today.

Ned and Diana Creighton
Publishers Emeritus

Photo from the Arizona News Service archives

Offices of *The Arizona Gazette*, 1903

In its 117 years of existence, the *Arizona Gazette*, later renamed the *Phoenix Gazette*, had twelve publishers (most Democrat, a few Republican) before finally, in 1946, finding a home with the Pulliam family. The publication first saw the light of day in 1880, in a small adobe just to the east of Second Street and Washington (where Symphony Hall is today). The *Gazette* ceased publication in January 1997.

When this photograph was taken, the operation was squeezed into 106-08 West Adams, a lively spot in O'Neill Hall, not far from Merryman and Holley, undertakers, and Melczer Brothers, wholesale liquors and cigars.

Between 1902 and 1904, Ned Creighton was listed as owner of the Gazette Printing and Publishing Company, a corporation which in later years Ned's brother, Hugh, who had bankrolled the outfit, described as a short-lived triumph of blind optimism over bleak financial reality. The bleak financial reality arrived in all its grimness in September 1904. To meet their last payroll, the Creightons put what was left of their cash assets on the faro table at the Palace Saloon. Luck was with them, and they were able to turn a debt-free operation over to Eli Perkins, a young newsman with wisdom enough, in later years, to depart journalism and become a successful sheepman.

Neither of the Creightons is in the photograph; however, the old gentleman in the background is Col. James Creighton, their father, who may have dropped in on his way to a meeting of the Phoenix post of the Grand Army of the Republic.

Joseph Shelton, the paper's editor, is at the desk. He later published newspapers in Oregon and Washington before returning to Arizona in the 1950s.

The man in profile, with the newspaper in his hands, is Joseph Laney. He was the entire reportorial staff of the *Gazette*. He moved to California and founded *The Inter-City Express*, a legal newspaper in Oakland, California, in 1909. Laney College in Oakland was named in his honor. His brother Lynn Laney practiced law in Phoenix and was a member of the Arizona Board of Regents.

There are still Laneys practicing law in Arizona, and until 2005 there were still Creightons in the publishing business. In 1946, Ned Creighton's son Robert founded *The Messenger,* which later became the *Arizona Capitol Times*. Robert's son, Ned, took over in the 1980s and in 2005 sold the paper to Dolan Media.

– Arizona Capitol Times

Community and Culture

Territorial Saloons

Often among the first businesses established in new communities, the saloon is at the center of much of the folklore of the frontier West. It was here that men gathered to boast about their newest ore strike, to commiserate about the backbreaking work that produced little in the way of monetary rewards, to pick up a prostitute or play a game of faro.

The saloon floor was often the only place a weary miner could find a spot to sleep, for a fee of course. In a society where men — most of them young and single — far outnumbered women, alcohol consumption tended to be very high, as much as a gallon a week per customer by some estimates.

Saloons provided considerable income to city coffers and held a central place in the social life of early communities. John Cady, an early Arizona pioneer and entrepreneur who ran several saloons at various times during his career, claimed in his reminiscences that, "the entire fabric of the Territory was constructed on liquor."

Saloons proliferated in mining communities and commercial centers like Phoenix and Tucson. Prescott's Whiskey Row sported a number of famous saloons as did Bisbee's Brewery Gulch.

In 1872, when Phoenix was four years old and with a population of less than 1,000, it boasted 15 saloons with two more on the outskirts of town. Many started in tents with signs painted on their canvas walls. Initially, owners manufactured their own brews —liquids of questionable quality — but quickly decided to purchase whiskies and wines hauled in by wagon from distributors in other parts of the country.

Competition was fierce, and savvy entrepreneurs advertised their establishments in newspapers. An ad in the July 1864 *Arizona Miner* for the Arizona Pioneer Brewery and Saloon in La Paz shows that the owner carried cool lager beer and fine California wines and had also built a bathhouse and shower room. Nearly every saloon that advertised also made certain that potential customers knew they carried genuine Havana cigars. Many installed billiard tables. Some brothels had their own saloons attached, where customers could find such delicacies as peach brandies and raspberry wines. Other saloons had chop houses and restaurants connected to them.

While some owners named their saloons after themselves, other names were more colorful. In Prescott, there was the Quartz Rock Saloon, the Pine Tree Saloon, the Tiger Brewery, the Monarch Cash House, the Oriental Bakery and Saloon, the Pacific Brewery, the Diana Saloon, the Plaza Bit Saloon, the Montezuma Saloon, the Snug Saloon, the Bit Saloon and Lodging House, and the Sazerac where you could buy a drink for 12 cents.

Globe boasted the Champion Billiard Hall, the Good Cheer Beer and Lunch House, the Pony Saloon and the Mount Hood Saloon, among others. In Yuma in 1873, Mrs. T. E. Williams advertised her Oyster Saloon as open every night until midnight, and where one could purchase stews and fries together with coffee, tea, chocolate, cakes and pies.

In 1881, Tombstone was home to the Crystal Palace, with its accompanying ice cream saloon, the Alhambra Saloon, the Cosmopolitan Saloon, the Oriental Saloon, the Occidental Saloon, the Grotto and the Music Hall Saloon, all of which provided libations to thirsty customers.

One of the most imaginatively named establishments was Gila Bend's Whis-(key) the Road to Ruin Saloon.

Over time, these saloons became far more sedate establishments, but their legend lives on in movies, novels and community folklore.

— *Dr. Melanie Sturgeon.*

Originally published: August 15, 2004

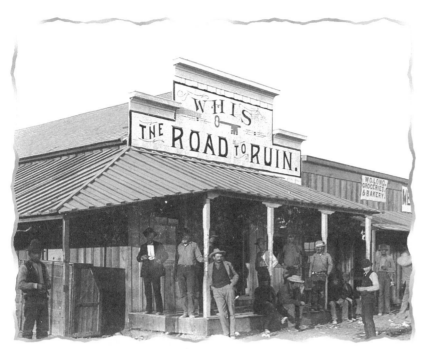

Photos courtesy of the Arizona State Library, Archives and Public Records; History and Archives Division

 ## *Award of Merit*

By Marshall Trimble

Official Arizona State Historian

Trying to pick out a favorite story from "Times Past" reminds me of the kid in the candy store. There is such a variety of topics to choose from, one doesn't know where to start. Should I choose a person? How about a town? A natural landmark?

There's something appealing about them all, so I decided to think outside the box, and I came up with this one. The photo of the Gila Bend saloon, with its "Whis," etched over a rendering of a "key" that hangs over the words "The Road to Ruin" has long been a favorite of mine.

For years that sign has graced the saloon at Pioneer, Arizona, on I-17 north of the Carefree Highway.

Saloons were social gathering places. Here, one could socialize, quench their thirst, play cards, spend time with a girl for hire, find out about the latest gold strike rumor, or get caught up on the news from the "states." Like society, saloons ran the wide gamut of frontier society, ranging from hog ranches that served the worst kind of rot-gut whiskey to high class establishments that offered imported wines and whiskey served in crystal glasses.

In a vast, empty land where women were scarce and loneliness was a constant companion, saloons satisfied one of man's most basic psychological needs —- to be around other people.

Charlie Brown

The top photo is a portrait of Charles O. Brown, photographed about 1870 in Tucson. The bottom photo, undated but believed to have been taken several years later, shows Charlie (left) standing with another gentleman next to the bar in his Congress Hall Saloon. At the time of these photos, Charlie had become a respectable businessman, but his early career was checkered at best.

He was born in Westport, New York, on October 27, 1829. As a young man, he caught gold fever and came west to California with the great wave of Forty-Niners. About 1858, he showed up at the Yuma crossing on the Colorado River and aligned himself with John Glanton, two of whose business ventures have made him notorious.

The Mexican government paid Glanton's gang a bounty of up to $150 each for Apache scalps. A tidy sum was made, but apparently not enough to satisfy Glanton. He took to supplementing his income by submitting the scalps of Opatas, Pimas and even a few Mexicans and passing them off as Apache. That got him in trouble with the Mexican government, and the arrangement was terminated.

Glanton's other venture was a ferry operation across the Colorado. He tolerated no competition. When a rival started a second ferry, Glanton killed him and assumed complete and unchallenged control of the river crossing. His fees were so outrageous they amounted to extortion, but countless gold-seekers passing through Arizona Territory en route to California had no choice but to pay them.

Finally, fate and the desire for revenge caught up with Glanton. The Indians rose up against the gang, which numbered about 25 and killed them all. Charlie survived only because he was in California on a trip at the time of the attack.

We next hear of Charlie during the Confederate occupation of Tucson in 1862. It is not known whether he collaborated with the Confederates, but indications are that at least he did business with them.

After the Confederates' departure, the California Column of the Union Army came to town. Charlie was called to a meeting by the military commander of Tucson, Lieutenant Colonel J.R. West. Fearing that he would be arrested, Charlie insisted that the meeting take place outside the presidio walls. His fears were misplaced, however. West offered him exclusive rights to Tucson's liquor and gambling trade, with the stipulation that he not sell liquor to intoxicated soldiers, and that he kickback $500 a month to West.

This arrangement made Charlie a wealthy man, and sometime in 1867 or 1868 he built the Congress Hall Saloon. By all accounts, it was one of the finest buildings in the Territory. It had wooden plank flooring shipped from Santa Fe at a cost of $500 and featured door fixtures that cost $12 each. The largest mirror in the territory hung above its back bar, and supposedly only the finest liquor and cigars were served its patrons.

Members of the Territorial Legislature liked the place so much, they held many informal meetings there. (Lawmakers avoided the Capitol building, with its dirt floors and mud roof, preferring to hold their caucuses at San Agustin Cathedral and using Charlie's hospitality whenever they could.)

By then Charlie had gotten respectable, and like most respectable men in Tucson, he married a woman from a prominent Mexican family and began producing offspring. He even sat on the city council and became a deputy sheriff.

But old habits die hard. He was a wild spender and squandered his money, staking prospectors whose claims were worthless. When he died in 1908 at the age of 79, he was broke.

His house still stands at 40 West Broadway Blvd. in Tucson. It's a fine example of Mexican Territorial style with Victorian ornamentation.

— *W. Lane Rogers*

Originally published: December 9, 1992

Photos courtesy of W. Lane Rogers

Old Main: No Running on the Balcony

This remarkable piece of architecture is Old Main on the University of Arizona campus in Tucson, photographed in 1894. The first story was constructed of gray stone, the second of red brick. The building's original floor plan consisted of six large rooms on each level. These were later partitioned to form 34 rooms on each level in which virtually all university activities took place. Concentrated in the building were classrooms, laboratories, dormitories, faculty quarters and a kitchen with a Chinese cook.

During the first session of the Arizona Territorial Legislature in 1864 — when not a single public school existed in the newly formed Territory — lawmakers authorized a university and wrote a constitution to guide its affairs. However, no appropriation was made, and the notion of an institution of higher learning sat on the back burner for more than 20 years. Not until 1885 was the University of Arizona formally founded by an act of the Legislature — the Thieving Thirteenth, as it came to be known — an act that pleased almost no one in Tucson.

In a division of institutional spoils, legislators voted to retain Prescott as the capital, and Phoenix got the coveted insane asylum. All that Tucson got, grumbled an angry Tucson editor, was a territorial university "that nobody asked for and which at best can only be realized in a far distant future." Tucsonans, hoping to regain the capital and unable to understand the value of a university to their community, expressed their displeasure by pelting their local legislative delegates with rotten vegetables.

Nonetheless, plans moved forward, albeit slowly. Land had to be secured for a campus, and a building had to be built. The paltry sum of money appropriated by the Legislature was insufficient to do both; thus, donations were sought. In one of history's delicious ironies, a saloon owner and two gamblers stepped forward and donated forty acres of desert land, then a far distance from the city. On October 12, 1887, ground was broken for Old Main.

Another four years would pass before the university opened its doors on October 1, 1891, with a faculty of six and a student body of 32. Determined to have a disciplined institution, administrators established a code of conduct. Absence and tardiness were not tolerated, and running on the balcony of Old Main was strictly prohibited.

Robert H. Forbes, professor of chemistry, who came to Tucson from Harvard the year this photograph was taken, offers a charming description of the building: "Old Main, as I first saw it on the morning of September 1, 1894, stood in lonely dignity far beyond the limits of the then little Mexican adobe town [of Tucson].... The architecture of Old Main was unique and, as time proved, admirably adapted to the climatic conditions of the country. The lower story, floored three feet below ground level, caught and held cool night air for the comfort of daytime workers; and the wide verandas of both upper and lower stories protected inside rooms from summer sun and gave convenient outside communications around the building." Old Main stands today as one of Tucson's enduring landmarks.

— *W. Lane Rogers*

Originally published on March 17, 1995

Photo courtesy of the Arizona Historical Society, Tucson

'Tombstone Prospector,' 1888

This is the first office of the *Tombstone Prospector*, the afternoon competitor for the morning *Tombstone Epitaph*, at the time the city's main newspaper. Barely visible at the desk inside is editor Stanley Chipman Bagg. The men standing outside the building are unidentified, but it is a safe guess that the one in the boater and vest is a lawman because he is wearing a badge.

The *Tombstone Prospector* was founded on March 7, 1887, by James Reilly, Andy Ritter and Joseph Pascholy, who opposed the editorial line of the *Epitaph*. James J. Nash of the recently defunct *Daily Tombstone* was the first editor, but he failed to live up to the expectations of the sponsors, who soon hired Bagg to replace him. Stanley Bagg was the son of John Sherman Bagg, founder of the *Detroit Tribune*, so newspapering came naturally to him. He was hired in October of 1887 and four months later bought out the owners and became both editor and publisher.

He was a defender of press freedom and a champion of clean politics. In August 1888, less than a year after he bought the paper, he got into a bitter dispute over the awarding of the Cochise County printing contract. Although the *Prospector's* bid was almost half that of the rival *Epitaph's*, the latter won the contract. Bagg was understandably upset and took the matter to court. The court found the county supervisors within their rights and dismissed the case, and when Bagg wrote a fiery editorial on the subject, they fined him $300 or 300 days in jail. Bagg chose jail. He was locked up for three days before friends raised the money to pay his fine.

Bagg's crusading obviously had a healthy effect on his newspaper's sales because in September of 1891 he bought the *Epitaph*, which by then had been reduced to publishing only weekly. Bagg made the *Epitaph* the Sunday edition of the daily *Prospector*. The next year he started the *Arizona Kicker*, a weekly which served as the *Prospector's* Wednesday edition.

In 1895, he sold his newspaper interests and turned his hand to the mining business. He opened the Katherine and Cyclopic mines in Mohave County. The *Prospector* continued to be published until March 7, 1924. Its Sunday Edition, the *Tombstone Epitaph*, was published until 1975, when it became the nationally circulated Western history publication it remains today. Stanley Bagg died in Santa Barbara, California on October 1, 1931.

— *Joan Metzger*

Originally published: January 21, 1987

Photo courtesy of the Arizona Historical Society, Tucson

Sedona's First Post Office

These are the Schneblys: Sedona and Theodore Carlton (known as T.C.). The building in the lower photo is the original Schnebly homestead on the banks of Oak Creek in what would become the town of Sedona.

The area was first settled in the 1870s by homesteaders drawn to the canyon and grasslands along the creek by the year-round water supply, abundant game and good climate.

The Schneblys didn't arrive until October 1901, coming from Gorin, Missouri to what was then called Camp Garden.

They came by rail, taking the Santa Fe to Ashfork and then the narrow gauge line to Jerome. They bought 80 acres of proven homestead on the banks of Oak Creek and built this two-story frame house. T.C. dug the irrigation ditch (at right in the photograph) to water a garden and small orchard he planted.

When he arrived, the settlement of homesteaders on Oak Creek was too small for a post office. Mail was delivered by way of Cornville, a neighboring community to the southwest. But in 1902, the settlement applied for and was awarded a post office. Many names were suggested — Oak Creek Station and Schnebly Station were mentioned— but those were too long for the cancellation stamp. At his brother's suggestion, T.C. submitted his wife's name, and the town was born.

T.C. was the first postmaster, and the Schnebly home was the first post office. It soon became a hub of activity, full of guests and a calling place for neighbors who stopped in to pick up news from the outside world.

In 1905, the Schnebly's little girl Pearl died in an accident. The loss was too great for the couple, and they decided to sell out and move back to Missouri. They would not return to Sedona for more than 25 years.

The property was sold, probably to another early day settler named Claude Black, and the two-story house became a hotel. In 1918, it burned to the ground and was replaced by a rock house that now stands on the grounds of Los Abrigados resort.

Over time, the post office moved to several different locations. It was at Indian Gardens in Oak Creek Canyon for a time and later in uptown Sedona, where it occupied a small stone building, which is still in use as a retail store.

At some point, the Jordan family acquired all or most of the northern end of the Schnebly property (the area north of the Y intersection at Jordan Road and 89A). They added to the existing orchards, and by the 1920s were growing apples and peaches as a commercial crop. Harvests were hauled up what is now Schnebly Hill Road to the top of the rim and on to market in Flagstaff.

Helen Jordan, wife of George J. Jordan, told an interviewer in the 1970s that, "Sedona had the perfect climate for the fruit grower, and our trees produced so much fruit that we needed a packing house other than the canvas-sided shed we had been using." That packing house later became the Sedona Art Barn Center in uptown Sedona.

In 1931, the Schneblys returned to Sedona permanently. T.C. worked as a CCC camp supervisor and handyman for the Jordan family, and Sedona Schnebly cared for the Jordan children and helped in the house.

Helen Jordan remembers life in Sedona as slow paced. Literary programs and dances in the schoolhouse were the highlight of the week. Most of the time was spent with the business of farming, harvesting and hauling.

Many rural areas had no electricity until the early 1950s. As land was cleared away from the creek, irrigating the trees became a problem. In 1949, George Jordan designed and built a water wheel to power an irrigation system that carried water from the creek to the orchards above.

By then, the Schneblys were near retirement. The town of Sedona threw a huge party for them on their 50th wedding anniversary in 1947. They lived out their remaining days in a modest house in uptown Sedona, near the site of the new city parking area at the corner of Jordan and Schenbly roads.

Sedona Schnebly died in November 1951. T.C. died two years later.

— *Joan Brundige-Baker*

Originally published: June 21, 2002

Photo courtesy of Sedona Historical Society, Sedona Heritage Museum

Photo courtesy of Special Collections, Cline Library, Northern Arizona University

Clifton-Morenci: The Baby Train

It was not unusual at the turn of the 20th century for orphanages to place wards in foster homes on the frontier. They were able to raise money that way because farmers and ranchers needed boys to help with chores, and their wives needed girls to help with housework. Usually the children were adopted into the families.

The top photograph appeared in *Leslie's Weekly* in October 1904 over a caption calling the orphans "the pretty American children who were recovered from hovels in Morenci, Arizona, where they had been placed for adoption."

The children were from the New York Foundling Home, a Catholic orphanage in New York City. They were sent by train to Arizona in October 1904 for placement with mining families in Clifton and Morenci, under an arrangement made by the local Catholic priest, the French-educated Father Constant Mandin (see lower photo). Father Mandin was considered by some accounts to be an odd person and a story in and of himself (he once was stabbed in a fight, one account said). He was serving in Clifton while the regular priest, Rev. Peter Timmerman, visited his native Belgium.

Father Mandin had received a letter from George Whitney Swayne, an agent for the foundling home, soliciting foster families for young orphans. Father Mandin spread the word, and 60 mining families in Clifton-Morenci applied.

He approved 33 of the families, and in doing so, he set the stage for a very tense confrontation. According to later reports by nuns at the New York home, Father Mandin told Swayne he wanted only Anglo children, while all but one of the families approved to receive the orphans were Hispanic. Why he specified Anglo children no one ever will know, and presumably the reason he wanted Hispanic families was because they were Catholic.

In any case, the prospective foster families paid $2 and up for each child, and back in New York the sisters at the foundling home chose 57 children, aged two to five, for the trip West.

The children were told they were going home to their parents, and on September 25, 1904, they boarded a train, accompanied by three nuns, four nurses and George Whitney Swayne. Along the way, 14 of them were placed with Catholic families in St. Charles, Missouri.

The group arrived in Clifton on October 1, and when the foster families showed up to claim the children, there was consternation all around because no one apparently had been told that the Anglo children were being placed with Hispanic families. Consternation turned into anger, and that night a group of Anglos formed a vigilante committee and confronted Swayne and Father Mandin, demanding that all the children be brought to Jake Abraham's hotel within the hour.

Angry and chagrined, the Hispanic foster parents brought the children back, and the next morning the children were parceled out among Anglo families. Tempers were still running high, and a crowd began forming to punish Father Mandin and Swayne. It took a sheriff's deputy, Jake Dunagin, to protect the two.

After three tense days, the New Yorkers took the train back East, leaving the children behind. Father Mandin went to Tucson to report the incident to Bishop Granjon. The press played the story for all it was worth, and that is where this photo came from.

At the end of October, the Anglo foster families applied for legal adoption through Judge P.C. Little at Solomonville. On November 16, Little granted guardianship of the children to the Anglos on grounds that the children had been abandoned and needed care.

The New York Foundling Home sought to recover the children and took the case to the Arizona Territorial Supreme Court. On January 17, 1905, the court decided it was in the best interest of the children to remain with their Clifton foster parents.

So, the children stayed in Arizona. Their records were sealed, and to this day, no one knows their true identities.

— *Jane Eppinga*

Originally published: March 29, 1996

Photo courtesy of the Arizona Historical Society, Tucson

Fr. Mandin in a photo dated at 1912.

Photo courtesy of the Catholic Diocese of Tucson Archives

Alianza Hispano-Americana

During the mid to late 19th century, Mexicans and Anglos were living side-by-side in many cities and towns throughout the Southwest. In Tucson, the first Anglos settled during the 1850s. They enjoyed a close association with their Hispanic neighbors, both socially and in business, and intermarriage was more common than not. During the 1870s, as the Anglo population rapidly increased, racial tension — especially among the labor classes — developed.

With the coming of the railroad in 1880, racism accelerated. It was exacerbated after 1890, when the American Protective Association was formed. The association was vociferously anti-Catholic, anti-immigration and racist. Anti-Mexican chapters were formed in the Southwest that exploited nativist fears.

In response to the growing hostility, Hispanics banded together in *mutualistas* — mutual aid societies that provided social as well as economic benefits. The movement began in Tucson and spread rapidly across the country.

Alianza Hispano-Americana, which became the largest *mutualista* organization in the nation, was founded on January 14, 1894, by Cahn Velasco, Mariano Samaniego, Pedro Pella and nearly 50 other prominent Tucson Hispanics. The organization grew quickly and by 1916 was able to build an attractive two-story headquarters building on Congress Street. At its height during the late 1930s, the Alianza counted more than 17,000 members in chapters throughout the West and in northern Mexico.

Velasco, a Republican, helped draft the Alianza's constitution and served as its first president. He was by no means a radical, but a man who espoused conservative views and guided the organization with moderation. His philosophy was summed up in a 1905 speech, in which he told fellow Hispanics that the laborer ... "can have no better shield than the mutual-aid association, which contains the practical doctrines of the social virtues: personal dignity, the love of work, respect for the law, the desire for recompense and all forms and means of mutual protection, moral and material." But even this organization was not free of racism. Its bylaws excluded from membership men who were unemployed, former convicts and "members of the African and yellow races."

As a non-profit fraternal aid society, the Alianza offered a rudimentary form of health insurance and provided death benefits for its members' families. A social organization as well, it sponsored dances, concerts, lectures and other activities that emphasized Hispanic culture and family unity.

The Alianza's mutual benefit insurance program, noble as the concept was, proved to be a thorn in its side. A major setback occurred in 1917, when, an official pilfered $15,000 from the fund and disappeared into Mexico. Significant losses occurred during the Depression and, over the years, there were frequent complaints of mismanagement.

By the close of World War II, new directions were taken by the Hispanic community, which demanded a voice in politics and began a lengthy battle against discrimination. Slow to follow this inevitable agenda, the Alianza suffered.

During the 1950s, it joined the fight against segregated schools and public facilities, but it was too little, too late; other stronger organizations had emerged. By 1966, membership had dwindled to about 2,000, and the headquarters building was razed. After that, the end came quickly, and the Alianza Hispano-Americana was soon relegated to history

— *W. Lane Rogers*

Originally published: August 20, 2004

Photo courtesy of the Arizona Historical Society, Tucson

Arizona School of Music, 1907

For many years, this building on Central Avenue north of Van Buren was a Phoenix landmark. It was one of the few cultural centers in a city that was otherwise just a raw Western town. The building was the home of the Arizona School of Music, founded by Abilena Creighton Christy, daughter-in-law of pioneer financier Col. William Christy and great-aunt of Ned Creighton, Publisher Emeritus of the *Arizona Capitol Times*.

The school opened for business in a small downtown office in 1904. There were only six students, but Mrs. Christy was determined that her school, the first of its kind in the Arizona Territory, should have its own building. Three years later her dream came true with the construction of the mission-style building in this photograph.

The Arizona School of Music was the first commercial structure north of Van Buren. According to historian James Barney, "people thought the school a foolish venture because it had been built too far from the business section of the city." Nevertheless, the school flourished. There were art and music studios and a 500-seat auditorium for concerts, recitals and stock company productions. There was also a ballroom where a redoutable lady named E. Paula Revare revealed the mysteries of the waltz and fox trot to the city's reluctant youth.

Mrs. Christy's influence on the culture of early-day Phoenix was profound. At a time when few women completed high school, she was a college graduate with degrees in classics and music. She also had studied abroad in Italy and Paris. She brought celebrities to Phoenix to perform, frequently inviting them to stay at the family ranch on West McDowell Road. She managed to hire a first rate faculty for her school. She found that Phoenix's dry climate was an attraction to those of stature in music who otherwise would not have left their established positions in the East. The school eventually boasted a 16-member faculty.

For almost a quarter of a century she operated the school, finally selling it in 1928, when her husband, Shirley, died. The school had been her life however, and she died the following year. In 1955, the building was torn down to make way for a parking lot.

— *Arizona Capitol Times*

Originally published: February 18, 1986

Photo courtesy of the Arizona State Library, Archives and Public Records; History and Archives Division, #97-2534

The Southwestern Society of Spizzifiers

According to a writer for the Great Depression's Arizona Federal Writers Project, Arizona's prospectors and miners have been famous for stretching the truth for many years. These raconteurs have spun marvelous stories about their diggings and exaggerated the value of their strikes, often for the sole purpose of entertaining friends.

On April Fool's Day 1936, the art of tall tale telling reached its zenith with the formal establishment of the the Southwestern Society of Spizzifiers. Art for art's sake was their slogan, and they touted their stories as rivaling those of the legendary Pecos Bill.

Now a spizzifier is not a liar, according to the Federal Writers Project author; rather, he "moulds his tale lovingly, garnishes it with bits of local color, and tops it with climax upon climax." Even if the listener is skeptical about the truth of the story, "he knows if the yarn isn't true it ought to be, for its sheer artistry."

One tall tale from a spizzifier told how he and his partner found a promising claim in the highest peaks of the Mazatzal Mountains and decided to stay there through the winter. They had plenty of food and powder, but not enough wood. So, one day they "took an old pick handle and went hunting for a super-venomous Mazatzal rattlesnake." They teased the nine-foot long reptile into "biting the pick handle, which right away swelled up to the size of a redwood log." They sawed up the log and had plenty of wood for the rest of the winter.

Soon, bitter winds started whistling down from the north, and the two men moved into a cabin and quickly started a fire. Unfortunately, the chimney did not draw well and the cabin filled with smoke. The smoke was so saturated with rattler "pi-zen" that the two prospectors were "plumb overcome." Lying on the floor, they agreed that the "little spilliken of whiskey" that remained in a bottle would save only one of them, so they "drew for the low card." The one that drew the Joker "drank the whiskey and was enough revived to crawl outside." He survived. No sooner did he bury his partner than a fierce snowstorm forced him back into the cabin where he nearly froze to death because he did not dare burn any of the rattler wood.

Even better was the tale of Arizona Slim, the first prospector to find gold in Yavapai County's Granite Creek. One day, while eating his lunch, he threw a rind of yellow cheese into the water. Immediately, a school of tadpoles went for it. Now Slim was very caring when it came to critters, so he cut some of his cheese into little pieces and threw it to them. "He noticed one pick up a shiny yellow nugget among the crumbs of cheese and spit it out disgusted-like." Well, he decided to train those tadpoles — it only took him a week — so that every time they brought him a nugget, he "would feed them a smidgen of cheese. He saw himself getting rich without doing hardly a stroke of work."

Soon all his cheese was gone, so he went to Prescott to buy more, but all the stores were sold out, and no freight trains were coming in for at least a month. Being an enterprising gentleman, he substituted yellow soap for the cheese. Well, it didn't take long for those tadpoles to figure it out, so they "called off the trade and stopped bringing him nuggets." Poor Slim had to go back to running sand through a rocker. Those tadpoles showed him. They scraped up "every speck of gold in that part of the creek, carried it off and hid it." Slim meandered up and down the creek for days and finally found the spot where they "stowed the staff." He found a big pile of nuggets and gold flakes in the bottom of a deep pool. He dived in, pulled out a handful or two and "quicker'n you could count the hairs on a Chihuahua dog" about a million tadpoles "toted the gold off to a new hid'n place."

Slim never found the new stash. He prowled through the trees and brush, away from the creek banks, so the tadpoles couldn't see him. Then he'd race down to the water, hoping to grab more gold before they moved it yet again. It didn't do him any good — "fact is his tactics proved fatal." He got careless one day and dove into that stream with his mouth open and swallowed some water. "His insides were unused to anything but forty-rod whiskey, and the shock killed him."

It is unknown how long the Southwestern Society of Spizzifiers spun their stories, but their tall tales have been entertaining people for years and have become part of the colorful history of prospectors and miners in the Southwest.

— *Melanie Sturgeon*

Originally published: April 30, 2004

*A prospector that was perhaps a member of the tall tale telling Southwestern
Society of Spizzifiers during the early 20th century.*

*Photo courtesy of the Arizona State Library, Archives and Public Records;
History and Archives Division, Phoenix #97-6844*

The Founder of Teatro Carmen

On May 20, 1915, Teatro Carmen de Tucson opened on South Meyer Street. It was founded through the efforts of the remarkable woman in this photograph, Carmen Soto de Vasquez. At the time, about half of Tucson's 15,000 population was of Mexican descent — old Hispanic families, new immigrants and political exiles from Mexico's revolution. There was a strong demand for dramatic theater, as well as a desire on the part of well-to-do and middle-class Mexicans to eradicate Hispanic stereotypes and Tucson's cow-town image with presentations of high-caliber artistic events.

Carmen Soto de Vasquez was the granddaughter of Tucson Presidio Captain Antonio Comaduran and was married to Tucson businessman Ramon Vasquez. Vasquez gave her a lot on Meyer Street for the theater, and she commissioned Manuel Flores to design and build it. It was large and well appointed, with a parquet orchestra pit, upholstered seating for 1,400, a bar and a wrestling arena — all under one roof. Although there were other Spanish-language theaters at the time — El Principal, El Clifton, El Lirico and El Royal, in its few short years of operation, Teatro Carmen came to be the most famous.

The theater's first production, "Cerebro y Corazon" (Head and Heart), was staged by La Nacional Company of Mexico City. Thereafter, live performances alternated with movies, and the theater also served as a meeting place for Club Neutral, an influential Mexican-American group.

In March 1918, the theater booked the music and variety show of the Brothers Areu. Many years later, in 1952, several old trunks were discovered at a dump near Jerome. The contents revealed 116 Spanish operettas bearing the owner's name — Manuel Areu. Mr. Areu had apparently retired in Jerome after many years of performing in Cuba, Mexico and the United States.

Four years after opening, Doña Carmen began to rent her theater to independent impresarios. They brought such classics as "The Merry Widow" and "Lucia de Lammermoor" to Tucson. But in 1921, just six years after opening, the theater was closed by the city for failure to meet safety standards. For several years the building served as a theater school and dance hall, until finally, in 1926, Doña Carmen sold it to Elena Cervantes, who turned it into a garage. The building's later incarnations include a movie theater, boxing arena and Elks Lodge.

— *Jane Eppinga*

Originally published: July 20, 1988

Photo courtesy of the Arizona Historical Society, Tucson

Loyalty Sunday, April 8, 1917

This photograph, taken from near Castle Rock above Bisbee, shows marchers in Bisbee's Loyalty Day parade on their way down Tombstone Canyon. Each participant carried a small American flag and was, according to the *Bisbee Daily Review,* "ready to do (his) share for Old Glory."

St. Patrick's Catholic Church is seen nearing completion at upper left.

The United States entered World War I on April 6, 1917, when Congress declared war on Germany. Arizona Governor Tom Campbell immediately called for a show of public support and designated that Sunday — April 8 — as Loyalty Day. He asked the people of Arizona "to fittingly acknowledge in public manner their sentiments on that date."

The marchers in this photograph were joined at Naco Road by another group of residents from Warren, Lowell and South Bisbee. Together they marched up Brewery Gulch and gathered at City Park where they listened to patriotic speeches and sang patriotic songs, including the "Star Spangled Banner" and "America, The Beautiful."

At the time, about a third of the population of Bisbee was made up of foreign citizens, and perhaps as much as half of the population was foreign born. People hailed from England, Ireland, Mexico, Finland, Austria, Serbia, Italy, Germany, Sweden and Switzerland.

The anniversaries and special holidays of foreign nations were tolerated and even celebrated. A 1912 article in the *Bisbee Daily Review* described the flagpole atop the Pythian Castle: "During the year, probably as many as half a dozen flags of foreign countries are displayed from that flagpole in observance of some anniversary or an event in the history of the several countries represented in Bisbee's cosmopolitan population, but an American flag equally large or larger is run up on the flag pole first so that it flies over the foreign flag."

Once at war, however, loyalty to the U.S. was demanded of all. On the day this photograph was taken, an unidentified citizen raised a German or Austrian flag on School Hill. Four members of the Arizona Infantry rushed the hill and tore down the flag.

The *Review* published an editorial criticizing citizens who failed to fly the Old Glory, especially the businesses on Brewery Gulch: "...there is NO excuse for not flying the colors of the United States and the more so when the proprietors of businesses are natives of countries whose interests at the present time are inimical to those of the United States."

Reaction was quick. The following day, the *Review* noted: "Brewery Gulch has more (American) flags flying at the present time than for months.... If yesterday morning's editorial in the *Review* had no other effect, it certainly aroused the business residents of that thoroughfare to the fact that the people of the Warren district are extremely jealous of all things American and especially the flag."

On several occasions, the newspaper reported neighbors fighting over flags, and at least twice, arrests were made for desecrating American flags.

Later that month, two overzealous school boys tore down the flags of Scotland and England, unaware those countries were U.S. allies. Although Mrs. McDougall, the owner of the flags, flew them together with an even larger U.S. flag, the boys vowed they would pull them down every time they flew. She appealed to the British vice-consul at Douglas who wrote the Bisbee chief of police for redress. The chief was unmoved.

In a letter published in the *Review*, he called the incident a "regrettable matter" but said he believed no law had been broken and suggested that to avert trouble, no foreign flags be flown in Bisbee.

— *Tom Vaughan*

Originally published: July 1, 1997

Photo courtesy of the Bisbee Mining and Historical Museum

Eldredge Museum and Taxidermy

In 1918, Dean Eldredge began construction of his museum and taxidermist building on Flagstaff's Santa Fe Avenue. The structure was made from local timber and took several years to build. It included a curio store, museum of Indian artifacts and a taxidermy studio.

A huge wishbone-shaped tree framed the entrance of the museum and served as a perch for a stuffed eagle, a perpetual reminder of Eldredge's taxidermy skills. On the first floor were the store and museum and a large fireplace. A private apartment was upstairs.

Eldredge successfully operated the store until the 1930s when the Great Depression killed business. In 1936, he sold the property to a local man, Doc Williams, who reopened the place as a nightclub. The building was never again used as a museum and has been the location for a nightclub ever since.

Williams was an excellent fiddler and probably sat in with the band when he wasn't tending bar. His nightclub soon became a popular hangout. His wife Thelma spent her evenings upstairs in their apartment while Williams was busy downstairs. Many wives visited her to complain about their husbands spending time at the club.

Apparently, Williams wasn't cut out for the nightclub business. He was an accomplished saddlemaker and leatherworker and may have decided to return to that trade. He owned the club only a year before selling it to Jim McGown who was experienced in the business and had previously owned another local place, the Tumblers Lounge.

In the '60s and '70s, Don Scott took over the club. Scott was a former member of the Bob Wills Texas Playboys. His connections in the music business brought in performers such as Waylon Jennings, Willie Nelson and Stonewall Jackson.

In 1978, Martin Zanzucchi, of the Flagstaff Zanzucchi clan, bought the club. Apart from the business value, Zanzucchi had a sentimental reason for doing it: his parents met there in the late 1930s.

Over the years various structural changes were made to the building: the front and side porches were closed to provide seating areas for dancers and space for the band; sections of the exterior walls were cut away to provide access to the dance floor. The large fireplace in the front of the main room remained.

Since 1989, Zanzucchi has been restoring the building to it original appearance and contacting former owners' next of kin to find old photos and get an oral history of the building.

Today the club is called The Museum Club, but because of Eldredge's stuffed animals and the deer and elk antlers collected over the years, it is often referred to as the Zoo. It remains one of Flagstaff's liveliest historical landmarks and continues to host rising stars of country music.

— *Bonnie Greer*

Originally published: March 29, 1989

Photo courtesy of the Arizona Historical Society, Pioneer Museum.

Jerome in the '20s

This is the mining community of Jerome in 1927. Hanging precariously on the side of Mingus Mountain in the Black Hills, Jerome is such a jumble of architectural peculiarities that it is unlike any other town in Arizona. With a 1500 foot difference in elevation between its highest and lowest levels, the town is constructed of buildings with basements you climb up to, roofs below street level and garages built on roofs.

Copper was mined by Indians on Mingus Mountain centuries before Anglos arrived. Just after the Civil War, John Ruffner and August McKinnon, ranchers from the Prescott area, prospected near the old Indian workings. Ruffner staked a claim to what later would become the United Verde Mine. Because ranching took up most of his time, Ruffner leased his claim to Frederick Trifle, a man who would become Arizona's sixth Territorial governor (1881-1885). He developed the mine with financial backing from New York investor Eugene Jerome on the condition that the mining camp would bear Jerome's name.

It was not, however, until 1882, when the Atlantic & Pacific Railroad opened a line to Ashfork that profitable exploitation of the ore deposit at Jerome was possible. Even then, there were obstacles. Trifle had to strike a road from Ashfork in order to transport his smelter to the mine. Coke for smelting came all the way from Wales via San Francisco and had to be freighted from the railhead. Later, coke was brought from New Mexico.

In 1886, Montana Senator William A. Clark bought the mining property and began a series of improvements. He installed a new smelter that could handle a half million pounds a month. He built frame houses to attract a stable work force. And in 1888, he built the Montana House, then the largest stone structure in the Territory and big enough to house 1,000 men.

In 1894, a narrow gauge rail line was built from Ashfork to the smelter, and Jerome began to flourish. Even major fires in 1897 and 1899 were, in the long run, no more than minor inconveniences. The town was incorporated in 1899. A year later, J.J. Fisher laid claim to the Little Daisy Mine in Bitter Creek; it was developed into the United Verde Extension Mine in 1910. Some say it was the spectacularly rich orebody of the UVX, as it came to be called, that was responsible for kicking Jerome's growth into high gear.

As the mines grew, so did the expectations of the miners. A strike was called in 1907, and miners succeeded in reducing their 10-hour workday to eight and increasing their daily wage to $2.75. In 1917, when labor unrest was spreading across the state, 67 striking miners — most were members of the International Workers of the World — were herded at gunpoint into boxcars and dumped in the desert near Kingman. The Jerome Deportation was a prelude to the more massive, and more famous Bisbee Deportation a few days later.

In 1925, blasting for the Black Pit weakened the underpinnings from Jerome, and the entire town began to shift downhill at the rate of about three-eighths of an inch a month. The concrete jail skidded slowly 300 feet across the highway and fell over onto its side below street level.

At first the subsidence was treated as just another inconvenience. Jerome's residents used braces, beams and concrete blocks to shore up the buildings and went on mining. But the stock market crashed four years later, after which the price of copper began a long decline. Ore reserves played out finally, and Phelps Dodge Corporation — which had assumed control of the United Verde — closed the mine permanently in 1953.

By then Jerome was a virtual ghost town. Today, the town has made a comeback. Abandoned buildings have been renovated, businesses are thriving, and tourists by the thousands visit each year. The U.S. Census Bureau estimated the town's population in 2006 to be 343.

— *W. Lane Rogers*

Originally published: January 31, 1997

Photo courtesy of W. Lane Rogers

Main Street, Payson

This is all there was of Payson, Arizona in the 1920s: a dirt street, a bankers and merchants trust and a general store. The thoroughfare was the center of the tiny community and the site of the "August Doin's," one of the first rodeos in the West.

Payson was called Union Park when it was founded in 1882 and was a mining and livestock camp. Two years later, a post office was established, and the settlement was renamed for the chairman of the U.S. Post Office and Post Roads Committee, Sen. Louis E. Payson of Illinois.

Because of the mining activity in the area, the town was as wild and wooly as any gold rush town in California's Mother Lode. It is said that until a proper jail was built, lawbreakers were chained to a large oak tree for safekeeping until they could be brought to trial.

The large building on the left is the Payson Commercial and Trust Co., the first stone building in town. The trust company was opened in 1921 and provided banking services for local merchants and ranchers until it failed in 1932 during the Great Depression. There was not another bank in Payson for almost 30 years. During that time, the general store and the post office provided basic banking services— cashing checks, selling money orders and holding important papers. In 1958, banking finally returned to town with the opening of a Valley National Bank branch.

The liquor business boomed in Payson before Prohibition. There wasn't much else for the local cowboys, loggers and miners to do; and a trip to town was a chance to celebrate. Local bars were the Tammany Hall, Cowboy's Home and the cryptically named 16-to-1, which referred to the exchange rate of silver to gold used by the miners.

Even during Prohibition, liquor flowed in the area. Payson, with its good quality creek water and remote location, provided perfect conditions for whiskey production. The area was known to have some of the most active bootlegging operations in the state, and Payson Whiskey was famous from Texas to the West Coast.

Gradually, progress caught up with the town despite its remote location. In 1908, the first telephone line was strung — from Roosevelt Dam to the Payson Commercial Store, linking it to the county seat in Globe. The line was paid for by citizens who bought stock in the Overland Company and did all the repairs on the line as well. The tiny utility prospered, until the Depression struck and the stockholders were forced to turn over the line to the U.S. Forest Service.

In the early days, Payson was reachable only by dirt road, either across the top of Roosevelt Dam or northeast from Phoenix. This latter route was paved in 1959, becoming the Beeline Highway that connects Payson to Phoenix. The original main street still exists today near the south side of the city.

— *Joan Brundige-Baker*

Originally published: August 22, 2003

Photo courtesy of Special Collections, Cline Library, Northern Arizona University

Shoot-Out at the 'Arizona Kicker'

This apparent shoot-out took place at the offices of the *Arizona Kicker* newspaper in Flagstaff around 1900. The *Kicker* was a short-lived, humorous weekly that was not above staging a phony hold-up to promote circulation and provide a little excitement for readers.

The building, which stood at the east end of today's Monte Vista Hotel on Aspen Avenue, later became the first offices of the *Coconino Sun*, the predecessor of the *Arizona Daily Sun*.

To carry off the Wild West theme, the *Kicker* enlisted the help of some famous Flagstaff pioneers, as well as a small boy and a local dog.

Stan Sykes is on the right with his hands in the air. He and Charlie McLain (far right, holding the rifle) were English immigrants who ran a small herd of cattle near Turkey Tanks, east of Flagstaff. Representing the law in the photograph is one of the Hochderffer brothers.

The Hochderffers and their father arrived in Flagstaff in June 1887. They had located a clay pit near Flagstaff and began the production of bricks. They also ranched near the San Francisco Peaks.

Over the next several years, the Hochderffers became involved in developing Flagstaff and held numerous positions of authority in the town. It's not surprising then that one of them was masquerading as the law for this photograph.

Fourth from the left is one of the Donohue boys, of the family that owned J.J.'s Senate Saloon. Sandy Donohue, who loved physical labor, dug the cellar for the saloon by hand with the help of one of the Hochderffer boys. The man standing in the doorway was named Stout.

The photograph, while humorous for the locals, apparently did nothing to increase the fortunes of the *Arizona Kicker*, which soon folded and left no record for historians except this photograph.

In the 1950s, the photograph was reprinted in the *Coconino Sun*, which challenged its readers to tell why and where it was taken.

Several pioneers, including Stan Sykes, came forward and told the story, saying "a bunch of the boys" pretended to "rob the joint" for the benefit of a local photographer, since it was a well-known fact that "printing offices always have lots of money."

— *Arizona Capitol Times*

Originally published: May 8, 1991

Photo courtesy of the Arizona Historical Society, Pioneer Museum

Phoenix: Down the Canal to Brophy

The Salt River Valley's Grand Canal crosses Seventh Avenue about a quarter mile south of Camelback. That is where the top photograph was taken almost 75 years ago. The photograph gives a sense of the agricultural quietude that once surrounded Phoenix. Notice the citrus grove at left, a commonplace near to town in those years.

Those who write of Phoenix in the 1920s and earlier often belabor the fact that before air conditioning the Valley's irrigation canals took the place of swimming pools. But that fact is worth mentioning, because swimming in the Water User's canals was a memorable feature in the life of Phoenix youth in those days.

With time, growth of population and, we suppose, common sense, the practice died. We think, however, that it was not until the advent of water-skiing, when some daring youngsters tried to ski the canals, towed by cars on the canal bank, that the city and county authorities and the Salt River Project got really hard-nosed about recreational use of the canals and chained off the canal roads.

Today, with fast-running currents and strong undertows, it is far too dangerous to swim in the canals.

In the center distance of this photograph you can make out the spire on the chapel at Brophy College Prep. The private Jesuit boys school on Central Avenue and Campbell was founded by Ellen Brophy in memory of her husband, William Henry Brophy, a financial and civic power in Arizona in the early days. Mrs. Brophy donated 25 acres of land and $275,000 in funds for construction of the school, which began in 1928.

The larger photo dates from the early '30s.

The smaller photo is taken from approximately the same spot in August 2008.

— *Arizona Capitol Times*

Originally published: October 23, 1985

Historic photo courtesy of the Arizona State Library, Archives and Public Records; History and Archives Division

Contemporary photo by Bill Coates, Arizona Capitol Times

Tucson Veterans' Hospital

This is the Tucson Veterans' Hospital, a landmark of pink stucco that has graced the city for 80 years. The immature foliage around the building indicates that the photo was taken several years after the hospital was built in 1928.

As early as 1888, Arizona's climate was touted for its therapeutic advantages. Extolling Tucson as a paradise for invalids, the *Arizona Daily Star* wrote that the city's weather was a "great resource" that would produce large returns, and that the city will soon be known as the sanitarium of the Southwest.

By 1890, tuberculars, called "lungers" in common parlance, were arriving in large numbers, having been told to seek a warm, dry climate by doctors who had little else to offer in the way of a cure.

That same year, an Eastern doctor wrote an article entitled "Arizona as a Health Resort." It was published in a medical journal and also circulated as a pamphlet. The air, wrote the doctor, "is a real aseptic with antimicrobic fluid freely invading and preserving every accessible part of the person.... I never met a case of phthisis [a wasting disease] in an old settler, and it is well known that tuberculosis is very rare among Indians and Mexicans."

As the rush of immigrants increased, an acute housing shortage developed in Tucson. By the turn of the 20th century, tent towns had popped up all over the desert. The largest was on land north of the university. World War I created a whole new generation of invalids and health seekers. Two years after Armistice Day, there were several hundred World War I veterans living in Tucson, many of them in squalid hovels.

The Red Cross did its best to care for them, but the job was too big. Finally, local veterans' organizations and the Chamber of Commerce joined forces to seek a solution. With a $4,000 donation from the Red Cross, the veterans were able to lease Pastime Park, where a beer garden, skating rink and dance hall had once stood. The wooden buildings at Pastime Park could house 40 or 50 patients, but that was a drop in the bucket compared to the numbers who needed help.

The Chamber sent a representative to Washington to confer with Arizona Congressman Carl Hayden. He got an appropriation of $25,000 to renovate and expand the Pastime Park facility to house 275 men. When the veterans learned of the expansion, however, more than 1,000 applications poured in. The good citizens of Tucson returned to Washington to ask for more help. Pressure was applied and, in time, the government was persuaded to build a permanent facility for veterans. The Tucson Veterans Hospital became a reality in 1928.

— *Arizona Capitol Times*

Originally published: April 8, 1994

Photo courtesy Arizona Historical Society, Tucson

Famous Visitors

Frank Holme at the Schorgl Ranch

Buffalo Bill Comes to Phoenix

Lindbergh in Tucson

The First Women to Run the Colorado

Marvel Crosson and the Powder Puff Derby

Frank Holme at the Schorgl Ranch

The top photograph was taken at the Schorgl Ranch near Phoenix in February 1903, shortly after John Francis "Frank" Holme arrived there. Mr. Holme is the man in the dark outfit seated in the first chair. The photographer at the right side of the photo is unidentified.

The Schorgl Ranch was one of a number of camps for tuberculars (commonly called "lungers' camps") built in the Arizona desert around the turn of the century. Because tuberculosis was highly contagious, healthy people feared infection and segregated the invalids on the outskirts of town. The tuberculars lived in tents because it was cheap, and they couldn't afford medical care in the local sanitoriums and hospitals. Also, it was believed that fresh air was therapeutic and helped in the cure.

Frank Holme, the only man we can identify in the photograph, was a Chicago newspaper reporter and artist. He became famous for, among other things, his courtroom drawings done during the Chicago murder trial of sausage-maker Adolph Leutgert in 1897. One of his drawings is shown at right.

Holme was a man of tremendous energy, described by his friends as never too busy or too tired to give a helping hand.

In 1893, he married Ida Van Dyke in Chicago. Because of the number of unfinished projects the couple always seemed to have on hand, Frank and Ida were nicknamed "Mr. and Mrs. Bandar-log" after the monkey-folk in Kipling's *Jungle Book*. When they set up a press in the attic of their home, they named it, fittingly, the Bandar-Log Press.

Frank worked constantly. Besides writing for the *Chicago Daily News*, he started the Palette and Chisel Club, established the Holme School of Illustration in 1898, where he taught both day and evening classes, and wrote instruction books for mail order classes he started. The constant work took its toll, however, and in January 1901 he was found to have tuberculosis. In 1903 he moved to the Schorgl Ranch to attempt a cure in the dry desert climate of Arizona.

In a letter to a friend, he described part of his daily schedule: "After supper we visit each other's tents and swap lies — or sit by the stove to read or write letters till bedtime which ought to be about 9 o'clock."

He set up his old press in an abandoned chicken house on the ranch, and the work of the Bandar-Log Press was resumed. During this time he made friends with the newspapermen of Phoenix and visited the offices of the *Arizona Republican* when he could. When his health began to fail again, he moved to Denver, but he lived only two more months. He died July 28, 1904, at the age of 36.

— *Joan Metzger and John Bret Harte*

Originally published: February 5, 1986

Photo courtesy of Arizona Historical Society, Tucson

One of Frank Holmes' drawings of the 1897 trial of Adolph Leutgert in Chicago.

Buffalo Bill Comes to Phoenix

William F. "Buffalo Bill" Cody was born near Davenport, Iowa, on February 26, 1846. In 1860, at age 14, he joined the Pony Express which advertised for "expert riders willing to risk death daily." During the Civil War, he served as a scout and enlisted soldier, and at age 21 was hired by the Kansas Pacific Railroad to hunt buffalo that would be used to feed construction crews. In 17 months, he claimed to have killed 4,280 buffalo, garnering his nickname in the process.

Buffalo Bill's fame, in part, started when he was asked to guide a buffalo hunt in Nebraska for the Grand Duke Alexis of Russia in January 1872. General Phil Sheridan arranged the hunt, which also included General George Custer. Arriving at the hunt, Bill was described as being "...seated on a spanking charger, and with his long hair and spangled buckskin suit he appeared as the feared and loved by all for miles around."

In 1872, author Ned Buntline persuaded Buffalo Bill to star in the play "The Scouts of the Plains," which was based on the fictional "Buffalo Bill" in Buntline's dime novels. As it turned out, Bill loved being a showman, and in 1883 he created "Buffalo Bill's Wild West Show."

Buffalo Bill brought his show to Phoenix at least twice in the early 1900s to entertain the people within the growing city. He traveled by train with more than 800 people and animals that were part of his show. The show ran two hours, rain or shine, under an "immense canvas canopy." Admission to the show was 50 cents for bench seating, $1 for grandstand chairs and children younger than 10 were admitted for half price.

In the early years of the show, Bill would stage a parade through the town he was performing in to drum up business. When the show arrived in Phoenix in 1908, he rode through the major streets of Phoenix to "...convince the public that the old scout is still in the harness, ready to appear as he positively will at every performance." The performers along with the animals walked from the train tracks up Fourth Street to the grounds of the performance area, which included a cowboy campsite and an Indian village with teepees.

Shows were given at 2 p.m. and 8 p.m. and included cowboys riding horses and bucking broncos, a game of football between cowboys and Indians on horseback using a ball that was 6 feet, 3 inches in diameter and an artillery drill with cannon firing. There was even a train holdup where "...a real railroad train consisting of an engine, tender and combination baggage and passenger coach, puffed across the far end of the arena on a wobbly set of rails. In the attack on the train, a safe [was] blown up at each performance with a huge charge of gunpowder."

The show also included the reenactment of the Battle of Summit Springs from 1869. Newspaper articles indicated "not only is the battle scene reproduced and that of the duel, but also the mode of the Redman's living at that period. All the Indians will be seen in their full war paint and feathers."

Another feature of the show was the reenactment of a buffalo hunt with a small herd of buffalo. News reports indicated "there is plenty of gun-play in the stage holdup, train robbery, buffalo hunt and several other features. The buffaloes are very interesting to see, as they are of the hundred or so bison still surviving." Buffalo Bill appeared six times during the course of the show. One of the spectators, a middle aged woman, commented, "'Why, isn't he young looking!... I saw him when I was a little girl and he looked older than that then."

Bill toured the world with his Wild West Show, and he invested the money he earned in filmmaking, tourism, ranching and mining in Arizona. However, these ventures did not return a profit for him, and the Wild West show eventually ended in 1913. His debts forced him to continue touring through 1916 as an attraction in other shows. In 1917, at age 71, he died in Denver of kidney failure.

— *Mike Miller*

Originally published: January 20, 2006

Photo courtesy of the Arizona State Library, Archives and Public Records; History and Archives Division, Phoenix #97-8055

Lindbergh in Tucson, 1927

Tucson's love of airplanes started early. Pilots raved about the great weather which gave them nearly unlimited flying time. And crowds on the ground would gather at almost any opportunity to see those magnificent men in their flying machines. No aviation event was bigger than the visit of Charles Lindbergh and his famous "Spirit of St. Louis" plane on Friday, September 23, 1927. He was on a nationwide promotional tour, following his historic non-stop solo flight across the Atlantic in May of that year. His stop in Tucson coincided with the dedication of Davis-Monthan Airfield — the first municipally owned airfield in the country.

Lindbergh's arrival was a major event in southern Arizona. Citizens wrote poetry in his honor, town bells were rung, and a florist named Hal Burns built a full-sized replica of Lindbergh's plane from cactus ribs and dubbed it the "Spirit of Tucson." The lower photo features Lindbergh (fifth from the left) posing with various local dignitaries in front of Burns' plane.

On the day of Lindbergh's arrival, Tucson schools and businesses closed at noon so that everyone could make the trip out to the airfield for Lindy's two o'clock touchdown. People came from all over Arizona. The Southern Pacific Railroad put on special trains for the event, dignitaries and officials traveled from Mexico, and the street from Tucson to the airfield and the fences all around the airfield were lined with the cars of sightseers.

A few minutes before two o'clock, the "Spirit of St. Louis" was sighted. Lindbergh circled the field several times before making a picture-perfect landing. Troops from Camp Little in Nogales quickly roped off the area around the plane to protect it from souvenir hunters. Lindbergh posed with the plane and with local celebrities, answered questions from the crowd and attended a couple of social functions in town.

Later that day, he formally dedicated Davis-Monthan (the field was named in honor of two Tucson aviators who had lost their lives while flying for the Army) at a banquet on the commons of the University of Arizona campus. Twenty thousand people attended the dedication ceremony. Tucson's population at the time was barely 40,000. Lindbergh told the crowd, "It is a real privilege to be the first to land on the new, magnificent Tucson field."

The field he was talking about was little more than empty desert — 1,240 acres southeast of the intersection of Alvernon and Aviation, just south of 22nd Street. Today, of course, Davis-Monthan is a sprawling Air Force installation — home of the 355th Fighter Wing with 6,000 airmen and 1,700 civilian personnel.

— Joan Metzger and Jane Eppinga

Originally published: September 19, 1984

Tucson dignitaries pose with Lindbergh at the dedication of Davis Monthan Airfield: (from left) Hal Burns (the Tucson florist who created the cactus plane), Pima County Sheriff Jim McDonald, Tucson Chief of Detectives Cliff Kronuer, attorney Kirke Moore, Lindbergh, banker Harry H. Holbert, and Undersheriff John Thomas. Tucson Chief of Police Jack Dyer is partially cropped out of the photo.

The First Women to Run the Colorado

The portrait is of Dr. Elzada Clover, scientist and adventuress. The other photo shows Clover (left) with her associates Edith Kolb (center) and Lois Jotter on the Grand Canyon's South Rim in 1938. Clover and Jotter were the first women to successfully run the Colorado River from the Green River in Utah to Lake Mead.

Clover was a professor of botany at the University of Michigan. In the summer of 1937, while collecting cactus specimens in southern Utah, she met Norman Nevills, a local river runner. He encouraged her to make the trip down the Colorado as a way to collect even more unusual cactus specimens.

Clover returned to Michigan and lined up two passengers — Lois Jotter, her 24-year-old lab assistant, and Eugene Atkinson of the university's zoology department. She financed the trip with a $250 donation from the university and a like amount from a friend in Colorado Springs.

The group left the Green River on the 20th of June and arrived at Lee's Ferry on the 4th of July. Clover recorded her thoughts on the trip in a journal. She found the experience exciting and frightening, and physically demanding. Everyone in the party suffered bruises and blisters from lining and portaging the boats around and through the rapids.

Nevills repeatedly warned the party to watch for pink rattlesnakes in the rocks along the river bank. Clover thought the snakes looked strangely innocent with their soft pink color.

The group was four days late arriving at Lee's Ferry, where the press was waiting to greet them. Two of the boatmen left the party there, so additional days were spent finding replacements.

The party left Lee's Ferry on July 13 and arrived at Bright Angel Trail five days later. They hiked out to the South Rim where they were met by Edith Kolb. She and her photographer husband, Emory, operated a small studio on the South Rim. She offered the women warm baths, a prepared lunch and iced tea. It was a welcome respite from the rigors of the river.

Launched once more on the river, the party set off for Lake Mead — this time accompanied by Emory Kolb, who was himself a knowledgeable river runner.

July 31st found the party slowed to a crawl with all hands rowing. That evening as they started to make camp, Nevills narrowly missed stepping on a rattler. The members of the party decided to sleep in the boats that night.

The next day they were up at 4 a.m. for an early start to Boulder Dam and their final destination. At midday, as they ate lunch, they heard the buzzing of a motor. Carl Lehnert, chief Grand Canyon ranger, and Guy Edward, superintendent of Lake Mead recreational area, with two other men, had motored up from Boulder Dam to tow them in.

They arrived in Boulder City at 8:30 that evening and were entertained by the Rotary Club.

Nevills and Clover planned another trip for the following summer, but were never able to put it together. The publicity that resulted from the Clover trip enabled Nevills to build a very successful business as a commercial river runner.

— *Bonnie Greer*

Originally published: February 28, 1990

Photos courtesy of the Emery Lehnert and Kolb Collection, Northern Arizona University

Marvel Crosson and the Powder Puff Derby

These are photos of aviatrix Marvel Crosson, taken sometime in the late 1920s. Women had been flying airplanes since the early days of flight, and by 1928, they had also piloted balloons, parachuted out of disabled planes, served as their own mechanics, set altitude and speed records, wing-walked and barnstormed. But they hadn't yet raced airplanes. A year later, however, they got their chance when the Women's Air Derby was organized — the first all women's transcontinental air race. The course was from Santa Monica to Cleveland with stopovers in Arizona. To compete in the race, each pilot was required to have logged 100 hours of flight time and to pilot an aircraft with horsepower "appropriate for a woman."

On August 18, 1929, 20 women, including the famous Amelia Earhart, showed up in Santa Monica for the air derby. Even before the race started, there was tragedy and trouble. The pilot who had flown with Amelia to Santa Monica was killed in a crash on his way home. Mary Haizlip's airplane had been damaged during her flight to Santa Monica, forcing her to start a day late and with an aircraft that had only two-hour fuel capacity. When Phoebe Omlie landed her airplane in a field near Santa Monica, she was hauled off to jail by the sheriff who thought she was a dope smuggler. To top it off, the race's sponsor changed the route the day before the race.

The morning of the race, Howard Hughes and Will Rogers came to wish the women well. Rogers noted that each racer took a last glance at her compact and gave her nose a puff of powder. He said, "It looks like a powder puff derby to me!" The name stuck, and at 2 p.m. when the radio-relayed pistol shot sounded; the flag dropped and the women roared toward San Bernardino in the first ever Powder Puff Derby.

Seven of the women flew Walter Beech's Travel Air, two racers flew enclosed cockpit planes and Amelia Earhart flew a Lockheed Vega. There were immediate problems. Amelia had to turn back for a repair when her starter stuck, and Mary von Mach got squeezed by racers on take-off and had to land for breathing room before taking off again.

The first to arrive in San Bernardino was Opal Kunz, with Amelia right behind her. Visibility was terrible because of all the dust that was stirred up by spectators driving their cars onto the field, and Opal pancaked, damaging her landing gear. When Amelia landed, she ran out of runway, forcing the crowd to part to give her room to stop. The other racers arrived without incident.

On day two, the racers flew from San Bernardino to Phoenix with a stop in Yuma. "This is the first real test of women's ability to fly," said Ruth Elder, a fellow racer. Again, the women faced more setbacks. Claire Fahy had to land her Travel Air near Calexico because of frayed wires and was out of the race. Mary Haizlip got lost and landed in Mexicali. Amelia Earhart nosed over while landing in Yuma and had to wait in the heat for delivery of a new prop. Ruth Elder accidentally dropped her maps over the side of her plane, and after finally landing was greeted by an unfriendly bull. Thea Rasche went down with engine failure and discovered her airplane's fuel lines had been contaminated. Bobbi Trout ran out of fuel near Yuma and cartwheeled her Golden Eagle onto a field in Mexico. She was able to get it rebuilt and resumed racing three days later.

By the evening of day two, 16 planes had landed in Phoenix. All the missing airplanes were accounted for, except for the one flown by Marvel Crosson. The following day, reports arrived that the body of 28-year old Marvel Crosson was found near a clump of bushes in Wellton. Crosson, an experienced pilot who had flown the entire course prior to the race, had died the day before when her plane went into a tailspin. Wellton spectators reported that she had attempted to jump to safety, but her parachute lay unopened two hundred feet from her plane wreckage.

Crosson's accident added weight to suspicions that some planes had been sabotaged to force certain women out of the race. Bobbi Trout, holder of the women's endurance flight record, and Opal Kunz said that their instruments had been misadjusted while still in California. Investigation into the death of Marvel Crosson and charges of sabotage were launched by the chairman of the National Air Meet, Floyd Logan, but were never proven.

Calls went out to stop the race because "these women have proven conclusively that they cannot fly." The women decided that the best tribute to Marvel would be to continue the race. On day four, the racers made stops in Douglas, Arizona; Columbus, New Mexico; and El Paso and Midland, Texas.

Blanche Noyes, who had been a pilot for only six weeks, got lost and landed her plane in Mexico. The following day, as she made her way across Texas, she detected a fire on her plane. She made an emergency landing in the desert and put out the fire with sand. Then, on take-off she damaged her landing gear but was able to repair it and departed again.

On the fifth day of the race, more women began to drop out. Pancho Barnes landed at Pecos, Texas, not realizing that a car had driven on the landing strip. She hit the car and totaled her airplane. She was uninjured but was out of the race. Margaret Perry had to drop out after she was hospitalized with typhoid fever in Abilene, Texas.

After flying through Texas, the pilots moved into different terrain where they could fly at lower altitudes. In Wichita, home of Travel Air, 10,000 spectators awaited the racers. After they landed, the women changed into wrinkled dresses and participated in the festivities.

During the final leg of the race, the racers followed the Missouri River until it led them into East St. Louis. Blanche Noyes and Neva Paris suffered landing gear damage, and despite flying a completely rebuilt airplane, Bobbi Trout continued to have mechanical problems. She repaired the plane with a tin can patch.

The ninth and last day of the race was from Columbus to Cleveland, Ohio. Louise Thaden crossed the finish line first with Blanche Noyes and Gladys O'Donnell right behind her. The frenzied crowd swarmed over Louise's blue and gold Travel Air. A horseshoe of flowers was placed around Louise's neck and around the airplane's propeller. Louise dedicated her trophy to Marvel Crosson, who had lost her life in the Arizona desert.

—Jane Eppinga

Originally published: October 29, 2004

Photos courtesy Library of Congress from the
New York World-Telegram & Sun Collection.

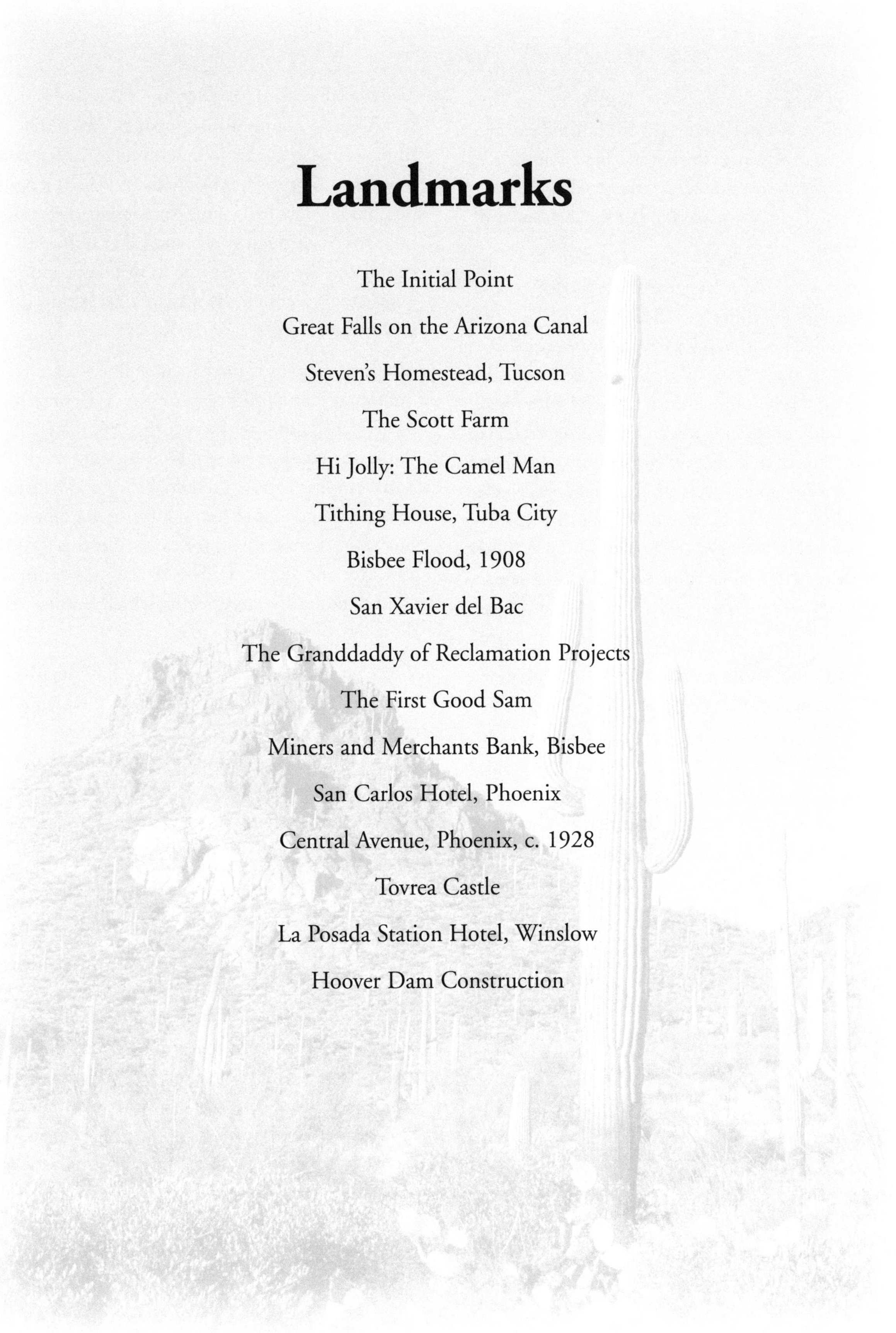

Landmarks

The Initial Point

Great Falls on the Arizona Canal

Steven's Homestead, Tucson

The Scott Farm

Hi Jolly: The Camel Man

Tithing House, Tuba City

Bisbee Flood, 1908

San Xavier del Bac

The Granddaddy of Reclamation Projects

The First Good Sam

Miners and Merchants Bank, Bisbee

San Carlos Hotel, Phoenix

Central Avenue, Phoenix, c. 1928

Tovrea Castle

La Posada Station Hotel, Winslow

Hoover Dam Construction

The Initial Point

East of Phoenix International Raceway, near Turn #4, there is a hill often used for hillside seating. Towards the top of the hill is a little known historical monument: a concrete "X" that marks the point where almost all private parcels of land in Arizona are surveyed from.

In late 1851, as part of a reconnaissance survey for the US-Mexican border under the 1848 Treaty of Guadalupe-Hidalgo, a survey party led by Andrew B. Gray and Lieutenant A. W. Whipple climbed this hill and built a circular monument with an eight-foot base made of nearby rocks. This original monument tapered upward to a height of eight feet with a four foot diameter at the top. A wooden pole, six feet high, was erected in the center and marked "United States and Mexico Boundary Commission, 1851." In 1865, John A. Clark, Surveyor General for New Mexico and Arizona, selected this monument as the initial point for future surveys in Arizona.

In January of 1867, William Pierce climbed the same hill with a seven-member survey crew. They had just crossed the Gila River that was over 200 feet wide and three-to-four feet deep to get to the point that would become the intersection of Avondale Blvd (115th Avenue) and Baseline Road. His field notes indicate, "I proceeded to perpetuate this corner [the center of the monument] as follows: I squared the post and marked it as a TP [township] corner."

Pierce had a contract for "the survey of certain lands in Arizona for the sum not to exceed seventy-five hundred dollars." His job was to mark off townships, six-mile square units that would be used to sell land. A township would usually be divided into 36 mile-square units called sections; each section had 640 acres. A section could then be further subdivided into quarter sections of 160 acres. The Homestead Act of 1862 called for a quarter section of public land to be given to each qualified settler who agreed to certain conditions.

Pierce's first order of business was to establish an east-west base line and a north-south meridian. He began at the Initial Point and surveyed a line 36 miles due east.

Much of this would later become Baseline Road. Pierce and his crew accomplished this task in just five days using a solar compass to determine direction and a 33-foot chain to measure distance (160 chain lengths equals one mile). They had to measure levelly over uneven terrain, rivers, through brush and other obstacles. They completed the east-west line in five days, and their efforts took them all the way to what is now called Power Road.

After measuring off the east-west line, Pierce returned to the Initial Point and began to survey a Prime Meridian for Arizona, a line that was to run 96 miles, or 16 townships, due north. This would be a point about 15 miles north of what is now Prescott Valley and halfway between Paulden and Jerome. Pierce was not to finish surveying the meridian, for in late February 1867 he asked for and received a release from his contract due to an impending Indian uprising which led him to fear for the safety of his survey crew.

Pierce wrote in his field notes that the Salt River, "at this season of the year, is a large stream … which renders it especially valuable for irrigation. I consider this valley … as containing some of the best agriculture land I have yet seen in the territory, and would recommend that it be subdivided at an early date."

Over the years, the Initial Point monument fell into disrepair through age and vandalism. Even though more than 62 million acres of Arizona had been surveyed from this point, it was largely forgotten.

In 1984, a statewide group of surveyors took it upon themselves to refurbish the monument. In an effort to preserve the history of this truly remarkable point, they placed a plaque on the monument that reads: "Dedicated to all land owners in Arizona by the Arizona Professional Land Surveyors." The monument stands precisely at 33 degrees, 22 hours, 37 minutes north latitude and 112 degrees, 18 hours, 20 minutes west longitude.

— *Mike Miller*

Originally published: October 21, 2005

Surveyors in northern Arizona, c. 1915.

Historical photo courtesy of the National Oceanic and Atmospheric Administration Central Library

Photo courtesy of the Arizona Professional Land Surveyors Association.

The Great Falls on the Arizona Canal

The Arizona Canal, the Salt River Valley's most important irrigation channel, was dug between 1883 and 1885. Thereafter, land and railroad promotional publicity aimed at prospective Valley settlers often featured imaginative drawings of the waterway and "the Falls on the Arizona Canal."

In a widely circulated advertising map drawn by C.J. Dyer (see opposite), called a "Bird's Eye View of Phoenix," the falls are shown in one corner. The canal bank appears to be at least 50 feet high and there is a correspondingly exaggerated fall of water. In another corner, Dyer included a fanciful drawing of the head of the Arizona Canal. Thus, an unwary Midwestern recipient of Mr. Dyer's map might have been forgiven for assuming that the new magic of irrigation was making Phoenix and its adjoining desert the beneficiaries of a conflux of water the size of the Mississippi at spring flood.

The truth was that the falls were but 12 feet high and the water in the canal only six feet deep, a mere trickle for anyone raised on a real river. Nonetheless, in those early years in a desert country, the falls were well worth a half-day's buggy ride to see. The family pictured in the top photograph probably made a social outing of the trip and had a picnic lunch when they arrived. What is left of the falls can be seen in the bottom photo. It is a short distance northeast of the intersection of 56th Street and Indian School Road, where the now abandoned concrete powerhouse diverts the canal just west of Herberger Park.

— *Arizona News Service*

Editor's Addendum

Not only did Dyer use artistic license in rendering the Falls, his prose was similarly exaggerated. Nevertheless, he accurately predicts that Phoenix will become the "leading city in Arizona."

The town is embowered in shade trees and shrubbery, has streams of living water through every street, is surrounded by orchards, gardens and vineyards, and is one of the handsomest in the West. The streets face the cardinal points, are broad and spacious and lined with trees. The County Courthouse, in the center of a square and surrounded by trees, is a handsome two-story brick, surmounted by a tower. The School House is a large and commodious brick structure, of two stories, almost hidden in a cottonwood grove. The Methodists, Baptists, and Catholics have tasteful places of worship. There are several large mercantile establishments, a steam flouring mill with daily capacity of 180 barrels, two ice factories and a planing mill. The Odd Fellows, Masons Workmen, Knights of Pythias, Good Templars and Chosen Friends have flourishing organizations. Two newspapers, the Herald and Gazette have daily and weekly editions. … Snow never falls and roses are in bloom in December. Phoenix is the center of an extensive and fertile valley almost 50 miles in length by 10 in width, and containing over 300,000 acres. Every variety of grain, grasses, fruits and vegetables give a prolific yield. For fruits, grape culture and wine making the soil and climate are especially adapted. Everything is grown by irrigation. Eight canals convey the water from the Salt river over the land. The Arizona canal is one of the largest works of this kind in the United States; it is over 40 miles in length, 80 feet wide on the bottom and 58 feet on the top, is 7 feet deep. It has reclaimed and made valuable over 100,000 acres of rich land. … The Territorial Insane Asylum is situated near the town, also the extensive and beautiful grounds of the Arizona Industrial Exposition. The Normal school is situated nine miles up the river. A branch road from the Southern Pacific will be completed to Phoenix by January 1, 1886. The town is rapidly growing, and its charming situation will yet make it the leading city of Arizona. Population about 3,500.

Originally published: July 1, 1981

Historical photo from the Arizona News Service Archives; modern photo by Bill Coates, Arizona Capitol Times

Stevens Homestead, Tucson

This is Hiram Sanford Stevens, a native of Vermont who came to Arizona in 1854 after a stint with the First United States Dragoons in New Mexico. He saw action against the Apaches in 1852 and 1854. The portrait was taken in 1875 when he served as territorial delegate to Congress.

During the intervening years, Stevens was a rancher, merchant, professional gambler and politician. He was elected to the Arizona Territorial House of Representatives in 1868 and served in the Territorial Council between 1871 and 1873. Before going off to Washington, he was successively elected Pima County assessor and supervisor.

He married Petra Santa Cruz, whose father and grandfather were born within the Tucson Presidio walls and had homesteaded the property shown in the other photograph. Stevens is the man on the right, nearest the corner of the building. The man next to him is his brother-in-law, Sammie Hughes. The homestead was located between Main and Court streets. At the time this photo was taken in the 1880s, Stevens was one of the richest men in the territory.

He had an interest in horticulture, and over the years his property became a kind of experimental agricultural station for all kinds of trees and shrubs. When he first arrived in Tucson there wasn't a tree in the city. By 1875, there were three pepper trees — two at the Elks Club and one at his home. The next year, Bermuda grass seed was imported from San Diego and planted at the corner of Court and Alameda as an experiment. With a little water, the grass thrived and soon several Tucson homes had lawns.

Stevens imported 25 trees from Kansas City in 1878. Most were mulberries, but there were a few figs, peaches, cherries and roses, as well as flowering shrubs. Only the mulberries survived. (We guess they are the trees behind the house.) The task of irrigating plants with hand-drawn well water (from a fifty-foot well) began to be too arduous, and Stevens sent for a windmill, the first in the Territory (at right in the photograph), which was bought in Indiana and freighted to Tucson by wagon. It was a delight and a curiosity to Tucson pioneers.

Having solved his irrigation problems, he sent once more for planting stock. This time he had success again with figs and roses. Pears, olives, grapes, pomegranates, English walnut and pecan also thrived. However, the peaches were hit by parasites, and the cherry trees died when their taproots struck calcite.

Several years later, Stevens' business ventures began to suffer reverses, and he fell on hard times. A prolonged drought killed off most of his cattle and destroyed his personal fortune. On March 21, 1893, despondent over his financial ruin, he tried to kill his wife and then put a bullet through his brain.

Today the area of the Stevens homestead is part of the Tucson Museum of Art Complex, which includes the Fish-Stevens house, the Cordoba house and the Romero house.

— *Jane Eppinga*

Originally published: March 2, 1988

Photo courtesy of the Library of Congress

Photo courtesy of the Arizona Historical Society, Tucson

The Scott Farm, 1892

On July 2, 1888, U.S. Army Chaplain Winfield Scott founded what today is Scottsdale, Arizona. That was the day he had an agent in Tucson file a claim and make an initial down payment of 50 cents per acre on 640 acres of land just below the Arizona Canal near the intersection of Indian School and Scottsdale roads. There he built the farm house and buildings pictured to the right.

Because the parcel was bought under the Desert Lands Act of 1877, he was required to irrigate the property once within the first three years of acquiring it. The Arizona Canal, which had been completed in 1885, crossed the north section of the land and diverted water from the Salt River to the area. Scott was able to irrigate all but 40 acres north of the canal. Those he relinquished, leaving him with title to 600 acres of patented land after final payment of two dollars an acre. He planted some of the first citrus groves in the Salt River Valley, and with his brother grew sweet potatoes and peanuts. However, the cost of delivering water to the crops was high. To cover expenses, he later sold some of his property to William Murphy, the builder of the Arizona Canal.

In 1894, a neighbor to the south unveiled plans to subdivide 40 acres into a town site and asked Chaplain Scott to take charge. The new town was originally called Orangedale, but the name was soon changed to Scottsdale, in honor of Scott.

He proved to be an able promoter and a hardworking community leader. Because he had a love of music and his wife, Helen, was an artist and poet, he attracted artists and musicians, as well as other clergymen to the new community.

He left a lasting influence on the city. In 1910, from his deathbed he wrote the following testament to the people of Scottsdale: "My dear Neighbors and Friends, I leave to you my work in Scottsdale. If you take this work and do it, and enlarge it as God gives you strength, you will receive my blessing and His, the blessing which maketh rich, and God addeth no sorrow with it."

The Scott farm was in what is now the center of modern, downtown Scottsdale. A statue of Scott near the northeast corner of Scottsdale Rd. and Indian School marks the approximate spot of the original ranch house.

— *Arizona Capitol Times*

Originally published: June 29, 1988

Photo courtesy of the Scottsdale Historical Society

Hi Jolly: The Camel Man

When the U.S. Army sent the first survey crews to northern Arizona in 1857 to survey a wagon road along the 35th parallel, it included in the contingent a herd of approximately 30 camels. The dromedaries were the brainchild of then-Secretary of War Jefferson Davis, who believed the camels could solve the Army's transport problems in the arid Southwest. In 1856, as many as 44 camels were procured from the Middle East along with eight camel drivers. One of the drivers was the fellow in this photograph. His name was Hadji Ali, but soldiers and civilians alike knew him as Hi Jolly. He had signed on at a salary of $15 a month. Tales of gold strikes no doubt lured him, too, and he was eager to come to the U.S. and make his fortune.

He became the lead camel driver on Edward Fitzgerald Beale's wagon road survey group. Despite some successes, the camel experiment was ultimately a failure. Donkeys, mules and horses were freightened of the much taller and strongly odoriferous animals. Soldiers also complained that the camels were ill-tempered and mean, claiming the animals would wait until the soldiers' backs were turned and then they would spit on them. In the 1940s, an old prospector said that Hi Jolly told him, "those camels were lonesome for the caravans of their home country, and every time they sighted a prospector's mule train they'd make a break for it."

The camel experiment continued until 1861, when the Civil War turned the attention of the Army to other matters. Some of the animals were sold and others were abandoned. Most of the drivers returned to their homelands, but Hi Jolly stayed on, acquired some of the camels and started a freight business hauling goods from Colorado River ports to mining camps in Mohave and Yuma counties. He also carried cargo from Yuma to Tucson. That business failed, and he released his camels into the desert to fend for themselves. He spent the next dozen years or so working for the military and prospecting for gold.

In 1880, at the age of 52, he became an American citizen, using the name Philip Tedro. That same year he married Gertrudis Serna of Tucson, shown in the photo in her wedding finery. He gave his nationality as Greek, probably because his bride was Catholic and he knew the church would not sanction a marriage to a Muslim.

The couple had two daughters, but in 1889 he deserted his family and returned to prospecting. Ten years later he became ill, came back to Tucson and asked to see Gertrudis and his children. She visited him briefly but refused his bid for a reconciliation. His final years were spent in Quartzsite, supported in part by his friends. He died in the desert in 1902, searching for a wild camel. His body was returned to Quartzsite for burial.

In 1935, the Arizona Highway Department marked his grave with a pyramid-shaped moument of native quartz and petrified wood. A casting of a camel stands atop the monument, and a large steel plaque mounted on one side reads: "Last Camp of Hi Jolly."

The last wild camel in Arizona was captured in 1946, and the last reported sightings of camels in North American occurred in Baja, California in 1956.

— *Jane Eppinga and Jim Turner*

Originally published: June 18, 2004

Photos courtesy of the Arizona Historical Society, Tucson

Tithing House, Tuba City

Navajo Indian agent, Leo Crane, identified this sandstone building as the Mormon tithing house in Tuba City. At the turn of the century, about 20 Mormon families lived in the Tuba City, Moenkopi Wash, Reservoir Wash and Moenave areas of northern Arizona. The families farmed and raised livestock and followed the church practice of tithing — giving one tenth of the increase in their income or goods each year to the church.

Families paid their tithing in wheat, flour, eggs, cattle and similar goods, or in work dedicating each tenth day to service for the church community, building roads, irrigation ditches, schools and church buildings. The tithing house was used to store foodstuffs, which were given out to those in need.

In one town, the following items were donated to the tithing house in one week: 12 eggs, 13-1/2 lbs. of meal, 6 lbs. of beef, 4-1/4 lbs. of butter and 34 lbs. of flour. The following items were given out by the bishop: 12 eggs, 13 lbs. of meal, 3-1/4 lbs. of pork, 34 lbs. of flour and 6 lbs. of beef.

In 1900, the federal government forced out the settlers in order to expand the Navajo Reservation. Only a few of the white settlers had clear title to the land; they were allowed to stay. Charles H. Algert, a young Pennsylvanian, who had been a trader at Canyon Diablo before opening a post in Tuba City, kept his trading post. Sam Preston, then training as a trader with Algert, also stayed. Two missionaries from the Gospel Union of Kansas City, Missouri, who lived half way between Tuba City and Moenkopi at a woolen mill, were also allowed to stay.

The remaining families had only squatters' possessory rights to the land, and they were forced to move. They were paid for their improvements, which included fruit trees, shade trees, irrigation ditches, drainage ditches, water rights, homes, chicken coops, corrals, wells and grapevines. One farmer was paid for nine Balm of Gilead trees. In all, the settlers were paid a total of $45,000.

In 1905, Algert sold his land and trading post to the Babbitt family of Flagstaff. Sam Preston, who by then was an experienced trader with the Navajos and Hopis, was retained as a partner and manager. He worked there for many years. Algert moved on to the Blue Canyon area and continued to work as a trader.

— *Bonnie Greer*

Originally published: March 25, 1994

Photo courtesy of the Special Collections, Cline Library, Northern Arizona University

Bisbee Flood, 1908

This is Main Street in Bisbee in August 1908, during one of the worst months of flooding in the town's history. In a three-week period, Bisbee was ravaged by three separate storms.

The first storm struck on August 4. The *Bisbee Daily Review* described it this way: "Bisbee was visited by a rain and cloudburst yesterday afternoon that did between $15,000 to $20,000 damage to property, wrecked the Post Office, (and) swamped the stores and saloons. A cloudburst and landslide from the mountainside back of Main Street was the cause of the damage.... Fifteen hundred to two thousand tons of rock washed behind businesses ... (At the Post Office) many letters floated away when the storm was at its worst and records of the office are covered with several feet of debris. The registered mail is also buried."

That is the Post Office on the corner in the photograph. The town library occupied the second floor of the building. At one point during the storm, water was flowing through the second story and pouring off the balcony onto Main Street. Fortunately the building's third floor was undamaged and provided temporary headquarters for the Post Office while repairs were being made.

The town had just started to dig out when a second storm hit on August 11. That one brought more rain but less damage. The *Review* headlined it, "Flood Again Hits Bisbee, Post Office Again Damaged, Second Time During The Week."

That was followed by two weeks of relative calm and then the knockout punch. On August 24, a third storm dumped more than two inches of rain in less than an hour. The wooden subways built to channel rainwater down Tombstone Canyon and under the businesses along Main Street gave way. Ten thousand dollars of damage was done to city property, and damage to homes and businesses exceeded $25,000.

That storm encouraged the city fathers to find a permanent solution to flooding. In 1909, a new subway channel was built of concrete and large timbers. It is still in use today. Combined with several small dams built above town during the 1930s, the channel has since prevented any serious flooding on Main Street.

— *Tom Vaughan*

Orignally published: August 5, 1987

Photo courtesy of the Bisbee Mining & Historical Museum

San Xavier del Bac, c. 1910

San Xavier del Bac, a few miles south of Tucson, is among the best preserved and most beautiful of the Spanish missions in North America. Today it looks virtually the same as it did when this photo was taken almost a century ago when the building, then already more than 110 years old, had recently been restored. The corncobs surrounding the Indian women in the foreground suggest the picture was taken at harvest time.

"Bac," an old Pima word for "well," was the name of the Indian settlement in this area that the Jesuit missionary Eusebio Francisco Kino first visited in 1692. He renamed the village for his patron saint, the famous missionary St. Francis Xavier, one of the original Jesuits, who had died 140 years before. On April 28, 1700, Father Kino laid the foundation of the first San Xavier, about two miles from the present building.

The original mission was abandoned several times because of Apache attacks and was severely damaged in a Pima revolt in 1751. When the Jesuits were expelled from the Spanish colonial domain in 1767, the Franciscans took over, and when the Spanish missionary Francisco Garces arrived in 1768, he made San Xavier his headquarters.

The Apache raids continued, but the Franciscans were undeterred, and in 1783 they began construction on the present church.

It took 14 years to build (the incomplete dome is a mystery to this day), and even after its completion, Indian depredations, plagues and crop failures brought periods of distress made even more difficult by a lack of military or church intervention. The mission was abandoned about 1823 when church lands were secularized during the Mexican control of the area. The mission was re-occupied in 1857, after the Gadsden Purchase.

By 1900, the mission had fallen into disrepair — judging from one account that says dormitories and one tower were nearly destroyed and the mortuary chapel was obliterated. In 1906, Bishop Granjon of Tucson undertook restoration, with the help of the Tohono O'Odham Indians (who were then referred to as Papago). Much of the cost of restoration was borne by Bishop Granjon himself.

Today San Xavier del Bac is still an active parish.

— *Joan Metzger*

Originally published: October 8, 1986

Photo courtesy of the Arizona Historical Society, Tucson

The Granddaddy of the Reclamation Projects

This is Roosevelt Dam, the oldest reclamation dam in the U.S. It was completed in 1911 and named for President Theodore Roosevelt, who was so pleased with his namesake, he made a trip out West for the dedication.

The dam was rededicated in 1996 after a five-year, $430 million construction project that added 77 vertical feet to the dam and expanded storage capacity by 20 percent. (See lower photo) Also, the project added flood control storage space for the first time.

Roosevelt Dam was an engineering wonder when it was completed in 1911. It was the highest masonry dam in the world, stretching more than a 1,000 feet across the mouth of the Salt River Canyon. Roosevelt Lake held 1.3 million acre-feet of water before the modifications, which added another 300,000 acre-feet of water-storage capacity and 557,000 acre-feet of dedicated flood-control space.

In the top photograph, taken shortly after construction was completed, the lake is filling behind the dam and the hand-cut blocks that face the dam are visible. The blocks were cut from the canyon walls by Italian stonecutters brought to the U.S. to work on the dam. The blocks weighed between six and ten tons each and were laid in a mix of mortar and large boulders, using a building method known as modified cyclopean rubble construction. Altogether, the masons cut 350,000 cubic yards of stone and used 350,000 barrels of cement to lay the blocks in place.

With the completion of the dam and the Salt River Project water delivery system, farmers in the Salt River Valley finally had an assured water supply. Cultivated acreage in the valley doubled, and Phoenix, then a city of 11,000 inhabitants, began to grow.

Today, Phoenix is the fifth largest city in the nation with a 2007 Census Bureau estimated population of 1,552,259. Roosevelt Dam is the largest single source of water for the metropolitan area.

This photograph is from the collection of C.W. Pomeroy, a relative of former State Rep. Bill Lewis's wife. Each week, Mr. Pomeroy took the train from Phoenix to Mesa and the stage up the Apache Trail to the dam site to deliver the payroll. He sent postcards and photographs to his relatives to share the wonders of the construction project he was witnessing, telling them, "You can't see the greatness of all these things in the picture."

— *Arizona Capitol Times*

Originally published: April 12, 1996

Photo courtesy of the Library of Congress

Photo courtesy of the Salt River Project

The First Good Sam

This is the original Good Samaritan Hospital of Phoenix — an apartment house on Third Avenue south of Van Buren Street.

The hospital was founded by Miss Lulu I. Clifton, a Methodist Deaconess who suffered from tuberculosis and came to Phoenix in early 1900 for her health. Her doctors advised against the trip, fearing she could not survive such a difficult journey. She not only survived but had enough stamina to gather together a group of Methodist men and begin planning the first hospital in Phoenix.

It was incorporated as the Arizona Deaconess Hospital and Home on October 13, 1911. The original incorporators were: G.H. Adams, Arizona's first Presiding Elder of the Methodist Episcopal Church; S.J. Rogers, Presiding Elder; Robert S. Fisher, Pastor of the First Methodist Episcopal Church; Lloyd B. Christy, layman and banker; and H.B. Wilkinson, layman and attorney.

The incorporators rented this building, the Carol Apartments, and were able to provide the city with 15 hospital beds. Immediately, the Board of Directors began planning for a permanent building. In 1917 they bought the property on Tenth Street and McDowell where the hospital stands today. Construction started that year, was interrupted by World War I, and was finally completed in 1923 when the hospital was moved from the apartments to its new quarters. Five years later the name was changed to Good Samaritan Hospital which is now part of the Banner Health system.

The apartment building was torn down in 1969.

The bottom photo from 1981 shows the tower under construction.

— *Arizona Capitol Times*

Originally published: March 11, 1981

Photos courtesy of Banner Good Samaritan Hospital

Miners and Merchants Bank, Bisbee

This is the interior of the Miners and Merchants Bank on Bisbee's Main Street around 1925. The bank had incorporated as an Arizona bank on June 12, 1900, with a capitalization of $50,000. Founding directors were Bisbee merchants L.C. Shattuck, Joseph Muheim, L.J. Overlock, Jakob Schmidt and J.T. Hood.

One of the first steps the founders took was to build a vault of concrete and iron with twenty-two inch thick walls. Next they installed a Mosier patent screw door bank safe, state of the art in preventing burglaries. It weighed several thousand pounds and was built of the finest steel. The round door contained a Yale & Towne three-movement time lock, which locked by means of steel threads that moved from the door to the vault. The design of the door without the usual hinges prevented bank robbers from using explosives to blow off the hinges and force the door open, one of the easiest ways to break into a safe in those days.

The bank was first located in a saloon building on the south side of Main Street. By 1904, however, the owners had purchased the Anheuser Saloon on the north side of Main Street, demolished the building and replaced it with an entirely new building that opened the following year. The address was 7 Main Street.

The bank expanded yearly during the early part of the century, and soon became the largest bank in Cochise County and fifth largest in the Arizona Territory. Besides the usual loans, payroll and savings, the bank added a trust department that managed trusts, life insurance and other fiduciary matters for customers.

By the 1920s, the bank had expanded its quarters again, acquiring the Hoffman Saloon to the west and using that space for its vault. That was about the time this photograph was taken.

The bank remained an independent Bisbee institution until 1956, when it merged with First National Bank of Arizona. The new bank again expanded, taking over the Bisbee Drug Store next door. But throughout all the additions and moves, one artifact survived: the original Miners and Merchants brass logo above the door. That artifact is still there today.

Throughout all the years as the Miners and Merchants Bank, there was never a robbery or hold-up at the bank. However, as First Interstate (the successor to First National) the bank suffered Bisbee's first bank robbery. In the mid-1980s, a man brandished a pistol at employees and customers and ran off with an undisclosed amount of cash. He surrendered to the Bisbee police a short time later.

First Interstate closed the Bisbee branch in the early 1990s before the merger with Wells Fargo. The building currently houses office and retail space.

—*Tom Vaughan*

Originally published: June 11, 1993

Photo courtesy of the Bisbee Mining and Historical Society

Hotel San Carlos, Phoenix

This is the Hotel San Carlos on the corner of Monroe and Central in downtown Phoenix as it looked when it opened for business in March 1928. Behind it is the Security Building under construction. The cars massed on the street are awaiting the start of a parade to Riverside Park for the annual pioneer's reunion.

The San Carlos had just been completed when this photograph was made. The hotel was built by Charles Harris and was the first high-rise, fully air-conditioned, elevator-equipped hotel in the Southwest.

It was a long time coming, however. The property had been vacant for more than a decade when construction began. The block had been the site of Phoenix's first school, a small one-story adobe built in 1874. That structure was replaced in 1879 with a two-story brick building of four rooms with a bell tower. In 1893, the schoolhouse was expanded to 16 rooms, and this structure continued to serve the school children of Phoenix for almost a quarter century.

By 1916, however, the building was beginning to fall apart and became unsafe. It was condemned, and the property was put up for sale.

The first buyer planned a large nine-story hotel of 300 rooms, but that scheme never materialized. Finally, near the end of the boom decade of the twenties, the San Carlos was built. The Security Building and Westward Ho, as well as the Luhrs Tower, were also built in those years.

The San Carlos opened to great fanfare. It was seven stories high, with 175 luxuriously appointed rooms. There was a restaurant — the Palm Room — an outdoor sun room, dancing and card rooms and a coffee shop on the main floor. There was circulating ice water in every room, and "automatic cooled air, changed in each room every three minutes." The hotel also had its own well, which had existed on the site since the time of the first schoolhouse.

For several decades the hotel was a major Phoenix attraction, and celebrities such as Clark Gable, Spencer Tracy and Carole Lombard stayed there.

Today, the San Carlos is the only historic hotel still being operated as a hotel in the downtown Phoenix area. (The Westward Ho is a retirement home; the Adams was demolished in the 1970s and a new hotel built on the site; the Jefferson was converted to an office building; and the Luhrs Hotel was demolished in 1981 and never replaced.)

Early in 2008, a representative of the Melikian family, which has owned the San Carlos for 35 years, said the family was interested in finding a "partner" to take over day-to-day operations of the hotel. Meanwhile, the owners have continued to restore and refurbish the property. The Palm Room restaurant has been replaced by the Copper Door, but it still serves its famous French onion soup. The well is still in working order though not in current use. The Melikians also own and have refurbished historic properties in downtown Tucson and in Scottsdale.

— *Arizona Capitol Times*

Originally published: January 9, 1991

Photo and research courtesy of the Melikian family

Award of Merit

— Phoenix Mayor Phil Gordon

I have always loved this photograph of downtown Phoenix. Not only does it feature the historic Hotel San Carlos, which celebrates its 80th anniversary this year, but it depicts the "hustle and bustle" of a central city. In this photograph, the activity was created by an annual parade. Today, of course, the activity downtown is increasing and will remain constant — due to universities, sporting venues, restaurants, museums, residential and retail. I love our history, but I am excited about our future.

Central Avenue, Phoenix c. 1928

The top photograph of Central Avenue in the 1920s shows the famous ash trees planted by pioneer developer William J. Murphy. The middle photo, taken in 1903, is of the home he built on Central in the Orangewood subdivsion, far north of the Phoenix city limits.

The ash trees, along with a row of olives, flanked Central Avenue from Bethany Home Road all the way to the Arizona Canal above Northern Avenue.

Murphy planted avenue trees all over the Salt River Valley both to promote his subdivisions and for his own pleasure. His son once figured he had planted 32 miles of trees during the years he was building subdivisions.

Murphy was a visionary who saw the potential for growth in the Valley of the Sun when it was still a sparsely populated desert.

In 1882, he secured the contract to build the Arizona Canal and sought financing for the project, traveling to Chicago, New York and Europe to find investors for his canal bonds.

In 1887, he and a group of associates created the Arizona Improvement Company, which began development of five areas: Glendale, Peoria, Marinette (in the Sun City area), Orangewood and Ingleside.

The Orangewood subdivision was laid out along Central Avenue north of present-day Glendale Avenue. Ingleside was developed south of the Arizona Canal between 56th and 60th streets.

Murphy built his own home on ten acres on the west side of Central Avenue across from what is today Orangewood Avenue.

While awaiting completion of the canal, he and a worker irrigated the ash trees by hand from a horse-drawn water tank. The path he used between the trees gradually came to be used for pleasure riding. In 1895, he dedicated a bridle path on the east side of Central Avenue and a 100-foot right-of-way to the Central Avenue Driving Association.

Murphy died in 1923, but he left a lasting legacy. In the 1940s, the Arizona Horse Lovers Club dedicated the bridle path to Murphy. Some 20 years later, the club prevailed on the city of Phoenix to maintain it and keep its unpaved character.

The home Murphy built on Central Avenue was designated a historic site by the Phoenix Historic Commission in the 1990s. The front yard, where the croquet game took place, has been subdivided, and new homes now block the view of the historic house from Central Avenue.

The ash trees Murphy planted along Central grew old and were finally removed in the 1970s. The city of Phoenix, after some prodding by Arizona horsemen and homeowners in the area, agreed to replace the trees, and the character of the street was maintained.

Murphy's Maricopa Bridle Path (bottom photo) is now a popular jogging and walking path.

— *Arizona Capitol Times*

Originally published: December 12, 2001

The above photos are courtesy of the State Library and Archives
and Arizona Historical Society, Phoenix

Photo by Bill Coates, Arizona Capitol Times

Tovrea Castle

This is Alessio Carraro (right) and his son, Leo, in front of the home they built on a knoll near Washington and 56th Street — the three-story Moorish looking-structure that Phoenicians call Tovrea Castle.

Alessio was an Italian immigrant who settled in San Francisco in 1906. He became a successful businessman, land developer and investor, and according to Leo was always adventurous. That may be why in 1928 he sold his San Francisco sheet metal business and moved to Phoenix. He bought 277 acres of desert between Van Buren and the Salt River, east of 40th Street, and planned to construct a luxurious resort hotel. At the time, 16th Street was the eastern boundary of Phoenix, and Van Buren was the only road to Tempe. Alessio believed that the hotel would attract the development of homes and businesses, allowing the city's boundaries to expand.

Alessio and Leo Carraro originally constructed the castle to be a resort hotel, but instead it became the home of Ed and Della Tovrea. Today, it is a Phoenix historic landmark undergoing a major renovation.

Without blueprints, Alessio, his son and a crew started work on the hotel. It took the shape of a three-tiered castle, complete with metal-covered parapets and battlements, and topped by a metal covered dome. It was built of lath and stucco, (the lath walls are visible behind the Carraros in the photograph) and river rock was hauled from the Salt River bed at 40th Street to be used for walls, landscaping, fountains and pools. A forest of saguaros and 300 species of cacti and other desert vegetation were planted around the hotel to create a spectacular garden.

Many of the materials used inside the castle were recycled. The maple flooring came from a recently demolished Phoenix home, mahogany and oak kitchen cabinets were salvaged from the Phoenix National Bank and a vault from the bank was transformed into the castle's wine cellar.

After all the planting and construction was completed, Alessio lived in the hotel for only six months. Shortly after he moved in, Ed Tovrea, owner of the nearby Tovrea Packing Co., purchased 40 acres adjacent to the hotel and began building sheep pens. The smelly sheep, coupled with the first stages of the Depression, made Alessio realize his idea for a resort hotel and a housing development was not viable. He sold the hotel and gardens to Ed and Della Tovrea in 1931 for $21,500, and the hotel became the Tovreas' home.

After the sale, Alessio and his son worked as miners in the Huachuca Mountains for a time. Alessio later became a successful "water witcher" and was hired to find wells in Arizona and California. He retired at age 75, moved to Yarnell and spent his remaining years building trails and rock walls for his own pleasure. The Desert View Lookout on Yarnell Hill was one of his projects. Leo opened the Liberty Buffet at 19th St. and Van Buren and spent the rest of his working years in the hotel business.

After Ed Tovrea purchased the castle, he lived in it for only a year before dying in 1932. Della Tovrea later remarried and used the home when she and her husband, William Stuart, publisher of the *Prescott Courier*, came to Phoenix. Stuart died in 1960, and his wife returned to the castle and lived there until her death in 1969.

Over the years, Della made improvements to the castle's grounds. She put in a reflecting pool, planted a rose garden, constructed a massive patio with a fire pit, built an aviary for her bird collection, and installed electric lights and concrete urns throughout the property. Della also brought in peacocks to roam the grounds. Della died at the age of 80, two months after being badly beaten by burglars who had broken into the castle and made off with $50,000 in cash, silver and jewels.

In 1993, Phoenix purchased the landmark castle and about 7.5 acres of the surrounding land in an effort to restore the castle and gardens. Since then, the city has purchased additional acreage, and in 2001, voters approved a bond issue that allowed the city to purchase the remaining land and continue restoration efforts. In 2003, Phoenix purchased an additional 15.6 acres, and former Phoenix Mayor John Driggs was appointed to manage fund raising efforts for the $12 million restoration project.

The building and grounds are scheduled to be rededicated and open to the public in February 2009.

— *Arizona Capitol Times*

Originally published: March 16, 1988

Photo courtesy of the Arizona Historical Society.

La Posada Station Hotel, Winslow c. 1930

This is La Posada station hotel in Winslow, as it appeared to train passengers in the 1930s. It was operated by concessionaire Fred Harvey, designed by architect and artist Mary Colter, and was one of the most expensive hotel projects undertaken by the Santa Fe Railroad. It was also one of the last of the southwest railroad hotels built as overnight stopovers on the Santa Fe line. (La Posada means resting place in Spanish.)

The hotel was designed and decorated in the style of a Spanish landowner's hacienda, with red tile roofs, pale pink walls, handmade furniture and elaborate gardens. Mary Colter was known to thrive on an assignment that allowed her to create not only a functional hotel, but an image of a time past as well. Romantic balconies overlooked verdant lawns and trees that formed an oasis out of the site that had once been the location of the railroad roundhouse. Tourists came by rail to relax at the hotel and to take in the local sights — the Hopi Villages, Petrified Forest and Painted Desert — on tours conducted by the Harvey staff.

The hotel had 70 guest rooms and several suites. All the rooms had special beds built to Colter's specifications and shipped to Winslow to be antiqued at the workshops on the hotel grounds. Some rooms featured New Mexico-style beehive fireplaces, and all the hallways were finished in a special linoleum that was quiet to walk on but had the look and feeling of Mexican tile.

The striking design of the lounge and dining room became the talk of northern Arizona. Large murals decorated the walls. Handmade and antique furniture, including church pews and altar candles imported from Mexican churches, gave authenticity to the Spanish theme. Niches were carved for two patron saints: San Ysidro of the Inn and San Pasqual, saint of feasts.

The hotel soon became the epitome of Fred Harvey tradition, providing comfortable sleeping accommodations for travelers and serving tourists and railroad employees elegant and hearty food in attractive surroundings. Local groups also made the hotel a popular spot; bridge clubs from Flagstaff would take the train to Winslow just to play cards for the day.

La Posada closed to the public in the early 1960s, a victim of the rise of auto travel and motels. For a time it served as the division offices of the Santa Fe railroad. But in 1994 the railroad announced it would demolish the building. UC-Irvine graduate student Allan Affeldt heard of the impending wrecking ball, visited the old hotel and fell in love with the place. It took three years for him and his wife, artist Tina Mion, to complete the purchase. In 1997 they actually moved into the abandoned 80,000 square foot, 37 room hotel and were its only residents for more than a year. They literally restored the hotel one room at a time. La Posada reopened in 1998, and Affeldt is still busy with renovation projects, always trying to make Mary Colter's original vision come alive.

— *Joan Brundige-Baker*

Originally published: January 10, 1990

Photo courtesy of Special Collections, Cline Library, Northern Arizona University

Hoover Dam Construction

This photograph of Hoover Dam was probably taken about 1935 when construction of the dam was almost complete. It took five years — from 1931 to 1936 — to build what was then the largest concrete dam in the world. It was built in the Black Canyon of the Colorado River, in northwestern Arizona on the border with Nevada.

The Lumberjack bus in the foreground had brought a group of students from Northern Arizona State Teacher's College in Flagstaff for a view of the huge project before the lake began to fill behind the dam. The bus is parked on the Arizona side of the river. Nevada is across the gorge.

The building of Hoover Dam was one of the first steps in the U.S. Bureau of Reclamation's long-running effort to harness the Colorado River and divide the water among the Western states it traveled through. Originally called Boulder Dam, it was renamed for president Herbert Hoover in 1948.

As soon as construction was completed in 1936, a power plant was added, and electricity was sold to defray the costs of construction. Even today, much of Las Vegas's famed neon and southern California's millions depends on Hoover Dam electricity.

Hoover is an arch-gravity dam. It rises 726 feet above the Colorado and is 660 feet thick at the base. U.S. Highway 93 curves along the top of the dam, which is 45 feet wide. The public areas of the dam have an art deco style characteristic of the 1930s. Sculptures adorn the elevator towers, and elsewhere there is an emphasis on sleek lines and smooth curves.

Hoover Dam impounds Lake Mead, the world's largest reservoir, which stretches upstream some 110 miles above the dam, all the way to Pierce's Ferry and the edge of Grand Canyon National Park. The lake was named after Dr. Elwood Mead, who was commissioner of the Bureau of Reclamation at the time the dam was built.

As the lake filled behind the dam, it covered the remains of two historic Mormon settlements — Callville and St. Thomas. Callville was the county seat of Pah Ute County, a governmental subdivision that was in existence only from 1865 to 1871, after which it was absorbed into Mohave County.

When the dam was first proposed to President Woodrow Wilson by journalist Anson Smith of the *Mohave County Miner*, he is said to have told the journalist the idea was 50 years ahead of its time. In fact, within 15 years, the dam was completed, as the U.S. government focused on development of the West.

Today, U.S. Route 93 — a major north-south intermountain highway — still uses the top of the dam to cross from Arizona to Nevada. This stretch of road has been plagued by serious traffic congestion for many years. In 2003, construction of a bypass bridge over the gorge was begun. Completion is scheduled for 2010.

— *Joan Brundige-Baker*

Originally published: January 13, 1993

Photo courtesy of Special Collections, Cline Library, Northern Arizona University

Lawmen and Outlaws

Texas John Slaughter: A Legend

To modern eyes, the full-length photograph opposite has an artificial, almost foolish, quality, with its stiffly posed shotgunner, finger carefully off the trigger, standing amid fake ducks and scattered leaves.

But there was nothing artificial or foolish about this man. He is John Horton Slaughter, who came to the Arizona Territory in 1879, when he was 38. He made a fortune and became a legend.

John Slaughter was born in Louisiana in 1841 and moved with his family to Texas when he was just a boy.

When the Civil War began, he enlisted with the Confederacy, but tuberculosis cut his enlistment short. When he recovered his health, he signed with the Texas Rangers, where he spent much of the 1860s.

In 1871, he married a Texas cattle rancher's daughter, Eliza Adeline Harris of San Angelo, and soon was buying and selling cattle all across Texas, New Mexico and Arizona. He also spent considerable time fighting outlaws and cattle rustlers.

He formed a partnership with cattleman Amazon Howell by posting a bond to obtain the release of a herd Howell had bought without a bill of sale. (The bond had been demanded by another legendary figure of the time, New Mexico's territorial governor Lew Wallace, the Civil War Union general who wrote *Ben Hur*.)

Eliza bore four children, but two died. And in 1877, after only six years of marriage, smallpox took Eliza. Slaughter was left a widower with two small children.

Two years later, he courted and married Amazon Howell's beautiful 19 year-old daughter, Viola. They lived for a time in Tularosa, New Mexico, but later moved to Arizona. Our photo may have been taken about that time, though it's hard to say; his unlined face contrasts with the salt-and-pepper moustache.

The Slaughters established a ranch near Hereford in the San Pedro Valley, where they prospered.

By 1884, Slaughter was able to buy the huge San Bernardino land grant of Ignacio Perez. This great ranch spread across 75,000 acres and straddled the Mexico-US border. Apaches had ruled it for years, and as a result, there were virtually no white settlers in the area before Slaughter arrived.

Over the next four decades Slaughter developed the San Bernardino Ranch into an operation that at its peak ran 50,000 head of cattle and employed as many as 500 people — ranch hands, sharecroppers and their families. It was like a little town, with its own store, school and post office. Slaughter became one of the richest and most influential men in the Territory.

Southeastern Arizona in the 1880s was a place and time that has become a movie staple. The tales about the wild lives of the Earps, Clantons, Doc Holliday and their like — most famously the October 1881 gun fight at the O.K Corral — have made them more famous than others, who like Slaughter were much more important to the settling of the West.

Also, the colorful last name aside, Slaughter's personal manner and appearance were not designed for Hollywood. He was quiet and small — just five feet six — but his reputation was such that in 1886 the Democrats who ran Tombstone politics put him up for Cochise County sheriff. He spent six years on the job, earning a reputation as a fearless and effective lawman.

His message to outlaws was straight and simple: "Get out of Cochise County, or I will kill you." That usually did the trick, although unprovable legend says upward of 20 men died at his hands.

He lived to see automobiles, airplanes and the end of the frontier. The portrait shows him as an older man, probably within a decade or so of his death at 86 on February 15, 1922.

— *Arizona Capitol Times*

Originally published: August 23, 2002

Photos courtesy of the Arizona Historical Society, Tucson

Criminal Justice in the Old Pueblo

This is the body of highwayman William Whitney Brazelton propped against a wall on Tucson's Main Street as a warning to anyone planning a career in crime.

Brazelton had been tracked down and killed on August 19, 1878, after having twice robbed the Tucson to Florence stage. That was one of many incidents in a long criminal career that started in New Mexico. Brazelton had moved on to Tucson when the law got too close.

In Tucson, he got a job at the mayor's livery stable and proceeded to bully another employee, David Nemitz, into giving him food, shelter and ammunition. He then began to prey on the stage line. He picked a spot 20 miles outside of Tucson and held up the stage with a Spencer carbine and a pistol. Although both Art Hill, the driver, and John Clum, one of the passengers and the editor of the *Florence Citizen*, were armed, they were no match for the carbine and decided not to fight.

A week later, on August 8, Brazelton did it again. When Hill saw him masked and waiting, he yelled, "There he is again." Brazelton is said to have replied, "Yes ,... here I am again. Now throw up your hands."

Clum was critical of Pima County Sheriff Charles Shibell for losing Brazelton's trail after both holdups. But it turned out that one member of the sheriff's posse was sharp-eyed. Juan Elias noticed that Brazelton's horse had a crooked hoof and tracked him to David Nemitz's place.

Nemitz was arrested and, with a little persuasion, revealed all he knew about Brazelton.

He agreed to set up a supply rendezvous with the wanted man, but did ask that the posse kill Brazelton outright rather than take him prisoner, because he feared Brazleton's revenge.

On the evening of August 19, 1878, Shibell with deputies Bob Leatherwood, Charles O. Brown, Charles T. Etchells and I.E. Brokaw set up an ambush. A short time later, Brazelton approached and gave a pre-arranged signal for Nemitz to come out of hiding. Instead, Shibell and his deputies opened fire, killing Brazelton instantly in a hail of gunfire.

The posse carried the body back to Tucson, where it was propped against a wall and a man named Henry Buehman made this photograph. After a couple of days, when the body began to smell, Brazelton was buried in a pauper's grave.

Buehman's photograph was a popular souvenir. At least one man used it on his personal calling card.

— *Jane Eppinga*

Originally published: July 29, 1992

Photo courtesy of the Arizona Historical Society, Tucson

Tombstone's Deadliest Gunfighter

The larger image, dating to the early 1880s, is the only known photograph of John Peters Ringo, better known as Johnny Ringo and dubbed Tombstone's deadliest gunfighter. The smaller photo is of Wyatt Earp in 1887, five years after Ringo was killed under suspicious circumstances which some say implicate Earp.

Ringo was born March 3, 1850, in Green Fork, Indiana. In 1856, Ringo's family moved to Missouri. Six years later, after two Confederate nightriders were lynched by Union forces on the Ringo farm, his father decided to move the family to San Jose, California, where his in-laws lived.

On the trail to California, Ringo's father died in a gun accident. As he was dismounting from a wagon, his shotgun caught in his bootstrap and discharged, killing him instantly. The family continued on to San Jose, where they lived with Ringo's in-law, Coleman Younger (uncle to the outlaw Younger brothers).

By 1875, he was involved in a Texas ranching dispute between German immigrants and local cattlemen that came to be called the Mason County or Hoodoo War.

In September of that year, he was probably involved in the reprisal murder of Bill Cheyney, who had killed Ringo's close friend, cattleman Moses Baird.

Ringo was never charged with the murder, but three months later he was arrested and charged in Burnet with threatening another man's life. He escaped, was later recaptured and taken to an Austin prison, where he was imprisoned with the famous gunslinger, John Wesley Hardin.

He was eventually acquitted of the charges against him (or they were dropped, the records are not clear), and in 1878, he ran for Constable of Llano County and was elected. He turned up next at a bar in Safford later that year, where he offered a whiskey to a man named Louis Hancock. The man, who was unarmed, declined and said he preferred beer; Ringo then drew his pistol and fired, nicking Hancock's ear. When the case came before a grand jury, Ringo did not appear. He wrote Pima County Sheriff Charles Shibell the following note, explaining why:

"I write this letter to let you know why I can not appear — I got shot through the foot and it is impossible for me to travel for a while. If you get any papers for me, and will let me know, I will attend to them at once as I wish to live here. I do not wish to put you to any unnecessary trouble, nor do I wish to bring extra trouble on myself...."

Apparently, the case was resolved because in 1880, Ringo became a delegate to the Pima County Democratic convention and served as an election official at San Simon.

In early 1881, he was in Tombstone, befriended by the Clantons. He probably avoided the gunfight at the OK Corral in October of that year only because he was visiting his sisters in California.

On December 28, 1881, Virgil Earp was severely wounded by unknown assailants, and Wyatt Earp claimed that Ringo was one of the men responsible. Rumors also circulated that Ringo had been involved in a recent stage robbery.

On January 17, 1882, he confronted Doc Holliday and Wyatt Earp on the street in Tombstone and got into a shouting match. Constable James Flynn stopped the fight and brought the men to police court. Holliday and Ringo each were fined $30. Earp was discharged.

A month later, Morgan Earp was killed while playing pool in Campbell and Hatch's billiard hall. The Earps began a vendetta against anyone they suspected of being involved in Morgan's assassination. Ringo was deputized by Sheriff Johnny Behan, perhaps in an effort to protect Ringo from the Earps by making him a peace officer. Within weeks, most of Ringo's friends were either dead or had been chased out of the area, and although he continued to deny any involvement in the death of Morgan, Ringo felt it expedient to go to California until things cooled down.

In mid-April the Earps left for Colorado, and by July Ringo was back in Tombstone. After a day of heavy drinking with friends near Antelope Springs, Ringo headed towards Sulphur Springs for more whiskey. He was seen in Galeyville on July 9.

On July 14, 1882, Ringo's lifeless body was found seated in the crotch of a large tree. There was a bullet hole in the left side of his head, his boots were missing, his coat had been torn and strips of his shirt had been used to bind his feet. His rifle rested against the tree close to him. In his right hand was a Colt .45 with only one spent shell. Ringo's horse was later found roaming the canyon area with his boots tied across the saddle. The *Tombstone Epitaph* wrote, "Many friends will mourn him. And many others will take secret delight in learning of his death."

A coroner's jury ruled Ringo's death a suicide, but many believed Wyatt had returned to Arizona and killed Ringo, a theory corroborated many years later by Wyatt's wife Josephine. She wrote in her memoirs that her husband and Doc Holliday were responsible for Ringo's death.

Ringo is buried near West Turkey Creek, near where his body was found. The location is on private property off Highway 181 in southeastern Arizona. His grave can be visited, but only with permission from the landowner.

— *Jane Eppinga*

Originally published: August 15, 2003

Both photos are in the public domain.

Bat Masterson

This is William Barclay Masterson — better known as "Bat." He was born on November 6, 1853 in County Rouville, Quebec. In 1871, he moved with his family to Sedgwick, Kansas. Over the next several years, he worked as a buffalo hunter, army scout, gunfighter, gambler and lawman.

The other photo shows Masterson (standing) next to his good friend Wyatt Earp, whom he knew in Dodge City and later in Tombstone during its heyday. But Masterson spent time all over the frontier —from Kansas to Colorado — before ending his career in New York City.

In 1876, he was living in Sweetwater, Kansas, a few miles from Dodge City, when he got into his first gunfight. He was involved with a prostitute named Molly Brennan, who also was involved with another man, Corporal Melvin King. On January 24, 1876, Masterson and King got into a confrontation over Molly. King drew a gun and fired two shots, wounding Masterson and killing Molly. Masterson returned fire, killing King.

Later that year, Masterson opened a saloon in Dodge City. There, he became a deputy city marshal, assisting his brother, Marshal Ed Masterson, by serving papers, rounding up jurors and arresting troublemakers. During his stay in Dodge City, he met the Earps, and they became lifelong friends.

In 1877, he became sheriff of Ford County. His brother was killed two years later during a saloon gunfight. Shortly afterwards, Masterson moved to Tombstone, and the Earps put him in charge of keeping the peace at the infamous Oriental Saloon.

During the early morning hours of February 25, 1881, two men — Luke Short and Charlie Storms — got into an altercation at the saloon's gaming tables. Masterson took Storms to his room to calm him down, but Storms lacked the good sense to stay put. Instead, he went out onto the street and confronted Masterson, who was trying to talk some sense into Short. Storms began to shout insults at Short, who pulled a gun and shot him in the heart.

In 1882, Masterson returned to Dodge City to help his brother Jim out of a business predicament. He then moved on to Colorado, where he stayed for a decade, working the gambling halls and saloons in Trinidad and Creed and doing stints as town marshal in both places. On November 21, 1891, Masterson married Emma Waters, a saloon performer.

In 1905, President Theodore Roosevelt appointed Masterson as United States Marshal of New York State's southern district. Two years later, Masterson resigned and took a job with New York's *Morning Telegraph* as sports editor.

For years he feuded with Bob Edgren, sports editor and cartoonist for a competing paper, the *New York Evening World*.

Edgren had attacked Masterson's journalistic ability and his knowledge of boxing and attacked Earp for his controversial 1896 referee's decision awarding Tom Sharkey the victory in a boxing match with Bob Fitzsimmons.

He charged Earp with taking a bribe to ensure Sharkey's victory. Masterson sent the column to Earp, who vehemently denied Edgren's allegations, including one that claimed Earp notched his pistols to mark his murder victims. Earp responded that he would like to cut 12 notches on Bob Edgren's lying tongue.

In 1911, Edgren's brother, Leonard, a sports writer for yet another paper, the *New York Globe*, attacked Masterson in a column. He quoted fight manager Frank Ufer's allegation that Masterson had gained his reputation as a gunfighter by shooting drunken Mexicans and Indians in the back. Masterson brought a libel suit for $10,000 against Ufer, charging him with false and defamatory remarks. A settlement for an undisclosed amount was reached out of court.

Masterson also filed suit against the publishers of the paper for $25,000. When the case went to trial in May 1913, Benjamin N. Cardoza, who would later become a U.S. Supreme Court Justice, represented the newspaper. He grilled Masterson at length regarding his reputation as a gunfighter. Masterson heatedly denied shooting anyone, drunk or sober. He admitted shooting Indians in battle, but could not say if any were drunk. He also said that he never shot a Mexican in the front or in the back. The jury agreed that Masterson had been defamed and awarded damages of $3,500 plus court costs.

Masterson also waged a war against members of the New York Boxing Commission. He criticized the appointment of Walter Hooke as boxing commissioner, claiming he was not qualified to hold the position. A few nights after the column was published, Masterson sat at his usual ringside seat at Madison Square Garden, while an angry Hooke swore at him. Masterson retaliated in his next column by calling the governor's attention to the commission chairman's unprofessional behavior and demanding his immediate dismissal. The governor fired Hooke and replaced him with William Muldoon, one of Masterson' closest friends.

Masterson wrote his final column on October 25, 1921. Shortly after finishing it, he collapsed at his desk and died of a heart attack, passing on without a sound. William S. Hart, the era's top Western movie star and a longtime friend of Masterson's, told Hollywood columnist Louella Parsons, "I play the hero that Bat Masterson inspired. More than any other man I have ever met, I admire and respect him."

Masterson's death was described by Damon Runyon as "a strangely quiet closing to a strangely active career."

— *Jane Eppinga*

Originally published: August 1, 2003

Photograph dated 1879

Both photos are in the public domain.

*Masterson & Wyatt
Earp as Dodge City
deputies, 1876*

Sheriff Owens and the Pleasant Valley War

The larger photo is of Apache County Sheriff Commodore Perry Owens. Some believe he came by his unusual name because he was born on the 40th anniversary of Commodore Oliver Hazard Perry's victory over the British in 1813 at the Battle of Lake Erie. But that was not the case. Owens was born on July 29; the battle took place on September 10. It was his father, Oliver Hazard Perry Owens, who was named for the war hero, and his mother honored both her husband and the naval commander by naming her son Commodore Perry.

Owens was raised in Tennessee and Indiana. He arrived in Arizona in 1881, worked on various ranches and ultimately homesteaded near Navajo Springs. He had long, reddish blond hair, worn in the manner of mountain men. He was elected Apache County Sheriff in 1886 and quickly got embroiled in what came to be called the Pleasant Valley War, one of the most costly feuds in American history, one that resulted in the almost complete annihilation of the two families involved. The two men in the smaller photo were employed by the Hashknife Outfit, a cattle ranch whose cowboys were swept up in the feud, and each became a bit player in the drama.

The conflict arose over disagreements pertaining to grazing rights, water rights and property boundaries between two ranching families: the Tewksburys and the Grahams. The former started running sheep on the open range, the latter got increasingly annoyed because sheep grazed the land clean, leaving little for cattle. Years of mutual dislike between the outfits escalated in February 1887, when Tom Graham shot and killed a Tewksbury ranch hand, a Navajo who was herding sheep in an area that until then had been understood as reserved for cattle.

Hostilities hit a peak in September of that year. First, a group of Graham partisans surrounded a Tewksbury cabin in the early morning hours one day and ambushed John Tewksbury and William Jacobs as they left the cabin to mount their horses. They died almost instantly. The remaining Tewksburys inside the cabin returned fire, and although shots were exchanged for several more hours, no more fatalities occurred that day.

A few days later, Andy Cooper (aka Andy Blevins), one of the Graham faction leaders, was overheard in Holbrook bragging that he had fired the fatal shots at Tewksbury and Jacobs. Sheriff Owens already had a warrant for Blevins on an unrelated charge and decided to ride out alone to Blevins' house to serve the warrant and to investigate the Tewksbury-Jacobs murder.

Upwards of a dozen people were at the Blevins house that day. When Owens called on Andy to come out, Blevins refused. One of his relatives, John Blevins, did come out of the house — with a rifle. He started shooting at Owens, who returned fire, wounding John and killing Andy, who had appeared at the door. A friend of the Blevins, Mose Roberts, jumped out a back window (some say to escape the bullets Owens was firing into the house; some say to ambush Owens). Owens heard the noise, ran to the side of the house and shot Roberts dead. Fifteen year-old Sam Blevins then ran out of the house with a pistol he had picked up next to the body of his brother Andy. Sam's mother followed and tried to drag her son back into the house, but Sam started firing at Owens, who returned fire and killed Sam. In less than one minute, three people were dead and one wounded. Owens was unscathed.

Local opinion turned against Owens, apparently because of the death of the young boy. There was talk of a murder charge being brought, but in the end there was no evidence to support a criminal indictment. Instead, the county supervisors simply relieved him of his duties and withheld whatever salary was due him. Owens didn't take kindly to the latter circumstance and held members of the board at gunpoint until he was paid. Needless to say, he left town soon after.

In 1895, Owens was appointed sheriff of the newly created Navajo County when it was formed out of Apache County. Two years later he retired and moved to Seligman where he opened a store and a saloon. He died on May 10, 1919, and is buried in Flagstaff.

After the shootout at the Blevins house, the Pleasant Valley War continued unabated. Over the next few years numerous lynchings and unsolved murders took place until only Tom Graham and Edwin Tewksbury remained from the families originally involved in the feud. In 1892, Tom was murdered in Tempe, and although Edwin was thought to have been involved, he was acquitted after several trials.

The smaller photo features Hashknife cowboys Jim Wilson (left) and Tom Tucker. On August 11, 1888, Wilson and two other men were taken from their cabin by a group of vigilantes, accused of rustling and summarily lynched. Some say rustling was a time-honored profession in that part of the state and that members of the Hashknife Outfit were frequent if not especially skilled practitioners.

Later, after one of the Graham patriarchs had disappeared under suspicious circumstances, Tucker took part in a reprisal raid on the Tewksburys. The Tewksburys killed two of the raiders and wounded three, including Tucker, who, after he had taken a bullet to the lung, used his horse as a shield. One of the Tewksburys later said he would have liked to have killed Tucker, but to do so he would have had to kill the horse, which was something he was loathe to do. Tucker escaped, recovered from his wounds and lived another 40 years.

— *Jane Eppinga and Barry Gartell*

Photos courtesy of Jane Eppinga

Buckey O'Neill and The Canyon Diablo Posse

The young fellow third from the left is Yavapai County Sheriff William O. "Buckey" O'Neill. With him are Carl Holton, special detective for the Atlantic & Pacific Railroad (the man with the beard) and deputies Jim Black and Ed St. Clair (left and right of O'Neill).

Buckey O'Neill had been a newspaper reporter with the *Tombstone Epitaph* when the OK Corral shootout occurred in 1881. The following year he moved to Prescott and worked as a court reporter and founded his own newspaper, *Hoof and Horn*, serving the livestock industry. He became captain of a local unit of the Arizona militia in 1886 and was elected Yavapai County sheriff in 1888.

Within two months of taking office, the A&P train was robbed. It had stopped for fuel at Canyon Diablo (about halfway between Flagstaff and Winslow) on the evening of March 20 when four cowboys from the Hashknife outfit came on board. They were William Sterin, John Halford, Daniel Harvick and J.J. Smith, and they weren't there for a pleasure trip. They held up the train, taking more than $7,000 in cash and jewelry, and then headed north towards Lee's Ferry.

O'Neill and Black were in Flagstaff when word of the holdup came the next day. O'Neill immediately formed a posse and took off after the robbers. At Lee's Ferry the lawmen were told the fugitives had passed through two days before, heading up into southern Utah. In Utah they learned the men had gone back south to Wah Weap in Arizona. At Wah Weap, after a chase that had taken nearly three weeks and covered over 500 miles, they finally captured the robbers.

To get the prisoners back to Prescott, the lawmen had to box the compass, first heading north to Marysville, Utah, to catch the train to Salt Lake City and then training east to Denver, south to New Mexico and back west to Prescott. Outside Raton, New Mexico, J.J. Smith escaped. He was later captured in Texas and returned to Prescott, where the robbers pleaded guilty and were sentenced to twenty-five years in the Yuma Territorial Prison. An additional five years was added to Smith's sentence for the escape.

In those days, a sheriff paid his own expenses and then was reimbursed by the county. It cost $8,000 to bring the robbers to justice. The Yavapai County Board of Supervisors refused to pay more than $5,800, so O'Neill sued them. He won a judgment in Superior Court, but the tight-fisted supervisors wouldn't quit. They appealed to the Territorial Supreme Court and won, so in the end Buckey had to pay after all.

Dorothy Goode, a niece of Deputy Jim Black, thinks this photo was taken in the spring of 1889, not long after the posse returned to Prescott with the prisoners.

All four criminals were pardoned in 1897, and the following year Sterin enlisted in the First United States Cavalry Regiment (a unit that was later known as the Rough Riders) under the name Henry Nash. He served as a sergeant under O'Neill, who commanded A Troop. O'Neill apparently was never aware of the man's past.

On July 1, 1898, during the Spanish-American War, the Rough Riders were below Cuba's Kettle Hill, an intermediate summit on the way up San Juan Hill, awaiting orders to advance. The unit was taking heavy fire from Spanish troops entrenched at the summit, and O'Neill was fatally injured. Shortly after O'Neill's death, regiment commander Teddy Roosevelt, without orders from brigade headquarters, ordered a charge that took Kettle Hill and then the main summit at San Juan Hill. By the end of the campaign, the Rough Riders had suffered a 76% casualty rate from battle and disease.

— *Bonnie Greer*

Originally published: March 26, 1986

Photo courtesy of the Arizona Historical Society, Pioneer Museum

Wham Payroll Robbery

On May 11, 1889, Major Joseph Washington Wham set out for Fort Thomas carrying a payroll of more than $28,000 in gold and silver coin. Some 15 miles northwest of Pima in Graham County, Wham and his Buffalo Soldier escorts encountered a large boulder obstructing the road. When soldiers dismounted to clear the way, gunfire rang out from the hills above. One man and several mules were hit. The soldiers scrambled for cover and returned fire but were unable to drive the attackers away. Within 30 minutes of the first shots, eight of Wham's 11 escorts lay wounded. The strong box was left in the open, and Wham, who was unarmed, watched helplessly as his attackers carried it off and disappeared into the brush.

Help arrived from a nearby ranch, and the men were carried to the hospital at Fort Thomas. Within 12 hours, some 1,700 men — soldiers, Indian scouts, sheriffs, deputy marshals and detectives — were scouring the area for clues.

The robbery was two weeks old when mass arrests shocked and angered citizens of Graham County. Seven men — all members of the Mormon Church — were suspects. They were Gilbert Webb, a prosperous cattle rancher and head of the Mormon Church Committee of Solomonville; his son Wilfred, an examiner of the district school committee; brothers Edward, Warren and Lyman Follett; Thomas Lamb; and David Rogers, a cowboy who worked for the Webbs.

Because agitation against Mormons was at its peak during the 1880s, some people reasoned that an impartial jury could not be seated in Graham County. Therefore, the trial was moved to Tucson. During the next 33 days, 165 witnesses testified. A Pima farmer claimed Marcus Cunningham hid a sack of gold pieces in his barn. Several witnesses noted that Gilbert Webb paid off long standing debts soon after the robbery. Soldiers, including Wham, identified various defendants as participants in the robbery.

Most observers thought the case appeared to be an open and shut case. But it was not. The *Arizona Daily Star* reported, "the jury was out less than two hours when they were brought into court and [the] foreman handed the verdict to the [judge]. There was a death hush in the court room and when [the judge] read the verdict, 'we the jurors find the defendants not guilty,' amazement and surprise was pictured on the faces of the entire audience."

Newspapers hinted ominously of bloodletting in Graham County as retribution against witnesses who testified for the prosecution. But cooler heads prevailed, and no one sought vengeance.

Two of the Buffalo Soldiers were awarded the Medal of Honor for heroic conduct during the ambush. After conducting an investigation of the incident, a U.S. Marshal said, "I am satisfied a braver or better defense could not have been made under like circumstance."

Wilfred Webb, the youngest of the defendants, inherited his father's large cattle ranch, which he expanded and made into one of the most successful in Arizona. He won three terms in the Territorial Legislature and in 1905 served as Speaker of the House.

In the 1920s, he converted part of his holdings into a dude ranch. A year before his death in 1938, Webb told a *Star* reporter, "I've never denied or affirmed that I was in on [the robbery]. In fact, over at my guest ranch they make me tell the story of the robbery all the time because it gives Easterners a thrill to be the guests of a highway robber. I was never one to spoil a good story."

Today the Wham Payroll robbery remains an unsolved crime.

— *W. Lane Rogers*

Originally published: March 22, 1989

Caption: Wham payroll robbery defendants and counsel. Standing, from left, are: Lyman Follett, Ed Follett, David Rogers, Thomas Lamb and Warren Follett Jr. Seated, from left, are: Marcus Cunningham, attorneys Mark Smith and Ben Goodrich, Gilbert Webb, attorneys B.F. Hereford and Frank Hereford, and W.T. Webb.

Photo courtesy of the Arizona Historical Society.

The Power Shootout

This is John G. Power, member of a reclusive Graham County family that was involved in one of the most notorious shootouts in Arizona history.

In 1890, Thomas Jefferson Power, Sr., his wife Martha and oldest son Charlie moved from Texas to Cliff, New Mexico, to homestead. Three children were born in New Mexico, John Grant (photo), Thomas Jefferson Jr. and Ola May. Martha was killed when a beam on a neighbor's house fell and crushed her. And in 1907, Thomas Power, Sr. decided to move on to Arizona.

The family eventually settled in Kielburg Canyon deep in the Galiuro Mountains of Graham County. The men ranched, but also gained a controlling interest in a mining claim variously known as the Jinx Mine, the Abandoned Claims and the Power Mine. Charlie decided to return to New Mexico.

For 10 years the family was content with ranching and mining. Then in 1917, the U. S. entered World War I and all young males were required to register for the draft. Thomas Power, Sr. refused to allow his sons to register.

That December, an incident occurred that has never been fully explained. Ola May, who lived apart from her brothers in a separate cabin, died. According to the Powers, who had gone to visit her, she had shouted the word "poison" and then suddenly died. Tom Sisson, a hired hand and former horse thief, was sent to Safford for a casket. The authorities became suspicious, and an autopsy of the body was ordered. No trace of poison was found, but foul play was suspected, and some claimed that Ola May's neck had been broken — possibly in a fight with her brothers.

On February 9, 1918, U. S. Deputy Marshal Frank Haynes, Graham County Sheriff Frank McBride, deputy Martin Kempton and deputy T. K. Wootan set out from Safford to bring in the Power boys. Marshal Haynes later testified he had a warrant for Tom Jr. and John for draft evasion; Sheriff McBride had a warrant for Tom Sr. and Tom Sisson for questioning in the death of Ola May.

The lawmen arrived early in the morning and posted themselves around the Power cabin. Tom Power Sr. came out, and both sides started shooting. When it was over, Sheriff McBride and his two deputies were dead; Tom Power Sr. was mortally wounded. Marshal Haynes escaped and went for help. Sisson and the Power brothers headed for Mexico.

The fugitives were followed by the largest posse in Arizona history — 3,000 men from Arizona and New Mexico. They hid out for a while in the Chiricahuas, but on March 8 surrendered to the 12th Cavalry at Hachita, New Mexico, rather than risk a lynching at the hands of the posse.

They were brought back for trial and were found guilty of murder, but were sentenced to life in prison rather than death, because Arizona had no death penalty at the time. They were sent to the state prison at Florence.

Over the years, families of the murdered lawmen fought any attempts at parole. Tom Sisson died in prison on January 23, 1957, at the age of 86. In the late 1950s, several people took up the Power cause. Finally in 1960, after relatives of the lawmen decided to "let matters take their course," Gov. Jack Williams pardoned the brothers. Tom died in 1970; John died six years later at Klondyke near the family mine.

— *Jane Eppinga*

Originally published: June 20, 1990

Photo courtesy of the Arizona Historical Society, Tucson

Stick 'Em Up... Just Kidding

George Smalley, editor of the *Tucson Citizen*, staged this photograph with the outlaw Billy Stiles in 1900. Smalley had sympathy for outlaws and a dislike for the local sheriff.

Smalley was a bit of a crusader. He came to the Arizona Territory in 1896, driven by poor health, having worked on his father's weekly newspaper in Caledonia, Minnesota. In Arizona, he served briefly as editor of the *Arizona Republican* and then joined the *Citizen* as editor.

In 1899, he ran a series of exposés on Tucson mining swindles. Companies were selling shares in nonexistent mines. Smalley began investigating the locations of the mines and, finding no activity, wrote articles accusing the companies of taking monies under false pretenses. His life was threatened. Three times he was shot at — apparently in warning. He never was wounded, and no one ever was arrested for the shootings.

Billy Stiles was a fugitive from the law when he posed with Smalley. The editor had heard that Stiles was hiding out near Tucson and printed a notice in the newspaper asking him to come in and pose for a picture. Stiles agreed, and the two men met behind Kurt Hart's gunshop on the corner of Church and West Congress.

Stiles was wanted for robbing a passenger train near Cochise with a gang of outlaws on the evening of September 11, 1899. Besides Stiles, the gang members were Bravo Juan Yoas, Matt Burts, Bill Downey, Three-Fingered Jack Dunlap and Burt Alvord (who had served as a deputy under Cochise County Sheriff John Slaughter earlier in the decade and was a constable in Pearce at the time).

On the evening in question, a railroad employee telegraphed the sheriff's office in Willcox with news of the robbery. A posse was formed. Constable Alvord was found in Schweitzer's Saloon innocently playing cards with Stiles and Burts. On being told of the crime, he broke up the game and deputized Stiles and Burts to join the posse. Over the next few weeks, Alvord and his friends behaved respectably and did not spend money obviously, but neither did they find the robbers. Then a saloon employee told the sheriff that the three men had spent only part of the evening in Schweitzer's Saloon on the night of the robbery.

Cochise County Sheriff Scott White became suspicious and finally arrested Alvord and another gang member, Bill Downing, and jailed them in Tombstone. Burts was caught in Tucson and returned to Tombstone. Bravo Juan also apparently was caught. Meanwhile, Stiles met Smalley and posed for this photograph. When Stiles was caught, he confessed and agreed to testify against his cohorts. He was allowed to roam free in Tombstone, a decision that would end badly.

In April, Stiles entered the Tombstone jail — on the pretext of visiting his friends — grabbed a rifle from jailer George Bravin and broke out the prisoners. In the struggle over the rifle, Bravin was shot and mortally wounded. Several prisoners stayed to help him, but Stiles, Alvord and the other gang members fled to Mexico. Sheriff White received a letter from the outlaws dated April 20, 1900:

Scott White, Esq.

We send you the keys to the jail ... We met the Mexicans that killed the gambler in Johnson Camp, but as we had no warrants we did not arrest them —and we were afraid they would shoot .... Tell the boys we are all well and eating regular. Tell the man I got the Studebaker saddle and will send it home soon.

Signed Bravo Juan, Stiles and Alvord

Alvord and Stiles were captured by the Arizona Rangers at the Young Ranch about a mile west of Naco, Sonora, on February 20, 1904. Alvord was wounded in the thigh and ankle. He was sent to the territorial prison at Yuma but was pardoned by the governor after three months. He was last seen working as a canal employee in Panama in 1910. It is unclear what happened to Stiles.

The other gang members went to prison after attempting to rob the Fort Huachuca payroll.

— *Jane Eppinga*

Originally published: January 29, 1999

Photo courtesy of the Arizona Historical Society, Tucson

The Getaway Train

This Southern Pacific steam locomotive was the getaway vehicle for a couple of criminals who broke out of the Yuma jail in 1901. That's the jail on the right.

The incident began when Thomas Hart, a drifter with a penchant for alcohol, stole a case of whiskey from Paul Moretti's saloon. Moretti reported the theft to Sheriff Gus Livingston. Not long after, Moretti spotted Hart on Main Street and pointed him out to a young deputy, Matt DeVanem, who confronted Hart and tried to arrest him. Hart shot the deputy at point blank range with a gun hidden in his pocket. The deputy died an hour later. Hart was taken into custody shortly after.

Feelings ran high in the community. Hart asked that his trial be moved, claiming that even the members of the Elks Lodge had tried to get up a lynching party. His request was denied, and he was tried, found guilty of murder and sentenced to hang in April 1901. He was put in the Yuma jail to await execution.

The jail was part of the Yuma Courthouse at Madison and 3rd Street, and, as the photo shows, the Southern Pacific main line ran directly in front of it. That set Hart to thinking.

His cellmate, Louis Leyvas, who was serving time for stealing a gold piece from a friend, had worked at the Southern Pacific roundhouse and knew how to run a locomotive.

Hart began to plan a break and encouraged Leyvas to join him. Leyvas made himself a knife out of a piece of packing-crate wood. On a Sunday afternoon, a friend brought Leyvas a watermelon. When Billy Neahr, one of the jailors, opened the cell door to roll in the melon, Leyvas pressed the homemade knife to his ribs. He and Hart took the keys and some weapons, locked Neahr in the cell, and, with Hart dragging along his "Oregon boot" (a 50-pound manacle designed to impede getaways). They headed for the rail yard.

There they commandeered a locomotive. Leyvas stopped Hart from killing Donald McIntyre, the shop foreman. He also freed Hart from the boot using tools in the cab of the locomotive. With Leyvas at the controls, they headed into the desert, bound for the Mexican border and followed by the inevitable posse whose most enthusiastic member was Neahr, furious at being tricked. Not far from the border, the engine quit, and Hart and Leyvas abandoned it. The posse rode up. Hart was unfamiliar with the .41 caliber pistol he had stolen and could not release the safety. He stood up and Neahr shot him through the chest with a .30-30, killing him.

Leyvas wisely surrendered and was returned to jail. His compassion for the shop foreman evidently worked in his favor; he was sentenced to three years for the jailbreak and won a release after two years and a month. Thereafter he went straight, and more than forty years later, on December 11, 1944, he was pardoned by Gov. Sidney Osborn.

— *Jane Eppinga*

Originally published: August 16, 1989

Photo courtesy Arizona Historical Society, Tucson

His Last Shot

The men in the top photograph are, from left, Lucien Creswell (partly visible), Hosteen Cli (a Navajo), Tom Hesser, Bill Campbell and Young Marley. They are standing at the grave of John Shaw.

The photograph was taken at Fred Volz's trading post in Canyon Diablo about thirty-five miles east of Flagstaff. The men, all cowboys from the Hashknife or other ranches in the Winslow area, had gathered there to dig up John Shaw's body and see that the dead man got the drink he paid for. Here is how it happened.

On April 8, 1905, a little after midnight, John Shaw and an accomplice named Bill Smythe entered the Wigwam Saloon in Winslow, ordered a couple of whiskeys and surveyed the gambling tables. Their interest was especially drawn to 600 silver dollars stacked on a dice table run by Frank Ketchum. The Arizona Territory was hard money country, and instead of chips, stacks of silver dollars were on the tables. The men held up the saloon, stuffed their pockets with silver dollars and took off heading west. Navajo County Sheriff Chet Houck and Deputy Sheriff J.C.N. Pemberton gave chase and cornered the robbers at the Volz trading post at sundown that evening. A shoot-out took place. Smythe was wounded, and Shaw was killed and buried on the spot. Two hundred and sixty-one dollars were recovered.

When word of the shooting got out, cowboys from the vicinity gathered at the Wigwam. They didn't like Houck, who was always interfering with their extracurricular activities (primarily cattle rustling), and they didn't like his methods.

They began to wonder whether Smythe and Shaw had paid for the whiskeys they ordered the night of the robbery, and whether or not they had drunk them. When the bartender confirmed the drinks had been paid for but not drunk, there was general grumbling about the propriety of burying a man who hadn't had a chance to drink his whiskey.

Sam Case spoke for everyone when he said, "it just ain't right, him not getting his shot of forty rod. We should go down to Canyon Diablo, dig him up and give him a snort, poor feller."

That sounded like a good idea, so about 20 men, including Ketchum, grabbed some whiskey and hopped the west-bound train. They forgot a shovel, however, and had to wake up Fred Volz to borrow one when they got to his trading post. He lent them the shovel, along with the camera that made this photograph, saying, "long as you no-goods are going to do it,… make some pictures. May be enough light to get some, time you have him out of the ground. Chet Houck wants one so he can find out who the dead man really is."

When the men unearthed Shaw, rigor mortis had set in and there was a faint grin on his face. The sobered cowboys stood him up and poured whiskey through his clenched teeth. Before putting Shaw back in the ground, they said a little prayer, and Ketchum posed with the dead man for the lower photo.

Volz told Creswell to give the film to Sheriff Houck, but Sam Case got hold of it for about a month and then gave it to W.H. Burbage, a former Navajo county attorney. The picture of the men actually pouring the whiskey down the dead man's throat disappeared after Burbage's death.

As for Smythe, who had only been wounded, he was sentenced to a term in the Yuma prison. He turned out to be William Evans, who had done time in 1897 at Yuma. John Shaw was never otherwise identified.

— *Jane Eppinga*

Originally published: May 17, 1989

Photos courtesy Arizona Historical Society, Pioneer Museum Gladwell Richardson Collection

Barbering Badmen

Emil Marks poses in the photographic gallery of W.E. Irwin in Bisbee about 1910. A barber by trade, Marks trimmed the hair and mustaches of Tombstone's most notorious gunfighters, including the Earps, 'Doc' Holliday and the Clantons.

Emil Marks arrived in the United States from Germany at the age of 16 and spent his first two months in New York City, working at his trade. He saved money, joined his brother Max in Tombstone and almost immediately secured work at the Barron brothers barber shop. He enjoyed the work but not the dangerous customers he served.

According to Marks, as quoted in a 1934 *Bisbee Daily Review* article, "Both members of the Clantons and Earps had a significant habit of removing their guns from their holsters and placing them conveniently on their laps while having their hair trimmed. As a member of the opposing gang passed by outside, there was a perceptible tenseness and an uncomfortable twitching of restless muscles on the part of the occupant in the barber chair."

Fearing that his customers might some day actually succumb to 'triggeritis' and cause blood to be shed in the peaceful little barber shop, Marks packed up his kit and moved farther down the street to a place where the patrons were chiefly peaceful persons "who weren't mad at anybody."

A few days after he moved, Marks witnessed the Earp/Clanton shoot-out at the OK Corral. He reportedly believed the Earps wore steel vests under their coats that prevented fatal wounds but gave no evidence to support the theory.

Marks moved to Bisbee in 1889, securing a partnership with another barber, Mr. Wittig. The Bisbee newspaper often referred to him in "Local Notes." In one column the newspaper reported: "E. Marks was slightly injured yesterday morning in a runaway — the buggy tipped over throwing Marks underneath. His companion rescued him from serious injury. As it was, he received cuts on the head and face."

In about 1905, Marks left the barber trade and opened a lumber yard in Lowell. He also invested in real estate, first building a hotel in Lowell and then entering into a partnership with James Letson and Antone Kline to build the KL&M building, which was completed in 1910. It still stands on Bisbee's Main Street today as the home of the Letson Loft Hotel.

Emil Marks died in Bisbee in 1947 at the age of 82.

—*Tom Vaughan*

Originally published: December 17, 1999

Photo courtesy of the Bisbee Mining & Historical Museum

Mayor's Award

Bisbee Mayor Ron Oertle

All towns have a history of unique and curious people. Mr. Emil Marks as a barber had the opportunity of cutting the hair of not only the well-to-do in Bisbee but also the notorious and dangerous individuals in Bisbee. It would be truly interesting to be able to research Emil Marks' letters to family and friends as to his perceptions of the various individuals he conversed with while cutting their hair. However, some of those families may wish for this information to remain lost history.

The Hanging Road

In the first decade of the 20th century, auto travel became popular, and Arizona responded with a program to develop highways and improve existing roads. Convicts from the prison in Florence were a ready pool of free labor.

Prison road gangs built the highway over the mountain pass between Bisbee and Tombstone, and when the project was completed an overzealous reporter dubbed it the "Hanging Road." The convicts also improved a stretch of the Douglas Highway and built a bridge at Fairbanks over the San Pedro River. No convicts were ever hung as far as we can tell, although four did escape to Mexico, where they joined the army, caused a disturbance in a Naco bar and were court-martialed and shot.

The convicts were housed in this tent prison camp in the Mule Mountains on the Tombstone side of the pass. This 1913 photograph looks south through the mountains along the Bisbee-Tombstone road towards Bisbee. The fence around the tents and a guard tower at center mark the convict camp. Other tents housed guards and civilian workers.

Seventy-five prisoners arrived by train in Bisbee in October of 1913 and were hauled over the pass in mule-drawn wagons to the prison camp in Tombstone Canyon. They set to work improving the Bisbee-Tombstone road, widening and grading it and building a macadamized road surface with culverts to divert water and prevent erosion. The road was closed each day from 8 a.m. to 5 p.m. for blasting and construction.

Some convicts were trusties who drove trucks and wagons into town for supplies. The unguarded excursions caused lifted eyebrows in Bisbee and prompted the *Bisbee Daily Review* to write: "(trusties) continue to come in town daily and are to be seen about the post office, stores and cigar stands during the time they are in town. Apparently, they take life easy."

Declaration of war in Europe put an end to the convict road crews in Cochise County. Copper prices took a nose dive, and in Bisbee 700 miners were laid off. Members of the Bisbee Commercial Club met with state officials and suggested that unemployed citizens replace convict labor. Governor Hunt agreed, and in late August of 1914 the convicts were returned to their prison cells in Florence.

Before they left, however, they saw the opening of the first section of the Bisbee-Tombstone highway. On August 21, the *Review* reported: "The road gang has now completed the first link in the highway and has built one of the most beautiful, and at the same time durable, highways in the West. The gangs are now working west of the convict camp, on the other side of the divide and are pushing the work rapidly towards the county seat."

A reporter drove over the road in September and waxed poetic: "Three and nine-tenths mile on the great 'Hanging Road' over the divide between Bisbee and Tombstone have now been completed. Next to the mines and smelters, this magnificent and picturesque mountain boulevard is easily the most interesting feature of Cochise County."

Today, a concrete monument commemorates the completion of the road, but the information on the plaque is wrong. The pass is not on the continental divide, which in fact is about 150 miles east of Bisbee. And the road was not built in 1912; 1914 is the correct date.

The road is still open but is used mostly by hikers, joggers and cyclists. Commercial and tourist traffic now takes the straight route through a tunnel constructed in the early 1950s.

— *Tom Vaughan*

Originally published: August 2, 1996

Photo courtesy of the Bisbee Mining and Historical Society

Eva Dugan

Eva Dugan, a woman unencumbered by modesty, probably disliked this mug shot. Better photos appeared in newspapers accompanied by jaunty prose composed by fawning reporters. One of her favorites appeared in the *Tucson Citizen*, showing her as an obese, middle-aged woman clad in a striking paisley dress, sleeveless and stylishly cut in the fashion of the time. Her flaming red hair was neatly coifed, and around her neck was a bauble that dangled to her midsection. Her appearance in the photo was in stark contrast to the bars looming in the windows behind her. It was Eva's last formal portrait. Days later, her life would end on the gallows in Florence, Arizona.

Eva was born in Missouri in 1878. Her fifth husband gave her the name Dugan, which is the name she used when she was hired as a housekeeper for Andrew J. Mathis, a reclusive chicken rancher on Oracle Road at the outskirts of Tucson. It was not a happy match and, after a couple of weeks, Mathis fired her. He told neighbors that Eva had tried to poison his meals.

In January 1927, Mathis disappeared. So did Eva and Mathis's nearly new Dodge coupe. The car eventually showed up on a used car lot in Amarillo, Texas, having been sold by a "Mrs. Eva Mathis." Eva was later found working as a hospital employee in White Plains, New York. She was charged with auto theft and extradited to Tucson. She was tried, convicted and sentenced to six years in the Florence penitentiary.

Mathis was still missing and believed to be the victim of a murder. Dugan was the prime suspect, but without a body, she couldn't be charged with the crime.

The following December, a California tourist selected a spot on the Mathis ranch to camp. Efforts to drive a tent post into the ground were stymied by a hard object. The tourist began digging up what he thought was a rock, only to find it was Mathis's skull.

Analysis determined that Mathis had been murdered, and Eva was charged with the evil deed.

Court convened Feb. 21, 1928. Five days later, Eva was convicted of first-degree murder — largely on circumstantial evidence. She was sentenced to death, and hanging was the state's method of capital punishment. When the sentence was read, she made no outcry or comment. Her stoic demeanor became legendary.

The press gleefully reported her every move, and women's groups and others who opposed the death penalty united across the state in an effort to stave off the execution. The protests may have helped for on Feb. 18, 1930, three days before she was to be executed, a sanity hearing was held, but Eva was judged sane and the hanging was not postponed.

Reporting on the events of Feb. 21, 1930, a *Citizen* reporter wrote, "Jauntily swinging her guard's hand as does a maid who goes a-maying with her swain, Eva Dugan this morning approached her rendezvous with death with a light step and a lighter laugh."

Dugan climbed the 13 steps to the gallows. Her shell-rimmed spectacles were removed, a black hood placed over her head and a noose adjusted about her neck. A few seconds later a steel trap was sprung, and then everything went wrong.

The weight of Eva's body caused her decapitation. Once detached from her torso, Eva's head rolled across the room, splattering blood on the feet of horrified spectators. Observers were stunned and four women fainted.

Eva Dugan remains the only woman to have been executed in Arizona, although as of August 2008 there were two women on death row at the state penitentiary in Florence.

— *W. Lane Rogers*

Originally published: July 4, 2003

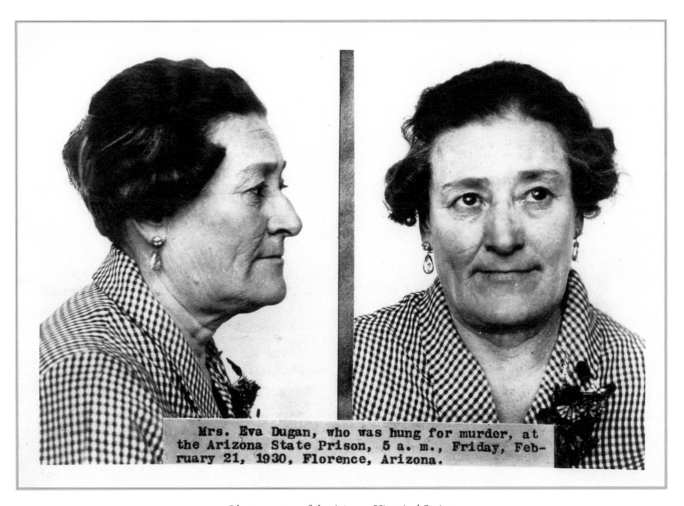

Mrs. Eva Dugan, who was hung for murder, at the Arizona State Prison, 5 a. m., Friday, February 21, 1930, Florence, Arizona.

Photo courtesy of the Arizona Historical Society

Dillinger Arrested In Tucson

The mug shots are of John Dillinger (he's the smirking one on the left) and two members of his gang. The booking photos were taken by the Tucson Police Department on January 25, 1934. Earlier that evening, Dillinger had been taken into custody by three Tucson police officers at the bungalow at 927 North Second Avenue pictured below. Here's how the incident went down:

In the early morning hours of January 21, a fire broke out in the Hotel Congress. Firemen swept through the building, banging on the doors of the sleeping guests. Oddly, a resident of the top floor seemed more concerned about his luggage than himself, and he put up a fuss when ordered to leave the building. Out on the sidewalk, he persuaded two firemen to re-enter the burning building to retrieve several expensive-looking bags.

Three days later, one of the firemen noticed a strong resemblance between the man who had been very protective of his luggage and a photo in the lineup section of a detective magazine he was reading. The face in the photo belonged to Russell Clark, a member of the John Dillinger gang.

Meanwhile, the same man and two of his friends had attracted the attention of a couple of tourists who had crossed paths with them the previous evening in a nightclub. He was boasting how easy it was to make a living robbing banks.

The tourists went to the police, who began an investigation. It was determined that Harry Pierpont (the man in the middle), "Fat Charlie" Makley (the one on the right) and Russell Clark — all notorious members of the Dillinger gang — had come to town. And police surmised that Dillinger himself was not far behind.

In quick order, Makley was arrested in a downtown radio repair shop. Pierpont, said to be the most dangerous of the gang because he killed for pleasure, was stopped at the intersection of Sixth Avenue and Nineteenth Street for a "routine" check of his automobile papers and arrested.

Clark was the most difficult to arrest. Traced to a rented house on North Second Avenue near the University of Arizona, he put up a vigorous fight that left him with a lacerated scalp. A search of the premises revealed the expensive looking bags firemen had rescued from the Hotel Congress. In them was an assortment of machine guns, pistols, ammunition and bullet-proof vests.

With the members of the gang in custody, the search now focused on the elusive Dillinger. Confident he would eventually show up at the Second Avenue house, the police placed it under surveillance.

Meanwhile, Dillinger had registered under an assumed name at a tourist court on South Sixth Avenue. At 6:30 p.m. on January 25, he came to visit his cohorts. As he made his way up the walk, three police officers sprang into action, and Dillinger was arrested without incident. Caught wholly off guard by the stakeout, his only words were, "Well, I'll be damned!"

Excitement swept the city and the nation at the news: without firing a shot, the Dillinger gang had been apprehended in a small Southwestern city. The public treated Dillinger more like a celebrity than a notorious outlaw. Fox Movietone News rushed in a camera crew from Hollywood. Some 2,000 people converged on the county jail, hoping for a glimpse of the man. His meals were catered by a nearby restaurant, and he was allowed to have his terrier puppy in jail with him.

Local authorities knew that wherever Dillinger was, trouble usually followed, and they were anxious to get him out of Arizona as quickly as possible. Among several states vying for the right to try Dillinger, Indiana was chosen, at least in part because it was holding a murder warrant for the killing of a man during a bank robbery in East Chicago. Dillinger was extradited on January 31 and delivered to the Lake County jail in Crown Point, Indiana. The jail was dubbed "escape-proof" by Sheriff Lillian Holley, but she soon had to eat her words. On March 3, 1934, he escaped from the jail. Accounts differ as to whether he was armed with a submachine gun or with a piece of wood painted black and carved to look like a gun.

Dillinger went back to robbing banks. In July of that year, he was shot and killed by FBI agents as he tried to escape from a trap they had set outside the Biograph Theater in Chicago.

— *W. Lane Rogers.*

Originally published: March 31, 1995

Photos courtesy of the Arizona Historical Society, Tucson

The Military

West Point's First Black Graduate

Buffalo Soldiers

Fort Grant

McClintock and Brodie in the National Guard

The Other Heroes of War

Border Duty, 1916

Pershing on the Border

Frank Luke, Arizona Greatest War Hero

West Point's First Black Graduate

This is the story of Henry Ossian Flipper, America's first black military officer. He was a man of multiple talents — a lieutenant with the 10th U.S. Cavalry, a civil engineer, mining consultant, special agent for the U.S. government and translator of Spanish texts.

He was born on March 21, 1856, at the Methodist parsonage in Thomasville, Georgia. His mother was Isabella Buckhalter, a slave owned by the parson. His father, Festus, was owned by slave dealer Ephraim G. Ponder. When Ponder moved his slaves to Atlanta sometime before the Civil War, Festus gave Ponder the money to buy his wife, Isabella, and son, Henry, from the parson. Henry was taught to read by one of Ponder's slaves.

After the war, the family remained in Atlanta, and Henry and a brother attended Atlanta University. Henry sought entrance to the U.S. Military Academy at West Point and was appointed by Georgia Congressman James Crawford Freeman.

He graduated in June 1877 as the nation's first black officer and was assigned to the 10th U.S. Cavalry — the Buffalo Soldiers — at Fort Sill, Oklahoma. His commanding officer, Capt. Nicholas Nolan, an Irishman who knew prejudice himself, liked Flipper and gave him responsibility for designing a drainage system. It came to be known as Flipper's Ditch and today is a National Historic Landmark

In 1880, he was assigned to Fort Davis in the Big Bend country of Texas as assistant quartermaster and commissary of subsistence. Col. William Rufus Shafter took command of Fort Davis in March of the following year and immediately relieved Flipper as quartermaster. Later, when he discovered that Flipper's office was missing funds, he had him charged with embezzlement.

Flipper was court-martialed on September 17, 1881 and found innocent of embezzlement, but "guilty of conduct unbecoming an officer and a gentleman."

Humiliated and dishonored, Flipper moved to El Paso and worked briefly as a clerk in a laundry. Within a year, however, he had begun a new career as a mining engineer and consultant. By 1886, he was chief engineer of the Sonora Land Company of Chicago, and the following year opened his own engineering office in Nogales, Arizona Territory.

He was hired as special agent for the Court of Private Land Claims and served as the government witness in the decision that disallowed the Spanish land grant claim to the Nogales area.

In July 1901, he joined the Balvanera Mining Company in Mexico as resident engineer at Ocampo, Chihuahua. He also worked as a mining engineer for other American-Mexican properties.

In August 1919, he was called to Washington, D.C. to translate documents and interpret testimony for Albert Fall's subcommittee on foreign relations investigating conditions of the Mexican Revolution. When Fall was appointed Secretary of the Interior, Flipper became his assistant. Later he was hired by William F. Buckley, Sr. (father of the founder of the *National Review*) as a consultant to the Pantepee Oil Company in Caracas, Venezuela.

Flipper died of a heart attack on May 3, 1940, at his brother's home in Atlanta. In December 1976, nearly 100 years after his court martial, Henry Ossian Flipper was granted an honorable discharge.

— *Jane Eppinga*

Originally published: October 11, 1996

Photo courtesy of the Arizona Historical Society, Tucson

Buffalo Soldiers

After the Civil War, the military formed six regiments of black soldiers: the 9th and 10th Cavalry Regiments and the 38th, 39th, 40th and 41st Infantry Regiments. Many of the men had served in the United States Colored Troops regiments during the war. They were generally former slaves who viewed military service as a steady job and as a source of food, shelter and medical benefits.

The 10th Cavalry Regiment was engaged in various campaigns against Native Americans, who referred to them as "Buffalo Soldiers" because they were as courageous as the buffalo, and they saw a similarity between the black soldier's hair and the buffalo's shaggy coat. The name eventually came to be applied to all black units.

In 1886, during the Apache wars, the 10th Cavalry pursued Geronimo and his renegade band into Mexico. During this time, there were long periods when the soldiers had nothing to do but wait. During one such period of inactivity, they constructed a stone memorial to President James Garfield, who had been assassinated a few weeks after being sworn in as president in 1881. Fifty-nine stones from the memorial were inscribed with dates, military rank and place names of the black soldiers. Today, the monument is part of a fireplace at Faraway Ranch in the Chiricahua Mountains.

On May 11, 1889, near Pima, Arizona, the entire payroll of about $29,000, for three army posts, was stolen from Major Joseph W. Wham's stage coach during a gun battle. Eight of the 12 black soldiers who served as escorts during the transport were wounded by the robbers. Two of the soldiers, Sergeant Benjamin Brown and Corporal Isaiah Mays of the 24th Infantry, were awarded the Congressional Medal of Honor for their "gallantry and meritorious conduct." (For more on the Wham payroll robbery, see page 100.)

By 1890 all Arizona forts had closed except Fort Huachuca, but there was still danger on the border as the Mexican Revolution erupted. Many Buffalo Soldiers were stationed along the border in temporary camps to protect United States interests. By 1913, Mexico was in virtual anarchy, and the United States tried to remain neutral as battles spilled over the border, endangering American lives and property.

On March 9, 1916, Francisco "Pancho" Villa and his army raided Columbus, New Mexico, killing 19 American citizens. An agreement between President Wilson and Mexican President Venustiano Carranza permitted both nations to pursue bandits across the border.

The punitive mission ordered by President Wilson was conducted by General John J. Pershing, who had the 24th and 25th Infantry and the 10th Cavalry accompany him across the border into the Sierra Madre Mountains of Chihuahua. The expeditionary forces spent the summer and fall of 1916 marching and counter-marching in the difficult terrain. (Pershing's military history, including his pursuit of Villa, is recounted on page 132).

Charles Young was one of the black soldiers in Pershing's expeditionary force. He was a graduate of West Point and served in military reconnaissance and intelligence in Haiti, the Philippines and Liberia. In Mexico he led the 2nd squadron against Pancho Villa's rebels at Agua Caliente. With the rank of captain in 1903, Young was appointed Acting Military Superintendent of Sequoia National Park — this was 13 years before the National Park Service was created — and later he became the first African-American to serve as a superintendent of a national park.

For the 40 year period from the end of the Civil War to the early years of the 20th century, Buffalo Soldiers were instrumental in taming the Western frontier and in securing the U.S. border with Mexico.

—Jane Eppinga

Originally published: January 27, 2006

Photo courtesy of the Arizona Historical Society, Tucson

Fort Grant

In 1885, when Geronimo and the Chiricahua Apaches were raiding in southern Arizona, the 10th Cavalry was transferred from Texas to Forts Grant, Thomas, Apache and Verde in the Arizona Territory. (The 10th was one of the cavalry regiments organized with black troops after the Civil War. Indians called the men Buffalo Soldiers). That's the 10th Cavalry on the parade ground of Fort Grant in the photograph at right, taken on January 31,1888.

The fort was at the north end of the Sulphur Springs Valley at an elevation of 4,000 feet, about 40 miles from Safford. Weather was mild, Mount Graham served as a backdrop, and there were fine adobe and stone buildings for officers' quarters. The fort even boasted a tennis court and a small pond for boating, both visible in the photograph.

The one drawback was the water supply. When Major Anson Mills took command of the post in 1887, there was talk of abandoning it because of the lack of dependable water. General Miles, his commanding officer, wanted to keep the fort operating and believed water could be obtained from the nearby mountains.

He secured funding and materials for Mills to construct a pipeline from Grant Creek. Adequate water could then be stored in cisterns and ponds on the post grounds. One of the ponds was the cement-lined 60' by 200' Lake Constance (named for Mills' daughter) visible in the center of the parade ground photograph.

With the new system in place, there was enough water pressure to run fountains on the post, one of which can be seen jetting out of Lake Constance in the top photo.

Among the other amenities at the fort was the First Infantry Band, which in addition to parade ground duty, performed minstrel shows at the fort chapel.

There was an ex-army musician working as a civilian at the fort named Anton Mazzanovich who organized shows and who probably was the source of the band shown in the lower photo. He collected photos of army life in the 1880s in the Arizona and New Mexico territories.

Mazzanovich was a musician from his earliest youth. He immigrated to San Francisco from Austria with his family in 1868, when he was eight years old. The next year, he and his father enlisted as musicians in the 21st Infantry. In those days, musicians were expected to fight as well as perform. Although Anton was too young to carry a weapon, he served as an orderly during the Modoc wars along the California-Oregon border. By the age of 14, he was mustered out and on his own.

Anton came to Arizona in 1881, re-enlisted and was assigned to the Regimental Band and Troop F of the 6th Cavalry. He was at Fort Apache after the Apache uprising at Cibicue and at the San Carlos Reservation when Geronimo and the Chiricahuas broke out in October 1881.

The next year he was discharged because of an eye ailment and went to work as a civilian at the Officers' Club at Fort Grant. There he pursued his love of theater and music, organizing and performing in minstrel shows. By all accounts they were a great success.

— *Arizona Capitol Times*

Originally published: June 10, 1987

Troops on the parade ground at Fort Grant in1888.

The Fort Grant Band in rehearsal.

Photos courtesy Arizona Historical Society, Tucson and Phoenix

McClintock and Brodie in the National Guard

This photograph of a group of officers at the Arizona National Guard Regimental Camp at the rifle range near Prescott was taken on September 15, 1904. Seated in the front row are James H. McClintock (left) and Alexander Brodie. Both men were Arizona Rough Riders and frontier leaders.

McClintock, born in 1864 in Sacramento, Califormia, emigrated to Arizona in June 1879 to join his brother, who was publisher of the *Phoenix Herald*. He worked as a newspaperman, rancher, Phoenix Postmaster, and became a published historian. He was also elected justice of the peace in Tempe.

In April 1898 he assisted William O. "Buckey" O'Neill in recruiting a cavalry regiment for the Spanish American War. This unit, known as the Rough Riders, saw action in Cuba, and McClintock was seriously wounded in action there.

In 1902, he became colonel of a militia, commanding the First Arizona Infrantry, which was called upon to keep order during large-scale labor unrest in Morenci. The unit was also involved in border security operations.

McClintock Road, McClintock High School in Tempe and McClintock Hall on the ASU campus are named after him.

Alexander Brodie was an Indian fighter under General Crook, as well as an engineer, miner, and at the time of the photograph, 15th Governor of the Arizona Territory. He had served in the Rough Riders as well as overall commander of the three troops of Arizona soldiers. The camp in this photograph was named for him — Camp Brodie — and he was there to inspect the troops.

For military history buffs, the photograph demonstrates a period of transition in army uniforms from the traditional blue of the Civil War to the new khaki of the Spanish American War. The two non-commissioned officers at right have combined the old and the new, wearing blue campaign shirts with the straight-leg khaki pants and canvas leggings worn in the 1898 fighting in Cuba. The cap cords on their hats are from an even later date — 1902 — and were added to designate rank.

McClintock and Brodie and the three captains standing in the back row are wearing the new uniforms. Rank is designated by the badge pinned to the outer end of the shoulder straps. The uniform includes cross-strapped leather leggings and brown shoes. The fellow on the end is wearing a new hat — the 1902 Bell Crown cap. The other men are wearing an older campaign hat.

— *Burnice Armstrong*

Originally published: April 22, 1987

Photo courtesy of the Arizona Historical Society, Phoenix

The Other Heroes of War

The soldier heroes of war are immortalized in bronze and stone, shouldering weapons, riding great steeds and urging their forces toward battle. Yet courage in war is not limited to adult males. Women and children also act in bold and noble ways in war. The Mexican Revolution (1911-1920) was no exception.

Many battles raged in and about Naco, Sonora, near the Arizona border. Men fought those battles, but children also carried and used weapons, and women nursed the wounded amidst flying bullets and exploding shells.

In 1914, a battle erupted between rebel troops of Governor Maytoreno and Mexican Federal troops led by General Benjamin Hill — who was Mexican despite his name. Hill's troops held Naco, constructed breastworks, dug trenches and equipped them with electric searchlights and piped in water. More than 8,000 soldiers took part in battles over a three month period.

Two American doctors staffed the small hospital at Naco assisted by several women nurses, including Mrs. Morelos, a Mexican-trained nurse. One day two wounded enemy soldiers, both Yaqui Indians, arrived at the hospital. Morelos and the doctors treated them as they did the other soldiers.

As the Yaquis lay recovering, two officers arrived and demanded the hospital release the soldiers. They were to be executed. Morelos protested, but the officers refused to listen and moved to take the men by force. Then, according to a story in the *Bisbee Daily Review*, Morelos "drew a small Derringer from her breast, placed herself in front of the helpless prisoners and said, 'If you take them, you'll do so over my dead body.'" The Yaquis remained in the hospital.

The *Review* also wrote about the bravery of a young boy called simply Chamaco. The lad overheard officers asking for volunteers to cross open ground and plant a bomb in the opposing army's camp. The men all refused to undertake the mission. Chamaco volunteered.

The *Review* reported: "To the shame of the grown men, the child was given the bomb to which a long wire was attached and set off in the direction of the Yaqui camp. He nearly reached his destination before he was sighted by the Yaquis. A volley of shots was fired… and he was instantly killed, a sacrifice to a cause about which he probably knew little."

Señorita Carmen Foss of Douglas also nursed soldiers in the small Naco hospital during the war. One day she ran out of bandages and cotton for the wounded. The only way for her to acquire more was to cross to Naco, Arizona. Mortar and artillery shells rained down on Naco, Sonora, but the diminutive nurse left the hospital anyway and walked toward the U.S. border as though she were shopping for dinner.

Soldiers on both sides of the battle lines hid behind trenches and walls for protection, but Foss boldly walked to her destination.

After crossing the border, an American officer warned her she was in mortal danger being so exposed, but she continued to the Naco Hotel and purchased medical supplies. Then, bandages in hand, she walked back across the border into the hellish rain of shrapnel, stopping only to help a wounded man and lead him to the hospital.

The *Review* reported: "She moved on to where a stretcher-laden procession [was] making [its] way from the trenches. She joined them and passed out of sight up a street into which the deadly aim of the Maytorena gunners were sending bursting shells with whir and bang almost deafening."

No statues or monuments have been built in the likeness of these women and children. Their names and deeds are for the most part lost in time. But they stared into the hell of war, touched it with a bit of humanity and, perhaps, steered men back toward peace.

— *Tom Vaughan*

Originally published: October 18, 2002

A young boy holds a rifle in Naco, Sonora circa 1914. Many boys died in the Mexican Revolution probably without ever understanding the political significance of what they were doing.

Photo courtesy Bisbee Mining and Historical Museum, McKinney collection.

Border Duty, 1916

Pancho Villa's attack on Columbus, New Mexico, in the early morning hours of March 9, 1916, set in motion a huge mobilization of the U.S. Army and the National Guard. By July 31, almost 111,000 Guardsmen were on the border, and an additional 40,000 awaited orders in mobilization camps around the country.

Among the first Guard units called into federal service was the First Arizona Infantry Regiment, which arrived by train at Camp Harry J. Jones, near Douglas, on May 12 and 13, 1916. More than 1,000 well-wishers had cheered the special train carrying most of the Guardsmen as it passed through Tucson at 6 a.m. on May 12.

As with most National Guard units called to the border, the Arizona contingent was undermanned. Arriving in Douglas with 49 officers and 837 enlisted men, it was 29 men short of its required peacetime strength and 1,029 short of the troops it needed to be accepted for federal service in wartime.

Upon arrival, each Guardsman was required to take an oath transferring his allegiance from the state to the federal government.

The mobilization efforts revealed the special character of several of the Arizona companies. Company F consisted of Papago, Pima, Apache and Hopi as well as Mission Indian students from the Phoenix Indian School. Newspapers around the state proudly boasted that it was the only truly all-Indian military unit in the country. Yuma's Company L, meanwhile, included 15 Yuma Indians among its members. Company E was composed exclusively of Mexican-American Guardsmen, most of them native Tucsonans. They spoke Spanish almost exclusively while in camp.

Arizona Guard units were quickly dispersed from Camp Harry J. Jones to locations along the border to relieve detachments of the First U.S. Cavalry.

On June 21, four companies left by train for Camp Stephen A. Little outside Nogales. Other units took up positions at John Slaughter's Ranch east of Douglas and at the rail stop of Forrest on the El Paso & Southwestern Railroad 12 miles east of Naco, Arizona. Later, deployment moved Arizona units to Fort Huachuca and to Roosevelt Dam.

In early September, the units were ordered to consolidate near Naco, and the troops began to hope they would soon cross over into Mexico to join General John J. Pershing and his troops fighting Pancho Villa. Failing that, they hoped to be released from federal service altogether. Instead, they spent another seven months in Naco, waiting and watching. Meanwhile, other Guard units were released from duty and returned to their home states.

The tedium of camp life was relieved by a variety of visitors: military officers from Washington D.C., out West to assess troop preparedness, and family, friends and sweethearts came to see what the soldiering business was all about. They peered into tents, sampled the food, experienced the heat and a few shouldered weapons and posed for the camera.

In an effort to boost morale, the regimental staff instituted regular dances for officers and their wives, many of whom regularly visited the Naco encampment. Other social activities included a Lincoln's birthday party, an enlisted men's Halloween party, a Washington's Day parade and a masquerade ball.

National and state elections on Nov. 7 provided a brief diversion, but the holidays proved especially difficult. To lift some of the Thanksgiving gloom, the regimental mess served a lunch of roast turkey, oyster soup, cranberry sauce, French fried potatoes, parsnips, dressing, celery, turnovers, pie, cheese and nuts, and finished with cigars, cigarettes and coffee.

In late November and early December, fresh lumber arrived for framing and flooring tents. Under other circumstances, the men might have reacted positively. But they understood that the upgrade to their living quarters meant their stay on the border was being extended.

Finally in late February of 1917, the troops got word they would be released from border duty on March 27. The men, eager to return to civilian life, began to prepare almost immediately. Military drills were suspended. Physical examinations, inspection of records by regular army officers and a 15-day paid furlough were all prepared for the appointed day. By March 26, all bed sacks, stoves and company equipment were turned in. The Arizona troops spent their last night in Naco sleeping under the stars.

The next morning as the regiment formed up for the formal mustering out, the men were greeted with a telegram from the War Department notifying them that because of the possibility of war with Germany, all National Guard units still in federal service were being retained in place. The staff reissued equipment, and by March 29, the men were once again sleeping in tents and trudging back to the firing ranges to continue training.

That fall the regiment moved to Camp Kearny near San Diego, where the troops received additional training, absorbed new recruits from other states and acquired a new designation — the 158th Infantry Regiment. They were deployed to Europe in August of 1918.

— *Dave Tackenberg*

Originally published: April 5, 2002

An Arizona National Guardsman in federal service on the border.

Photo courtesy Arizona Historical Foundation, ASU and Arizona Historical Society

Pershing on the Border

The top photo is a portrait of General John J. Pershing in 1917, just before being placed in command of the combined conscript and volunteer National Army organized to fight in World War I. Between 1916 and 1917, before America's involvement in hostilities in Europe, Pershing participated in the failed Mexican Expedition against Francisco "Pancho" Villa. The two other photos show him during this campaign: the one at the entrance to the tent was taken on the Arizona side of the border; the one of him sitting on a camp stool was taken at his encampment at Casas Grandes in Chihauhua.

This was a tragic time in Pershing's life. In August 1915, while he was setting up headquarters in southern Arizona, he received news that his wife and three daughters had died in a fire in San Francisco.

Pershing was born on a farm in Laclede, Missouri, on September 13, 1860. He spent his young life working on the farm and attended the local public school. But in the spring of 1882, he saw an announcement for a competitive examination for appointment to the U.S. Military Academy at West Point. He took the exam, passed and embarked on a career that would lead him to the highest rank in the U.S. Army.

At West Point, he was an average student, graduating 30th in a class of 77. However, he had a rare quality of leadership, recognized by both officers and his classmates, who elected him class president in 1886. After graduation, Pershing served as a cavalry officer at Fort Bayard, New Mexico, during the Apache wars.

In 1891, Pershing took a position as professor of military tactics at the University of Nebraska. When he arrived, he found little interest in the military among his students, lax discipline and a university faculty opposed to the establishment of a cadet corps. Within a year, he had created a well-trained company and had turned around attitudes at the university. While teaching there, he earned a law degree as well.

In June 1897, Pershing was assigned to West Point as a tactics instructor. Cadets there who disliked his strict discipline began calling him Black Jack after the leather-covered club used as a weapon. The name would stick with him throughout his military career.

In 1898, he left West Point to fight in the Spanish-American war and then spent several years in the Philippines leading a campaign against the Moros on Mindanao Island.

He returned to the U.S. in 1903, to Washington D.C., where he met Helen Frances Warren, the daughter of an influential Wyoming senator who was chairman of the Senate Committee on Military Affairs. He married Helen on January 26, 1905; the next day the couple left for Tokyo where Pershing was to act as military attaché during the Russo-Japanese war.

In 1906, shortly after the birth of the couple's first child, Pershing was promoted to brigadier general, ahead of 862 senior officers. Critics were furious, charging it was a political promotion influenced by his father-in-law. President Theodore Roosevelt responded, "To promote a man because he married a senator's daughter would be an infamy; to refuse him promotion for the same reason would be an equal infamy."

Shortly after his promotion, Pershing was sent again to the Philippines, where he assumed command of Fort McKinley near Manila. A second daughter was born at Baguio.

From 1906 until 1913, with several periods spent in the U.S., Pershing would work to subdue the Moros and bring peace to the Philippines. During that time, a son and a third daughter were born to the couple.

Pershing returned permanently to the U.S. in December 1913. That same year, General Huerta overthrew the Mexican government in a military coup, and the United States severed diplomatic relations with Mexico. Pershing applied to the War Department for an active duty assignment. In 1915, he was sent to Arizona.

In 1917, the U.S. declared war on Germany, and Pershing, by then a major general, sailed for Europe. There he organized the U.S. Army. He insisted that U.S. troops be led by U.S. officers, to the bitter opposition of the French and English who wanted the American soldiers under their own command. In September 1918, Pershing led U.S. troops to victory at the battle of St. Mihiel Salient, the first solo-victory for U.S. troops in the war.

In September 1919, Congress created the rank of General of Armies for Pershing, making him the highest-ranking military officer in U.S. history. He retired in 1924, at the age of 64.

When the U.S. entered World War II, Pershing offered his services to his country from his permanent room at Walter Reed General Hospital. He died on July 15, 1948, at the hospital. He is buried at Arlington National Cemetery.

— *Jane Eppinga*

Originally published: January 12, 2001

Photos courtesy of Library of Congress

Arizona's Greatest War Hero

These are photos of Frank Luke, Jr., the World War I flying ace. In the top photo he is standing by one of the SPADs he flew during the war. He was born in Phoenix, one of nine children, and attended Phoenix Union High School where he was an indifferent student but an outstanding athlete. His football coach, Francis Geary, called Luke the "nerviest and coolest headed... player I ever saw."

He graduated from high school in 1917 and soon after enlisted in the Army. He completed the nine-week aeronautics training course in seven weeks, won first place in assembling a machine gun while blindfolded, and later, while completing additional training in San Diego, was chosen first in his class to fly solo. He immediately put his Curtiss Jenny into a loop. For that rule infraction, he was grounded for three days. In March of 1918, less than a year after his high school graduation, he was sent to France.

There he was attached to the 27th Aero Squadron to support the drive on St. Mihiel that began on September 12, 1918. In 17 days of combat he made his reputation forever.

Luke's flying specialty was balloon strafing, an aerial warfare technique he originated. Hydrogen balloons were used by both sides as battlefield observation posts. The balloons were tethered to trucks on the ground and could be winched up and down or towed to new locations as necessary. Because they were well protected by planes in the air and by anti-aircraft and long-range machine guns on the ground, they were considered very dangerous targets.

After Luke's close friend and fellow pilot, Joseph Wehner, was shot down and killed on September 18,

Luke's commanding officer, Major Harold Hartney, ordered him to take a leave. Instead, Luke begged to be allowed to fly alone. Hartney refused, but Luke disobeyed and from that day on he flew solo. He preferred to wait until dusk when the light was poor and the balloons were being hauled in for the night. He would then swoop down out of the cloud cover to attack, sending the spotters parachuting for the ground.

Since pilots were credited with a kill only when it had been observed by two witnesses, and because Luke preferred to fly alone, there is no definitive record of the actual number of balloons and enemy aircraft Luke shot down. Luke soon developed the habit of dropping a note over the troops in the field to let them know he was in the air.

On the last day of his life, September 29, 1918, Luke took off without his commander's knowledge. He dropped his usual message on ground troops, "Look for burning balloons, Luke," then shot three out of the sky. In the action, he was hit in the shoulder and his plane badly damaged. Landing behind enemy lines near the village of Marvaux, he was able to get out of his aircraft and walk about 50 meters towards a stream before being approached by German soldiers. Instead of surrendering, Luke drew his weapon and held the enemy at bay until he died of his wounds.

Frank Luke was given the Congressional Medal of Honor posthumously on May 19, 1919. His body is interred at the Meuse-Argonne Military Cemetery at Romagne-sous-Mountfaucon, France. Today, a memorial in his honor stands at the east entrance to the Capitol. Luke Air Force Base is named for him.

— *Burnice Armstrong and Jane Eppinga*

Originally published: December 30, 1987

Top photo courtesy of the Arizona Historical Society, Phoenix; lower photo courtesy of the U.S. Air Force.

Mining & Logging

Arizona Mining Pioneer

The man in this photograph is noted Arizona mining engineer and businessman James S. Douglas, who developed the Copper Queen in Bisbee and ran the Phelps Dodge operations in Arizona. The town of Douglas was named for him.

He came to mining in a roundabout way.

He was born November 4, 1837, in Quebec, Canada, the son of a prominent physician, Dr. James D. Douglas, a retired ship's surgeon and the director of an asylum for the mentally ill. His parents did not trust the public schools in Quebec, so James's early education was under the private tutelage of a German schoolmaster.

In 1855, he enrolled at Edinburgh University in Scotland where his father had studied medicine and where he chose theology as a course of study. Within a year he was forced to return to Canada because his mother was ill. After her death, he remained in Canada and completed a Bachelor of Arts degree at Queen's University at Kingston, Ontario.

He still was intent on studying theology, however, and re-enrolled at Edinburgh University. Again family affairs confounded him. After two semesters of study, his brother died, and he was forced to return to Canada. There he discovered that his father had suffered serious financial losses on investments in gold and copper mining properties.

In 1860, he went back to Scotland and married Naomi Douglas (no relation), the daughter of Captain Walter Douglas, Commodore of the Cunard Fleet. The couple made their residence in Canada, but returned to Scotland after a year so that James could be formally admitted to the Church of Scotland as a licentiate. He passed the examination but never was ordained.

In Canada once more, he began studies in medicine at Laval University, perhaps with the intention of helping his father administer and care for the mentally ill in the family-run mental hospital.

Thomas Sherry Hunt, a chemistry professor at Laval University, apparently saw a talent in James and persuaded him to study metallurgy. That, and the young man's interest in saving his father's mining investments, led the young Douglas to a career in mining. Douglas developed new techniques for processing low grade copper ore and published his first paper, "The Gold Fields of Canada," in 1863.

That same year the family lost the lease on the mental asylum and with it a steady source of income.

Several years later, the elder Douglas mortgaged what was left of his property to purchase the Harvey Hill Copper Mine in Canada from a group of English entrepreneurs. With what little money was left, James and his father built a new reduction plant at the site. Before the plant could be brought into pro-duction, fire destroyed the reduction works.

Douglas moved his family, including his aging father, to Pennsylvania, where he organized the Chemical Copper Company and worked on processing ore. About 1869, he and his former professor, Thomas Sherry Hunt, formed a partnership and perfected a technique for processing ore. The pair designed leaching processes for mines in Utah and Montana.

Each year, Douglas's reputation as a metallurgist grew. In 1880, he traveled to Jerome in the Arizona Territory to assess mining properties in the area. Although the ore was promising, Jerome was almost 200 miles from the nearest railroad, which in Douglas's opinion rendered the properties useless.

Douglas then took the stage and traveled by horseback to Bisbee. He looked at a mine property there and persuaded Phelps Dodge, a New York mercantile house, to purchase it for $20,000. The mine became the Copper Queen and developed into a world famous enterprise and one of the largest copper producers in Arizona.

Of his first opinion of the Copper Queen, Douglas wrote in 1912:

> *"I could not have thought well of it at the time, because we professional men thought that [ore in] limestone was invariably a fake and simply placed there by Providence in order to delude us. [But]... I have a certain faith in Providence and feel that it doesn't play jokes ...[in the end] I took quite a liking to the Copper Queen."*

James Douglas spent the rest of his career working for Phelps Dodge. He oversaw development of mines at Morenci, Globe and Jerome, as well as mines in Nacozari and Caranea in Sonora.

He did not confine his activities to mining. He served as the president of El Paso & Southwestern Railway and gave large sums of money to colleges, hospitals and charities. He was especially interested in the General Memorial Hospital in New York City, which at the time was experimenting in treating cancer with radium.

He also made generous endowments to the University of Arizona.

Over the years, he made many innovations in the mining, processing and transportation of ore. He was elected president of the American Institute of Mining Engineers (AIME) in 1899 and 1900 and was awarded the John Fritz Medal at the International Engineering Congress held at San Francisco in September 1915.

James S. Douglas died June 15, 1918, at the age of 81. He left an estate worth $20 million.

— *Jane Eppinga*

Originally published: July 20, 2001

Photo courtesy of the American Institute of Mining Engineers

The Travels of a Singing Stone

This undated photograph was discovered in the files of the Bisbee Mining Museum. It shows two Bisbee miners, posing with a huge, crated mineral specimen. The base is more than 5000 pounds of malachite (which is green); the top is 800 pounds of azurite (which is deep blue). Both pieces were mined at the Copper Queen Mine in Bisbee. There is circumstantial evidence that the crate was bound for the Arizona Territorial exhibit at the Chicago World's Fair of 1893. And this is the story of how that determination was made.

The story begins with an article in the *Tombstone Prospector* in 1890 that said, "The Copper Queen of Bisbee will exhibit two cars of ore from their mines at the World's Fair."

The World's Fair nearest to the date of the article was the 1893 exposition in Chicago. Subsequent research yielded a story in the *Chicago Tribune* that referred to a photograph of a huge mineral specimen that had appeared in an edition of the *Tombstone Prospector*. The article seemed to describe the rocks in this photograph.

The *Engineering and Mining Journal* for 1893 showed a drawing of the two rocks. The article read in part: "The accompanying illustration is from a photograph showing the very handsome exhibit made in the Main Hall of the Mining Building of the Territory of Arizona, which in its general appearance is one of the most attractive of the state exhibits... The large trophy in the center is a square block of azurite from one of the Arizona mines, which is supported by a base of malachite, making a beautiful contrast of color."

The question arises concerning the post-exhibition fate of the specimens. At the Arizona State Library and Archives, a report of the Arizona Mineral Exhibit of the 1893 World's Fair by T.R. Sorb, Commissioner, states that "a three-ton sample of Azurite Carbonate of copper from the Copper Queen resided at the Museum in New York." That places the specimens in New York after the fair and implies that the large specimen was azurite, when all the other descriptions referred to malachite.

Calls to the American Museum of Natural History in New York, turned up the larger specimen which is malachite/azurite. It is on display at the museum and is the largest single mineral specimen in the hall. The smaller azurite obelisk on the top in this photograph has disappeared.

When American psychic Edgar Cayce visited the museum, he happened to pass by the great rock and said he heard music. Its powers inspired him to call it the "Singing Stone." According to the Museum's curator, Joseph Peters, however, the sounds Cayce heard are due to the porous nature of the specimen and changes in weather and humidity.

— *Tom Vaughan*

Originally published: January 21, 1994

Photo courtesy of the Bisbee Mining and Historical Museum

Breaking Camp, Flagstaff

This is moving day at one of Arizona Lumber and Timber Company's lodging camps in the early part of the 20th century. The loader is lifting a one-room cabin onto a railroad log car for transport to a new location. The cabins, which served as the sleeping quarters for the logging crews, were set on skids so they could easily be moved to the tracks for transport. Arizona Lumber and Timber Company cabins typically were built with rounded roofs like those of the three large cabins visible in the photograph.

Logging camps were common in Northern Arizona from the earliest days of the industry. Tracks were laid into an area where the company had timber rights, and cabins were taken there for the workers. When the area was logged out, the cabins were removed and the tracks were taken up and re-laid in a new area.

The logging railroad was a lumberjack's only contact with town. Each day, the train brought supplies and messages from Flagstaff and returned with a load of logs for the mill. In the event of serious injury, the locomotive served as an ambulance car. In addition to the town locomotive, there were usually one or two at the logging site for shunting cars.

Each camp had its cook and cook shack, where the workers took their meals. For many years, hogs were raised at the work camps to supply the cook shack. The animals feasted on scraps and grew to a huge size before being slaughtered.

A good cook helped to ensure a good crew. Arizona Lumber and Timber and its successor, Saginaw, were known among crews for good camp food. Even as late as the 1950s, employees from town thought it a treat to get a meal at camp.

Arizona Lumber and Timber also ran a company commissary in Flagstaff until it was destroyed by fire in the 1930s. Loggers could send their orders in with the train crew and would receive whatever they ordered the next day, provided it was available. If not, the commissary would order the item and send it out as soon as it arrived.

— *Bonnie Greer*

Originally published: June 7, 1989

Photo courtesy of Special Collections, Cline Library, Northern Arizona University

Photo by Markey: Bisbee Miners

This group of Bisbee miners visited D.A. Markey's photographic studio for a portrait shortly after their shift ended in 1895. Their shirts and pants are splattered with wax from their candles. Some of them clasp their candle holders — their only lighting while working in the pitch black underground tunnels and stopes. In the foreground are their lunch buckets.

David A. Markey immigrated to this country from Ireland as a teenager. Little is known of him, however, until he and a photographer named Mitton opened a photographic gallery at Fort Grant in 1885. Together they photographed the army post, enlisted men and officers. Markey also traveled to other army posts and Indian reservations making portraits of soldiers and Native Americans.

Markey visited Bisbee as a traveling photographer with a partner named Beckstein in 1895. Beckstein departed but Markey stayed to operate a successful gallery. In addition to photography, he succeeded as a crayon artist. Crayon or charcoal was used to enhance the imperfect photographic enlargements made in that period. In 1896, he exhibited some of his large crayon portraits at the Bisbee post office.

Once established, Markey's business attracted competition from other itinerant photographers. The Bisbee writer for the *Tombstone Prospector* defended Markey when he wrote, "Another photographer has just arrived in town to try and take the picture customs away from our local photographers. We are sorry to see the way which our people take to these outsiders and ignore established [photographers]. We have our town photographer, Mr. Markey, as accomplished a man at this business as any who have ever visited our town...."

At the turn of the century, Markey quit the photo business and opened a lunch stand. Shortly afterwards, he opened the Swim Saloon of Lowell, which became a popular hangout for the Irish of the Bisbee area. Markey moved to Courtland in 1910. After that date, we can find no further information about him.

More than fifty photographs by D.A. Markey are in the archives of the Bisbee Mining and Historical Museum. Among them are studio portraits, views of Bisbee from the hillsides, street scenes, social events, and individual houses. Markey's photographs are always of excellent tonal quality, exceedingly sharp and well composed.

— *Tom Vaughan*

Originally published: May 26, 1995

Photograph courtesy of the Bisbee Mining and Historical Museum, Power Collection

Bringing Culture to Bisbee

In 1881, Canadian-born mining consultant James E. Douglas recommended that Phelps Dodge & Company invest in Bisbee mines. From that early investment, the fortunes of both Phelps Dodge and of Bisbee grew exponentially over the next decades. Douglas went on to guide the corporation for the next 35 years. And although he never resided in Bisbee and never became a U.S. citizen, Douglas assumed an active role in the welfare of the miners and their families living there.

He traveled to Bisbee three or four times a year, inspecting mines, consulting with managers, engineers and foremen and taking an interest in the health and culture of the town. He helped establish Bisbee's first hospital, library and school.

Douglas photographed and collected images during his travels. Some of them were glass slides which could be projected onto a screen for viewing by large audiences. The projector was called a magic lantern and derived its light source from gas. It was bulky and a fire hazard. But despite the difficulties, Douglas energetically would set up a program in any convenient building in town — then invite the locals to a free evening of entertainment, culture and education.

His early lectures concerned health and sanitation. Joe Chisholm, a child contemporary of Douglas's wrote: "Every summer in the early eighties, the folk of the mining camps died off like flies from dysentery and the other dread maladies that came along with typhoid. And Professor Douglas would come hurrying into the Mules and induce the miners to come to the little school house and lecture them about adopting the best methods of sanitation known in those days."

He also lectured on history, geography, religion, art and travel. In the Bisbee section of the *Tombstone Prospector* of February 1896 a report stated: "Professor Douglas gave another of his interesting lectures on Sunday evening ... The views presented of Paris were of the finest order and the description given by the professor extremely interesting."

From February 7, 1898, we learn: "Professor Douglas gave an instructive and learned lecture at the church last evening on the early settlement of the Atlantic coast colonies."

And again in a 1903 article, the *Review* wrote: "The lecture on Ancient and Modern Egypt by Professor James Douglas was accompanied with stereopticon views of ancient and modern Egypt, and with views along the River Nile, of villages, castles, etc., and his explanations of all the pictures were given in such a lucid and novel manner that his audience was carried right along with him and in imagination could believe that they had left Bisbee far behind and were in reality making a trip down the Nile."

Other lectures given by Douglas before his death in 1918 included Bisbee history, investment in Mexico, the World's Fair, Japan, the Holy Land and railroads and transcontinental travel.

— *Tom Vaughan*

Originally published: May 3, 1995

Mining engineer James Douglas

Photo courtesy of the American Institute of Mining Engineers

A panorama of Bisbee, c. 1916

Photo courtesy of the Library of Congress

Ralph Cameron:
The Man Who Ran Bright Angel Trail

Both photographs are of Ralph Cameron. In the larger photo, taken in 1904, he is at the entrance to one of the mines he owned in the Indian Gardens area of the Grand Canyon. The studio portrait is Cameron when he was U.S. senator from Arizona in the early 1920s.

Cameron and his brother Niles were among the early settlers of the Grand Canyon. They arrived in Flagstaff in 1883, but soon moved to the Grand Canyon, where they acquired mining claims and went into business.

In 1891, Ralph helped Peter Berry improve an old Indian trail into the canyon, which became Bright Angel Trail and was operated as a toll road. The Camerons acquired Berry's interest in the early 1900s and operated the toll road for five years under an agreement with Coconino County, thus effectively controlling the main access trail to the canyon.

The Cameron brothers also built the Cameron Hotel at the head of Bright Angel Trail to accommodate tourists and to serve as a jumping off point for mule trips down the toll road.

One of the mining claims the brothers filed became the Last Chance Copper Mine, just below Grandview Point. Peter Berry had also built the Grandview Trail in 1892 to make the mine more accessible. The brothers worked the mine regularly and even built a small stamp mill at Grandview Point. Ore was hauled to the nearest railhead and shipped to smelters in Texas, Colorado and New Jersey. The mine was sold in 1902.

The Cameron's other mining claims were at the head of Bright Angel Trail and at Indian Gardens, giving them effective control of the only reliable trail and water source on the South Rim.

When the Santa Fe Railroad completed a rail spur in 1901 to the South Rim from the main line at Williams, it bypassed Cameron's hotel and ended at the newly built Bright Angel Hotel.

Cameron was convinced that the National Park Service had conspired with the Santa Fe to run him out of business. Some contemporary accounts agree with his assessment, mentioning that the Santa Fe was trying to force him to release his holdings at the canyon. This began a long dispute between Cameron and the Park Service that lasted a qaaurter of a century.

In 1907, he filed a blizzard of mining claims in an effort to retain control of Bright Angel Trail. The claims cost him almost nothing to file and develop and were well worth the effort, since he was charging $1 per person or animal to use the Bright Angel Trail. However, the Park Service challenged the validity of his claims, and in 1909 a court ruled against Cameron. Thwarted by the judicial system, he ran for and was elected as a delegate to Congress from the Arizona Territory.

He went to Washington to lobby for his interests, while his brother and others looked after business at the canyon. Over the next several years, he became interested in hydroelectric power and began to lobby for several dam projects he proposed for the canyon. He also is credited with getting the funds to build a bridge across the Little Colorado River at a small community and trading post which later was named for him — Cameron.

After an unsuccessful run for governor in 1914 against George W.P. Hunt, Cameron was elected to the U.S. Senate in 1920 and immediately set out to attack the National Park Service in a serious way. He lobbied to have its director replaced and even managed to have the Grand Canyon budget deleted from the Park Service budget for a period of three months. The budget finally was reinstated, but the dollar amount was reduced by one-sixth to $75,000.

When Coconino County, which needed money to improve a dirt road from the community of Maine (east of Williams), negotiated with the Park Service to exchange Bright Angel Trail for a payment of $100,000, Cameron backers forced the issue to a vote, and the proposal lost.

In 1926, Cameron lost his re-election bid to Carl Hayden, and with it much of his influence. Two years later, he moved to the East Coast.

Once he was out of office, the Park Service successfully negotiated the exchange of Bright Angel Trail for a road from Williams to the Grand Canyon. The federal government was to maintain the road in perpetuity, but after a few years turned it over to the state.

Today Bright Angel Trail is operated and maintained by the Park Service.

— *Bonnie Greer*

Originally published: May 16, 1990

Photo courtesy of the Kolb Collection, Northern Arizona University

Photo courtesy of the Library of Congress

The Coconino Giant, 1920

This is the largest tree ever cut in the Coconino National Forest — 65 feet tall, six feet in diameter and nearly 19 feet around at the base. It was felled in June 1920 by loggers for the Arizona Lumber and Timber Company, who posed for this photograph when they had finished the job. The tree was cut into four 16-foot logs and was scaled at 10,500 board feet — enough lumber to build a modest home. (A board foot measures 12 inches by 12 inches by 1 inch.)

According to Forest Service records, no tree larger than this has been cut in the intervening years, and only one other tree in the Coconino has come close in size. That was a five-foot diameter pine logged about 1942 by the Saginaw Manistee Lumber company, successor to Arizona Lumber and Timber. It was so large, it damaged the green chain, the conveyor that carries logs from the pond to the second story mill saws, and workers had to hand trim the log sections before they could be sent up to the mill.

Of course, trees the size of this one are frequently cut in other forests. Lumbermen from Montana, Idaho, and the Pacific Northwest laugh at the size of the trees in the Coconino, which today rarely exceed thirty inches in diameter. The Forest Service uses selective cutting procedures, permitting logging of larger trees to make way for smaller growth (the understory in forestry terminology) and cutting of smaller trees to allow larger trees to mature without competition. The trees used for lumber run only 20 to 25 inches in diameter, mere fence posts to out-of-state lumbermen. The smaller trees run 9 to 12 inches in diameter and are used for paper pulp.

A six-inch section of the Coconino Giant was cut and shipped to the University of Arizona for preservation. A.E. Douglass was there doing research on tree rings, although the famed Laboratory of Tree Ring Research would not be officially established until 1937. According to a curator at the Lab, the specimen from the tree in this photo is undoubtedly still around, although it is probably stored in an area of the warehouse that no one has been in for years.

— *Bonnie Greer*

Originally published: October 21, 1987

Photo courtesy of the Arizona Historical Society, Pioneer Museum

The Man with No Last Name

This photograph, taken around 1920, shows Lou of Oatman, Arizona, standing in front of the building that served as his place of business. Most of the information on the sign appears to be a listing of real estate he was selling or renting. Old-timers remember him going up and down the street with a megaphone that was inscribed "International Cigars," giving the stock market quotes, the news of the day and offering to list anything you wanted to buy or sell. He always ended his spiels with: "The wind blew, the bull flew, for information, see Lou the Jew." Those words fall harshly on modern ears, but that is what he called himself.

No one is certain of his last name, although it may have been Grossman, and sadly, no one seems to know where he came from or what happened to him. He was one of the many men who showed up in boom towns on what was still a frontier — even as late as 1920 — and then moved on. He was probably drawn to Oatman by the gold discoveries in the area.

The rich ore vein at Oatman was discovered by a Mohave Indian named Ben Taddock, who is said to have discovered gold ore glittering on a trail sometime around 1900. He filed a claim which he later sold to the Vivian Mining Company. The mine gave its name to the first town in the area.

In the three year period from 1904 to 1907, more than three million dollars in ore was mined in the area. The town's name was changed from Vivian to Oatman in 1909. It is said that Harry Knight and L.P. Hansen gave the community the name of Oatman to honor Olive and Mary Ann Oatman, who were captured by Indians during the massacre of their family in 1851. Mary Ann died in captivity, but Olive survived and was rescued from her captors in the Oatman area. Another story is that a wealthy Mohave Indian named John Oatman, who claimed to be Olive's son and who was active in mining in the area, influenced the name change.

Additional ore bodies were discovered in 1910 and 1915, and two smaller communities — Mazona and Old Trails — sprang up in the area. From the first discovery until 1931, the district produced $36 million of gold ore. At one time more than 10,000 residents lived in Oatman, but by 1958 only 60 remained. Mazona was destroyed by fire in 1918, and by 1925 only a few people lived in Old Trails.

Today, more people live in Oatman than in 1958. With its close proximity to Bullhead City, it has become a popular tourist stop.

— Jane Eppinga with help from Loren Wilson and Ed Edwards of the Mohave County Historical Society

Originally published: January 15, 1992

Photo courtesy of the Mohave County Historical Society

Phelps Dodge Mercantile, Bisbee

This is the Phelps Dodge company store on Bisbee's main street in 1939. It had just been rebuilt after a disastrous fire. The store was part of a company-owned chain that included branches in the mining towns of Ajo, Clifton, Douglas and Morenci, Arizona; in Dawson, Hidalgo, Playas and Tyrone, New Mexico; and in Nacozari, Sonora, Mexico.

The Bisbee store had its origins in 1886 when the Copper Queen Consolidated Mining Company (which later became Phelps Dodge) bought a dry-goods store on Main Street from a Mrs. Crossey. They named the store the Copper Queen Mercantile, but most people knew it as simply The Mercantile. Three years later when the railroad arrived, the company built a separate building for the store a short distance away. That building gave managers enough space to house all the goods brought by rail that had previously been unavailable in town.

The Mercantile grew from a slant-roofed stone building to a sprawling two-story brick department store. It carried everything a family could want: food stuffs, meat and fish, drugs, hardware and clothing. Because it was a company store, miners were given credit as soon as they were hired at the Copper Queen Mine. There was no interest or carrying charges, although all purchases could be deducted from miner's pay packets. In spite of the advantage of being a company store, the mercantile had plenty of competition. In the early 1900s, there were as many as 50 grocery stores and five to seven clothing stores in town.

Through the boom days of World War I, the roaring '20s and most of the depression era '30s, the Mercantile store was a fixture in Bisbee. But on the night of September 23, 1938, the familiar brick two-story structure burned to the ground in a fire of unknown origin that was so fierce the Bisbee, Lowell and Warren fire departments could do little but try to keep it from spreading to other buildings.

What was left of the structure was demolished, and the following year this modern two-story, art deco-style building was completed. The contractor on the project was a young unknown named Del Webb, who would later make his mark in the post-war building boom in Arizona, first as a contractor and later as a developer whose most notable achievement was the creation of an adults-only retirement community — Sun City.

The Phelps Dodge Mercantile Store operated until June 1976, when it closed for good. The building was purchased by Bisbee's Industrial Development Authority in 1980. Recently it was sold to a private investor who has rented the interior spaces to a restaurant and several small shops.

Phelps Dodge gradually sold off all its mercantile properties to third parties. The last of the mercantile stores to be operated by the company was the one in Morenci. It is now a Bashas' supermarket. In 2007, Phelps Dodge was acquired by New Orleans-based Freeport McMoRan Copper and Gold. After the sale, Freeport moved its corporate headquarters to Phoenix.

— *Tom Vaughan*

Originally published: November 21, 1990

Photo courtesy of the Bisbee Mining and Historical Museum, Phelps Dodge collection

Native Americans

Emory Meets the Pimas: All 'Honesty and Virtue'

This excellent sketch of the Gila River Valley was rendered by Lieutenant (later General) William H. Emory of the Army Corps of Topographical Engineers, as he accompanied General Stephen Watts Kearny's Army of the West and guide Kit Carson on the 1846 trek across the Southwest enroute to California. His journal of that expedition later appeared in book form as *Notes of a Military Reconnaissance*. The lower photo shows Emory as a much older man in an undated studio photo perhaps taken by Mathew Brady.

The first known contact between Pima Indians and Anglo-Americans occurred in the 1820s, when fur trappers worked the Gila River taking beaver pelts. Even so, in 1846, when the Kearny expedition arrived in the area, little was known of the Pima way of life. Emory, who conducted the first scientific study of the natives and their land, left a striking portrait of the culture.

On November 11, 1846, Emory entered the main Pima villages near present-day Sacaton.

We were at once impressed with the beauty, order and disposition of the arrangements for irrigation and draining the land," he recorded. "Corn, wheat and cotton are the crops of this peaceful and intelligent race of people. All the crops have been gathered in and the stubbles show they have been luxuriant. The cotton has been stacked for drying on the tops of sheds. The fields are sub-divided, by ridges of earth, into rectangles of about 200 x 100 feet for the convenience of irrigating. The fences are of sticks, wattled with willow and mesquite, and in this particular, set an example of economy in agriculture worthy to be followed by the Mexicans, who never use fences at all. The houses of the people are mere sheds, thatched with willow and corn stalks.

With the exception of the chief …who was clad in cast-off Mexican toggery, the dress of the men consisted of a cotton serape of domestic manufacture and a breech cloth. Their hair was very long, and clubbed up. The women wore nothing but the serape pinned about the loins...

To us it was a rare sight to be thrown in the midst of a large nation of what is termed wild Indians, surpassing many of the Christian nations in agriculture, little behind them in the useful arts, and immeasurably before them in honesty and virtue. During the whole of yesterday, our camp was full of men, women, and children, who sauntered amongst our packs, unwatched, and not a single instance of theft was reported.

The Pima are closely related to the Tohono O'Odham, and anthropologists believe both groups are descended from the Hohokam, thought to have arrived in central Arizona as early as 300 B.C.

Because the Gila River was located on the extreme northern frontier of New Spain, the Pima were little touched by Spanish and, later, Mexican influence. It was not until the arrival of Anglo-Americans that Pima culture suffered from outside influence. A little over a decade after Emory's report, the gentle, agrarian Pima were sent to the first of Arizona's Indian reservations—the Gila River Reservation, established in 1859.

Emory is best remembered in history for having led the boundary survey of the land acquired from Mexico after ratification of the Gadsden Purchase in 1854.

— W. Lane Rogers

Originally published: May 25, 1996

Photo courtesy of the Arizona Historical Society

Manuelito

These photos are of the Navajo leader Manuelito. The one with his wife Chiquita is dated 1881. The other was taken in 1887, when the chief was 68.

In the mid 1800s, Manuelito led the Navajos in some of the fiercest battles of the Indian wars with the U.S. Army.

He was born near Bear's Ear in Utah and belonged to the Bit'ahni clan. His father, Cayetano, was a prominent Navajo leader. At 16, he married Chiquita, the daughter of Narbona, a Navajo peacemaker, and traveled with him on peace missions. He soon grew tired of peace negotiations, and despite Narbona's teachings, became a warrior, believing the answer to the Navajos' problems was to fight.

His first battle was in 1835 against about 1,000 Mexicans and Pueblo Indians. For protection in battle, he painted snakes on the soles of his moccasins and carried a shield stretched with the hide of a mountain lion. When the battle began, he charged the enemy, shouting wildly, and jumped one of the Pueblans, clubbing him to death. Later, he cooked the warrior's scalp and brought it back to his companions, chewing on it to prove his fierceness.

He continued warring against Mexicans and other Indian tribes for the next ten years. By the 1840s, U.S. settlers in the New Mexico Territory were threatening traditional Navajo lands. Manuelito joined Barboncito in a series of raids against the settlers and began building a network of sub-chiefs who specialized in various aspects of war. Eventually, he became one of the Navajos' leading war strategists.

In 1846, Manuelito and thirteen headmen signed the Bear Springs peace treaty to end fighting with the U.S. The peace, however, did not endure. Due to a misunderstanding and arrogance on the part of the U.S. commander at another peace conference three years later, Narbona was killed. Afterwards, Manuelito threatened to drive all white men out of Navajo country, saying, "These Americans are arrogant and untrustworthy. I want nothing more of their bargains."

He began raiding in New Mexico, attacking ranches and driving off hundreds of sheep and cattle. In July l853, Major Henry Lane Kendrick told the Navajos that the U.S. would wage war against them if they continued their raids. Navajo peace leaders persuaded Manuelito to return the sheep and cattle he had stolen. Two months later, he attended a meeting in Santa Fe, where he listened to pleas by Navajos and warnings by the U.S. government representatives. By July 1855, another treaty had been drafted. Although he disagreed with the terms, which included turning over all wrongdoers to the authorities, he signed the document.

The following year, the Navajos were ordered to remove all their livestock from the grazing lands around Fort Defiance. Manuelito objected, telling the Indian agent Henry Dodge, "Your army has horses and wagons, mules, and many soldiers. They are capable of hauling in feed for their own livestock. We must take our sheep and cattle wherever there is good grazing, and that land around the fort has been ours for many years." He threatened the agent, saying he could muster a thousand warriors in less than a day.

He told the fort commander, Major William T.H. Brooks, "The water there is mine, not yours, and the same with the grass. Even the ground it grows from belongs to me." Brooks replied that the Army would defend its rights to the hay camp, and he replaced Manuelito as headman. Later that night, U.S. troops slaughtered all of the Navajo livestock that remained at the hay camp.

Hostilities continued for more than five years. In February 1860, Manuelito and 500 warriors burned all the haystacks around Fort Defiance, and two months later, he and Barboncito, along with a 1,000 warriors, attacked the fort. After another year of fighting, an exhausted and weary Manuelito and 32 headmen agreed to another treaty.

Three years later, General James H. Carleton ordered the Navajos and Apaches to be rounded up and taken to Bosque Redondo, in eastern New Mexico. Thousands of Navajos were captured and forced to walk 300 miles from their homelands in northern Arizona and New Mexico to the reservation. More than 8,000 Navajos made the "Long Walk." Many died.

Manuelito and his band avoided capture by hiding in the Grand Canyon, but by 1866, frequent attacks by Utes, Hopis and New Mexicans had worn them down. On September 1, 1866, weakened, wounded and facing another winter, Manuelito and 23 companions rode to Fort Wingate and surrendered.

On June 1, 1868, a final treaty between the U.S. and the Navajos was signed. General William Tecumseh Sherman appointed Barboncito head chief, Manuelito sub-chief of the eastern Navajos and Ganado Mucho sub-chief of the western Navajos.

After signing the treaty, Manuelito became convinced that education was the key to gaining Navajo independence and pride. In 1882, he became the first Navajo to send his children to Carlyle Indian School in Pennsylvania. But when one son became ill and died, Manuelito decided that he had been wrong in encouraging education for his people.

In 1894, at age 75, the great Navajo warrior contracted measles and shortly afterward died of pneumonia.

— *Jane Eppinga*

Originally published: June 25, 2004

Photos courtesy of the Denver Public Library, Western History Collection; X-32995 and X-32996

The Boss with the High Forehead

This is John P. Clum, Indian Agent for the San Carlos Apaches, founder of the *Tombstone Epitaph*, and the first man to take Geronimo captive. He is standing with a group of "good Apaches" in a photograph that may have been made at the Philadelphia Exposition of 1876. Clum and a group of Apaches attended the Exposition, performing in a Wild West show to raise funds along the way and traveling to Washington, D.C. for a look at the government.

John Clum was a New York native who came west in 1871 at the age of 20 to work for the U.S. Weather Service in Santa Fe. Two years later he was appointed Indian Agent on the San Carlos Reservation in the Arizona Territory. There he determined to give the Indians a square deal, encouraging self-government by appointing and training Indian judges and policemen. He made a distinction between the bad Apaches (Geronimo, Victorio and the Chiricahuas) who were attacking settlers in the southeastern part of the Arizona Territory and the cooperative Apaches of the San Carlos Reservation, who were providing scouts for the U.S. Army then fighting the Indian Wars.

The Apaches returned his respect, making him a full brother and giving him an Apache name that meant Boss-With-The-High-Forehead, because of his baldness.

In 1877, Clum and the San Carlos scouts were sent to New Mexico after Geronimo. They captured him and brought him back in chains, along with the leader Victorio and approximately 4,000 Chiricahua Apaches. In a letter to James McClintock, Clum said the San Carlos Reservation would have been "as calm as a New England village" without the addition of the 4,000 Chiricahuas.

At the same time, Clum realized the savings to the U.S. government resulting from keeping the Apaches on the reservation and at peace. He proposed that, for a modest additional outlay, the Indian Bureau could increase his salary of $1,600 a year, purchase equipment for two more companies of Apache scouts, and put him in charge of the Apaches. The army could then go home. The authorities in Washington thought the idea ridiculous, and territorial merchants, who made their living supplying the army, bitterly opposed it. A disgusted Clum resigned his post.

Two weeks later, Geronimo was released from jail and the Indian Wars resumed.

Clum moved to Tucson and bought the *Arizona Citizen*, which he eventually moved to Florence. In 1880, he moved to Tombstone, then booming with the discovery of silver, and founded the *Tombstone Epitaph*. He was elected mayor of Tombstone. Virgil Earp was his chief of police and Wyatt Earp the deputy marshal. The fight at the OK Corral took place during his tenure.

Clum's wife died in Tombstone, leaving him with a young son. He moved to Los Angeles, where he later remarried and took a job with the U.S. Postal Department. In 1898, he was sent to Alaska to organize the mail service there. He died in Los Angeles at 80 in 1932.

— *Burnice Armstrong*

Originally publshed: August 23, 1989

Photo courtesy of the Arizona Historical Society, Phoenix

Hualapai Leaders

These three native Americans were leaders of the Hualapai Tribe of northwestern Arizona in the late 1800s. Cherum (center), the head chief, lived in the Mineral Park area with a small band of three men and 14 women and children. The men earned money by working in the mines in the area and chopping wood; the women washed clothes and gathered hay.

Hualapai Charley (left), Cherum's brother, was war chief and an enemy of the whites. However, after serving a prison term at Alcatraz in California, he decided the whites outnumbered the Indians and that war was harmful to the tribe. He opposed the effort by the U.S. government to move his people to a reservation on the Big Sandy River south of Kingman, where there was disease and fever. He spoke fluent English and the military considered him "tricky."

Levi-Levi, (right) half brother to Cherum and Hualapai Charley, lived in the Hualapai mountains. During peace negotiations in April of 1869, Levi-Levi took the lead in suing for peace to save his people, who lived at Canyon Station.

These three men also were organizers of the Ghost Dance in Arizona. The Ghost Dance was the central ritual in a messianic religion founded by a Paiute prophet named Wovoka (who was also known as Jack Walker) in the late 1800s. The religion prophesied the end of the westward expansion of the whites and a return of the land to the Indians. Certain rituals, including a dance performed in a circle, were performed on five successive nights. During the dances, participants went into trances and saw visions. Clashes between the Ghost Dance practitioners and soldiers culminated in the massacre at Wounded Knee Creek in South Dakota in 1890.

Early in 1889, Mohave County residents were informed that Cherum had joined the Paiute leaders who were participating in Ghost Dances, and that he was bringing the ritual to Arizona. The *Mohave County Miner* on June 18, 1890, reported that most of the "Walapai" Tribe had gathered on the Thompson ranch, where they carried on the Ghost Dance for nearly two months, growing more excited and wrought up every day. Several deaths were supposed to have occurred from over-exertion. In the fall, the *Miner* again reported, "The Wallapai Indians are holding another 'ghost dance' in Free's Wash in the Walapai mountains." (The *Miner* seemed to have trouble with the spelling of the tribe's name.)

Hualapai Charley died on May 11, 1906. When word spread that he was about to die, Indians traveled great distances to participate in the death rituals. Until a few hours before his death, Charley directed the activities, which included a war dance and the wailing of the old women. After his death, his house was burned, his body cremated and several of his horses killed. The *Miner* announced, "The corpulent figure of this picturesque Indian will no longer be seen on the streets of Kingman."

We do not have records of the death of Levi-Levi or Cherum.

— *Jane Eppinga*

Photo courtesy Mohave County Historical Society

Award of Merit

By State Mine Inspector Joe Hart

I chose the Times Past issue that featured Hualapai Charlie because of the connection to mining in Mohave County and also to my family. Hualapai Charlie worked for my great-grandfather, Charles Sherman, on his turquoise mining claims on Ithaca Peaks located in Mohave County. My great-grandfather sold his turquoise claims to Tiffany's of New York around the turn of the century for $6,000. My grandmother (daughter to Charles Sherman), Katherine Sherman, married Isaac Newton Hart and taught school on the Hualapai reservation in Valentine, Arizona.

There was not much mining activity at the Ithaca Peaks location until 1962, when the mine was purchased by the Duval Mining Corporation. My father-in-law Riley Reeves was the operational manger for Isabell Construction, which was the construction company that did the exploration and equipment set-up for the mine to begin operation. My father, two brothers and myself worked for Isabelle Construction and later for the Duval Corporation. I was the safety/shift forman at the Duval mine until it closed in 1983. The mine has been mostly inactive since that time. However, it has recently reopened and is expected to be in full operation again in 2009.

Tuba Trading Post

The building in the top photo is the famous old trading post at Tuba City, sometime in the 1940s. The photo of the corn field was taken by Ansel Adams at the trading post in 1941 during fulfillment of a commission by the National Park Service to make a photo mural for the Department of Interior Building in Washington, D.C.

The trading post was built in the late 1880s — the only store in the then-Mormon settlement of Tuba City. Tuba was an English approximation of the name of the friendly Hopi chief Tlvi).

The first store was in the small shed-like structure at the left of the photograph. The larger octagonal building wasn't completed until Babbitt Brothers Trading Company bought the post from owner Charles Algert in 1905, two years after the federal government took ownership of the town in a reservation boundary settlement that displaced the Mormons.

The Babbitts hired veteran Indian trader Samuel Preston as manager, and in 1906 he designed and supervised the construction of the unique two-story, eight-sided main building. The massive metal-roofed, native stone structure combined the best of two cultures, adopting the symbolic east-facing door and circular design of Navajo architecture, and adding an innovative clerestory above the trading floor that provided natural light and ventilation for the building.

Early historian and explorer Sharlot Hall remarked that the space was functional, with the stock of goods all disposed on shelves along the wall in plain sight, but behind a high counter that ran all around the large room.

"The Indian can see anything they want to buy, but they cannot handle it as the clerk is behind the counter and his customers out in the octagonal court in the center."

The trading post stocked the usual merchandise of interest to customers on the remote reservation: tinned foods, bolts of cloth, medicine for both humans and livestock, tobacco, tools, tack and kerosene. In the 1920s, the post was well known as a market for wool and sheep, evidenced by the prominent corral north of the main building (center right in photograph).

A trip to the post was a social event of some consequence. The business of trading kept customers there for most of the day, as each awaited a turn at the counter. A strict rule of behavior was observed — only one customer was waited on at a time. Each transaction was carefully thought out, then livestock or native crafts such as weaving, silverwork and basketry were exchanged for the coveted goods of the 20th century.

In 1985, James E. Babbitt, grandson of one of the original Babbitt brothers and brother of former Arizona Governor Bruce Babbitt, took on an ambitious restoration project of the post to correct a misguided 1950s remodeling. A false ceiling was removed, allowing natural light to fill the interior once again. The entrance was relocated to the east again (under the gabled entry wing) and a fresh coat of paint was given to the tongue and groove interior paneling.

The Babbitt Brothers Trading Company sold the Tuba Trading Post to the Navajo Nation in November 1999.

— *Joan Brundige-Baker*

Originally published: February 8, 1989

Photo courtesy of Chuck Abbott

Photo courtesy of the National Archives

Lorenzo Hubbell Jr. with Julia Joe

This is Indian trader Lorenzo Hubbell, Jr. with a Navajo woman thought to be Julia Joe of Greasewood, the weaver of the giant rug on which the two are standing. The 16 by 27 foot rug weighed nearly 130 pounds. It was put on display outside of Hubbell's trading post in Oraibi around 1912 for this promotional photograph.

Lorenzo Jr. was the son of the famous Indian trader Don Lorenzo Hubbell, whose trading post complex at Ganado on the Navajo Reservation is now a national historic site. Lorenzo Jr. was educated at Notre Dame, but returned to northern Arizona to continue his father's trading business. Young Hubbell operated several trading posts in remote locations on the Navajo Reservation, at Keams Canyon and Oraibi on the Hopi Reservation and in the town of Winslow.

Like his father, he stocked foodstuffs, canned goods and cloth to trade for Indian arts and crafts — primarily dyed wool, finished rugs and pottery. A story is told of his buying a rug from a very old woman whose failing sight and trembling hands had created a less than perfect piece of work. When asked why he paid for such a poorly executed rug, Hubbell explained that the woman had once been the best weaver in that part of the country. Her family was gone, and she was reduced to earning her keep by herding other people's sheep. Hubbell felt that preserving her dignity was worth the small amount she would spend in trade for the rug.

Lorenzo Jr. gained a measure of fame in the early 1950s for another rug woven by Julia Joe. It was even larger than the one in this photograph, measuring 26 by 36 feet and weighing more than 250 pounds. It was woven in a grey, black and white pattern. Hubbell displayed it at his big trading post in Winslow and also used it in several local parades, draped on the back of a flatbed truck. The rug was featured in full page ads for the Hubbell trading post that appeared in many publications. Julia Joe traveled to Winslow to view the rug around 1956, when she was very old. She said she wanted to see her work once more before she died.

Today the Hubbell trading post in Oraibi is gone, and the post in Winslow is now the headquarters for Homolovi Ruins State Park.

— *Joan Brundige-Baker*

Originally published: March 14, 1990

Photo courtesy Arizona Historical Society, Pioneer Museum

Hopi Snake Dance

This is a photograph of a re-creation of a Hopi Snake Dance. The Hopi believe that photographs capture part of a person's spirit and generally do not permit photos to be taken during their ceremonials. Archive photos of actual Snake Dances are considered culturally sensitive and are not allowed to be published.

The Snake Dance is one of the elaborate religious dances performed by the Hopis to propitiate the gods and to ensure fertility and regeneration of life. It is held in late August and is one of the most spectacular of Hopi rituals. The snake, with its undulating movements, symbolizes lightning and is a messenger to the spirits of Hopi ancestors in the world below. Other Hopi religious dances are performed by Kachinas, but the Snake Dance is the responsibility of the Snake and Antelope clans. The ceremony takes nine days.

During the first few days, the men prepare themselves by praying, making prayer sticks, and setting up altars in the kivas. Every morning for four days, the clans leave early to collect poisonous and non-poisonous snakes for the ceremony. The snakes are kept in the kiva. On the eighth day, a symbolic marriage between a girl representing the Snake Virgin and a boy representing the Snake Hero takes place. The men of the Antelope Clan then dance around the plaza carrying early harvest fruits such as melons, squash and beans. They stamp their feet to get the attention of the gods.

On the ninth day, the snakes, which have been washed with water and dried in sand, are brought from the kiva and draped on a *kisi*, a specially built bower. Hopis believe the reptiles have the ability to tell if a man has a true and worthy heart, and that the snakes will drape themselves over the bodies of the most worthy men and fall asleep.

At sunset, the Snake Clan dances while the Antelope Clan chants. The dancers circle the village plaza four times before they pick a snake from the *kisi*. They then dance around the plaza carrying the snakes in their mouths. Each dancer is accompanied by a guard or "hugger" who carries a snake whip of eagle feathers. The eagle is the enemy of the snake, and it is believed that the strokes of the feathers terrify the snake and keep it from striking.

When the dancer has completed a circuit of the village, he takes the snake out of his mouth and places it on the ground where a "gatherer" picks it up, drapes it over his arm and hands it to a member of the Antelope Clan, who has been chanting an accompaniment to the dance. The ritual is repeated until all the snakes have been used in the dance.

Finally, the snakes are placed on the ground in a circle of cornmeal that has been marked out by the chief snake priest. The snakes are then returned to the desert and the Snake clansmen swallow an emetic, which causes them to vomit, thus purifying their bodies.

The Snake Dance is still performed today, and visitors may observe the ceremony, but no cameras or tape recorders are allowed.

— *Jane Eppinga*

Originally published: November 28, 1990

Photo courtesy Pimeria Alta Historial Society, Nogales

When Gambling Was Outlawed

The Navajo men in this photograph taken in the 1920s are burning their gambling [playing] cards as the handwritten title describes. The men appear to be near a school, perhaps at Leupp or Tuba City on the Reservation. There is an Anglo in a suit at center, possibly a government agent. The federal government had begun to crack down on Reservation gambling as Prohibition swept the country.

Gambling by Native Americans had been outlawed in 1825 with the passage of the Assimilative Crime Act, even as the rest of the nation and the Western territories in particular had wide open gambling. Scholars speculate that the prohibition was an effort to prevent Indians from being tempted by base pastimes, a plan enthusiastically supported by missionary groups working among the tribes. Even so, games of chance were a common tribal pastime.

Early games consisted of dice pieces made of sticks and bones. A Navajo game of chance played in the late 1880s included pieces of stick, which represented each player, and forty stones. The stones were tossed in the air with points assigned by how they landed. Stewart Culin, author of the definitive work *Games of the North American Indians* was told that the game was called *set-tilth* by a Navajo man attending the World's Columbian Exposition in Chicago in 1893.

Women had their own special game, which was photographed by a Catholic priest at St. Michael's Mission in the late 1800s. *Tsidil* required that sticks be placed on a blanket stretched above the playing area. The sticks would fall or be shaken from the blanket onto the playing surface and be counted by their position.

Another pastime was a form of the moccasin game played by men, which involved guessing the location of an object hidden among three or four similar things.

Anthropologists have speculated that Native American gambling was rooted in spirituality as well as entertainment. Games of chance may have been a form of communication with deities who could send luck — good or bad — to an individual.

By the early 20th century, the federal government had begun to take rules against gambling more seriously. Prohibition of alcohol went hand-in-hand with prohibition of gambling. In 1924, the federal government added gaming prohibitions to the code of Federal Courts and the Court of Indian Offenses, taking the anti-gambling fervor to a new level. Agents took on the responsibility for eradicating all forms of gambling and games of chance on government property, which included Indian reservations. The result was events like the one shown here.

Among the Navajo, the stricter enforcement of rules against gambling carried over into the culture, so that games of chance became almost taboo. Medicine men were revered for the very reason that they lacked vices such as gambling and drinking.

After two failed referendums to allow casinos on the Big Rez, Navajo voters approved a gaming resolution in 2004. Two sites are currently being developed: one near Sanders, Arizona, and one near Shiprock, New Mexico.

— *Joan Brundige-Baker*

Originally published: March 9, 2001

Burning their Gambling Cards

Photo courtesy of Special Collections, Cline Library, Northern Arizona University

Code Talkers, 1943

These are the instructors at the Navajo Communications School Training Center at Camp Pendleton — the men who trained the famous Navajo code talkers of World War II. They are from left: John Manuelito, John Benally, Rex Kontz, Howard Billiman and Peter Tracey, all Navajos, and Philip Johnston, an Anglo who grew up on the Navajo Reservation.

In 1941, shortly after the Japanese attacked Pearl Harbor, Philip Johnston read that an armored division was trying to develop a spoken communications code using Native Americans. He thought the Navajo language, which had no modern-language equivalent, would be perfect as the basis for a code. He presented his idea to the Area Signal Officer at Camp Elliot near San Diego, and by March 1942, Marine Corps recruiters were on the reservation to select 30 men as the first trainees.

The men spent their training choosing 211 words for the first code and learning to use communications equipment. Once in the field, they realized the code was too limited and added another 200 words. Philip Johnston followed the progress of the code talkers. When permission was given to expand the program and train an additional 200 men, he asked to enlist and work with them. He entered the Marine Corps as a staff sergeant in October 1942, and taught his first class in December. When the class ended, the five men in this photograph were selected as instructors, and Johnston took over administrative chores.

More than 450 men attended the communications school. Only 30 failed to qualify as code talkers, and they served honorably elsewhere in the armed forces.

Code talkers were used in every war zone, but were especially important in the Pacific Theater. When the flag was raised on Mount Suribachi after the battle of Iwo Jima, it was the Navajo code talkers who sent the news.

— *Bonnie Greer*

Originally published: April 6, 1988

Photo courtesy of Special Collections, Cline Library, Northern Arizona University

The Hohokam Legacy: Pueblo Grande

On the north side of the Salt River near the Papago Buttes in Phoenix are ruins associated with an ancient culture known as the Hohokam. For 1,500 years, this society of desert farmers occupied the area, developing complex irrigation systems and adobe structures, crafting ornate jewelry and creating a trade network with other prehistoric cultures of the Southwest. For reasons still unknown, their culture collapsed in the 15th century, shortly before Columbus arrived in the New World.

Some 500 years later, Hohokam ruins began being explored and excavated by archeologists near present day Washington and 44th Street. Omar Turney, a city engineer who had spent many years studying the Hohokam irrigation system, named the area Pueblo Grande (Spanish for "large town"). The name referred to the site's prominent platform mound, which was one of the largest structures built by the Hohokam.

Thomas Armstrong, former president of the Arizona Archaeological and Historical Society, purchased the Pueblo Grande platform mound and surrounding three acres in 1924 and donated the property to the City of Phoenix. The same year, Turney convinced the city to purchase an area south of the platform mound known as Park of Four Waters. This land contained the preserved remains of major irrigation canals that supplied water to most Hohokam villages on the north side of the Salt River.

The city wanted to develop the Hohokam site into a museum and archaeological park, and in 1929 it hired Odd Halseth as city archaeologist (the first one in the nation). Halseth's plans for Pueblo Grande included building an outdoor museum next to the platform mound along with an archaeological laboratory with exhibits and ongoing archaeological investigations, all surrounded by a park and botanical garden. His vision for the museum was to "incorporate professional archaeological investigations of the site, coupled with education programs for schools and visitors."

Beginning in 1933, Halseth started construction of a pueblo-style museum. With help from volunteers, he was able to construct the building out of salvaged materials and adobe blocks made from the backdirt left from excavations. The museum was completed two years later for a total cost of $14.95 (all of it spent on nails). A photo of the original museum appears at right.

Halseth's next move was to obtain exhibit materials and information for the new museum, which he did by using federal work programs to fund excavations. From 1934 to 1940, archaeology was conducted under the sponsorship of the Public Works Administration, the Civilian Conservation Corps and the Works Progress Administration. Julian Hayden, Albert Schroeder and Paul Ezell — individuals who later became well known for their contributions to Southwestern archaeology — supervised the excavations. The results, known as "Relief Archaeology," produced thousands of artifacts used in museum exhibits and exposed portions of the platform mound, which would be developed into an outdoor exhibit. It also generated hundreds of boxes of field notes and sketches, analysis sheets and photographs.

The information gained from those excavations was never fully analyzed and little was published about Pueblo Grande. Halseth considered the museum's public programs more important than the scientific research. He wanted to focus his limited city resources on the development and promotion of Pueblo Grande as a museum.

After Halseth's retirement in 1960, Donald Hiser took over as city archaeologist and museum director, and four years later, Pueblo Grande was declared a National Historic Landmark. Hiser expanded the park's boundaries by nearly 75 acres, and in 1974 replaced the old museum building with a new facility.

In 1984, David Doyel became the museum's third director and new city archaeologist. He continued to emphasize the museum's public programs but also began promoting the publication of archaeological research. He initiated a major study in 1989 of the archaeological records on file in the Pueblo Grande Museum, and the Arizona Department of Transportation began an excavation of the eastern portion of the Pueblo Grande site, which is located within the Hohokam Expressway corridor (State Route 143). The excavation was the largest ever conducted in the Southwest and recovered more than 1,500 archaeological artifacts and a wealth of data.

Doyel resigned in 1990, and the city decided to create separate positions for museum director and city archaeologist. Roger Lidman became the museum's new director and Todd Bostwick became the new city archaeologist. Since 1995, the museum has added two more buildings, a community room and permanent collection storage, doubling the size of the complex. Today, Pueblo Grande offers outdoor exhibits of Hohokam houses and artifacts along a 2/3-mile interpretive trail and an indoor gallery featuring exhibits on a variety of topics.

— *Tracy Keller*

Originally published: October 17, 2003

Original Pueblo Grande Museum Building, c. 1936

Odd Halseth, Phoenix's first city archaeologist and Pueblo Grande's first museum director, gives a presentation to a Creighton School eighth-grade history class in 1939, with the original museum and platform mound in the background.

Photos courtesy of the Pueblo Grande Museum and Archeological Park, City of Phoenix

Notable Personalities

Mark Aldrich & the Confederate Territory of Arizona

Mark Aldrich, the man in this portrait, abandoned a wife and family in Illinois, went west to San Francisco and ultimately landed in Tucson to become active in Territorial politics and honored as one of the town's leading citizens.

The record of his early life is sketchy. He was born in New York State in 1801, a member of a family that had settled in the U.S. before the Revolutionary War. Apparently, he attended college, although it is not known which one.

In 1829, he took employment with the American Fur Company and was dispatched to a trading post at what is today Keokuk, Iowa. That same year, he took Margaret Wilkinson as his wife.

Three years later he was sent to Fort Edwards, where he opened a store and helped lay out a townsite, which later became Warsaw, Illinois. He became a prominent citizen. In 1836, he was elected to the Illinois Legislature and won a second term in 1838, serving with Abraham Lincoln and Stephen A. Douglas. In 1844, he was one of five men implicated in the murder of Mormon leader Joseph Smith and his brother in Carthage, Illinois. All five were acquitted by a jury.

In 1850, he left his wife and six children and set out for California. It is widely suspected that he had been smitten by gold fever, but he never gave a reason for his departure. He did not return to Illinois, nor did he ever make contact with his family again.

The record then becomes obscure. Apparently, Aldrich spent five years in San Francisco, although virtually nothing is known of his activities there.

By 1855, Aldrich was in Tucson; he was one of the first American citizens to settle there after the Gadsden Purchase of 1853, and he was to live in Tucson the rest of his life.

In quick order, he became one of the wealthiest men in town and was appointed mayor. He became known for a most unorthodox form of justice. Tucson had no jail, but it did have a whipping post in the public plaza. When a defendant was found guilty, Aldrich would order that the prisoner be given a certain number of lashes from a leather strap. Only half the number would be administered, at which time the mayor would order the guilty party to return the following day for the remainder of his punishment.

The prisoner, of course, would never return, choosing instead a hasty departure from Tucson.

Beginning in 1856, citizens in Tucson and in Mesilla (a town near present day Las Cruces, New Mexico, but considered part of what was referred to as Arizona) began working towards splitting the New Mexico Territory into two sections, roughly along the 34th Parallel. They argued that the capital at Santa Fe was too distant for effective representation, and that the Territorial Legislature ignored Arizona concerns. Aldrich chaired the Tucson meeting, at which a memorial to Congress was drafted, urging that a separate Arizona Territory be created. The document was signed by 260 Arizona citizens.

In 1860, residents of Tucson held a mass meeting — some have called it a constitutional convention — to write a code of laws under which the Arizona Territory would be governed. Aldrich was elected judge, but he soon resigned in disgust, citing a "want of moral courage" on the part of Tucsonans "for the arrest and trial of those who commit a breach of the peace." The meeting, of course, had no official sanction, and its resolutions were ignored by the government in Washington.

The tensions surrounding slavery and states' rights contributed to the drive for an Arizona Territory. On March 16, 1861, less than one month before the Confederacy fired on Ft. Sumter in far-off South Carolina, Aldrich chaired a second convention in Tucson. The delegates approved a resolution, identical to one ratified earlier in Mesilla, calling for the territory of Arizona (still not a legal entity) to secede from the Union and join the Confederacy.

After Ft. Sumter fell, the military commander for the New Mexico Territory ordered all federal troops to be concentrated at posts along the Rio Grande for operations against Confederate forces in Texas. This action exacerbated secessionist sentiment because it left Arizonans without any military protection from marauding Apaches and Mexican bandits.

When the Territory of Arizona was finally created by Congress in 1863, the census listed Aldrich as the wealthiest man in the Territory, with assets of $52,000. In 1864, he was elected to the First Territorial Legislature and was re-elected twice. In 1865, he was named Tucson's first postmaster.

Although the census reported no family, it was widely known that Aldrich shared his home with Teofila Leon, with whom he had a daughter, Faustina Leon.

In his will, dated July 16, 1868, he left his estate to Teofila and Faustina, adding a clause that should the two expire in an untimely manner, what remained should be given to his "lawful heirs" in Illinois.

Aldrich died September 21, 1873.

— *W. Lane Rogers*

Photo courtesy of the Arizona Historical Society, Tucson

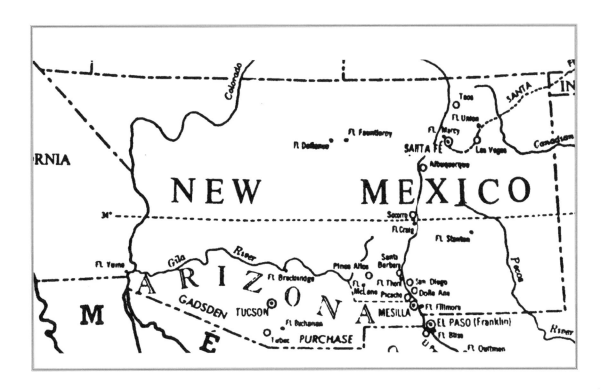

The Seven Sisters of Carondelet

The famous saying "How the West was won" often conjures up images of frontier marshals fighting ruthless outlaws and lonely cowboys struggling to protect their herds. The real settlers of the West, however, weren't vigilante lawmen but simple farming families and religious missionaries who came to Arizona to help build communities.

The first of these missionaries were the Spanish Catholics, then the Mormons and American Catholics by way of St. Louis after the Gadsden Purchase in 1854. There also were many Methodists, Presbyterians and Baptists serving remote missions throughout Arizona.

In *Death Comes for the Archbishop*, Willa Cather tells a poignant story of Catholic missions in New Mexico and Arizona. A similar account comes from a small diary written by Sister Monica Corrigan, one of the seven sisters of Carondelet, who made the dangerous trek from San Diego to Tucson to set up St. Mary's Hospital in May of 1870. The sisters are shown in the top photo.

They rode in light wagons with canvas tops and traveled mostly at night to avoid the heat. It took them a month to travel from San Diego to Yuma — a trip that would take only four hours today. They began the Arizona leg of their trek at 4 a.m. on Saturday, May 21.

After several days riding alongside the Gila River, they reached a ranch where they washed and change their clothes — a rare opportunity for desert travelers. Weeks later, they finally arrived at the Pima Villages, 30 miles south of present-day Phoenix. From there, soldiers escorted the nuns the remaining 80 miles to Tucson.

Those last four score miles were not without incident. Just after midnight, the group had made their way to Pichacho Peak, an area where Apaches often waited to attack travelers. As they passed the peak, the caravan's horses began to neigh, a sign of Indians close by. The soldiers whipped and spurred their horses, shouting "The Indians! The Indians!" to frighten them off. Then, they "went like lighting," Sister Monica wrote, and "the novelty of the scene kept us from being afraid." The nuns thanked God for getting them through the ordeal and stopped for coffee the following morning.

As the sisters arrived in Tucson, women and children watched from their rooftops. Sister Monica wrote:

> "At about three miles from the town we were met by the procession which was headed by four priests on horseback; but as we came in sight, they dismounted, and ran rather than walked, to meet us; the crowd, in the meantime, discharging firearms. Before we reached the city, their number had increased to about three thousand; some discharging firearms, others bearing lighted torches; all walking in order, and heads uncovered. The city was illuminated — fireworks in full play. Balls of combustible matter were thrown in the streets through which we passed; at each explosion, Sister Euphrasia made the sign of the cross. All the bells in the city were pealing forth their merriest strains."

With the active help of the entire community, the seven sisters established Tucson's first hospital, St. Mary's. The middle photo at the lower left shows Sister St. Martin Dunn standing in front of the hospital with the wife of Dr. Michael Spencer, who joined the staff during the 1880s. The lower photo dates from the same general time and shows the hospital campus after a windmill had been erected. Later, the Sisters also established St. Joseph's Academy, the first school for girls in Arizona.

Note: Sister Monica Corrigan's complete diary is available online at http://dizzy.library.arizona.edu/swetc./projectsa.html, along with illustrations and a map; excerpts courtesy of the University of Arizona, Southwest E-Text project.

— *Jim Turner.*

Originally published: January 6, 2006

Photos courtesy Arizona Historical Society, Tucson

John Hance, Canyon Pioneer

This is John Hance on the trail that bears his name in the Grand Canyon, sometime in the early part of the 20th century. John and his brother George were early Arizona pioneers. They arrived in the territory in 1868 to begin farming and to run a small sutler's store in Camp Verde. John worked with his brother until 1881, when he made his first trip to the Grand Canyon. After that, he was hooked.

He built a cabin on the South Rim as a homestead and staked out copper and asbestos mines. He also built a winter homestead in Red Canyon, one of the side canyons of the Grand Canyon, which provided more temperate weather and winter forage for his cattle.

He built the first reliable trail into the canyon by improving an old Havasupai trail he found. That trail came to be called the Hance Trail and served him for more than a decade. During that time, he began to take tour groups into the canyon. He charged $12 a day per group and $1 per person for use of the trail. He set up tents at his homestead on the rim for tourists and made his cabin in Red Canyon headquarters for the groups he guided.

In 1894, a storm caused rockslides that destroyed much of the trail. Rather than rebuild, he began improvements on another Indian trail which came to be called the New Hance Trail. That trail, also called Red Canyon Trail, is still used by canyon hikers today. Although traces of his original trail, now called Old Hance Trail, are still in existence, only the most experienced canyoneers can reliably follow its course.

By 1900, the center of activity at the canyon moved west of Hance's ranch to the area around the Bright Angel Trail, where Bright Angel Lodge was built. Hance sold out and moved into the lodge. There he spent his days entertaining tourists by telling tall tales. One such story, reported in the *Coconino Sun* in 1912, was of a rattlesnake he killed that had eight rattles and a whistle. It seems there were so many tourists in the canyon that summer, the snake wore out the rattles on its tail and in desperation got itself a whistle.

The Fred Harvey Company, owners of Bright Angel Lodge, provided a room for Hance until he died in 1919. The smaller photo shows Hance at the Lodge in his later days, perhaps getting ready to launch into one of his stories.

The Hance family has continued to have an impact on northern Arizona. John's grand nephew, Terence, was elected Coconino County Attorney in 1996 and served three terms in office.

— *Arizona News Service*

Originally published: March 21, 1990

*Top photo courtesy of the Emery Kolb Collection, Cline Library, Northern Arizona University;
lower photo courtesy of the National Park Service.*

Charles Williams, Tucson Pioneer

Charlie Williams, known in Tucson as Banjo Dick, was one of only 26 black people in the Arizona Territory when he arrived in 1871. He came from California, where he had worked as a laborer, and settled first in Yuma, where he was hired by L.A. Smith.

When the Smith family moved to Tucson in 1872, so did Williams. During the day, he worked as a handyman for the Smiths. He was paid $25 a month plus room and board. Smith's daughter recalled that Williams helped raise the children, washed, ironed and tended the livery.

At night, and any other time he could, Williams played the banjo. He is remembered for his sweet music — serenading in Alex Levin's park and playing and singing as he went about town running errands during the day.

In 1891, Williams moved to Nogales and opened a shoe shine parlor. In this undated photograph, he appears to have prospered. His swastika tie pin, often seen in Navajo weavings, was a common ornament of the time. (Not until the rise of the Nazis in the 1930s did it take on negative associations.)

The migration of black people to the West began after the Civil War. Black cowboys tended herds of longhorns on ranches in Texas; other blacks settled in the plains states and the Indian Territory (Oklahoma) and gradually some drifted further west into Arizona.

The 1880 census recorded 155 African-Americans in the Arizona Territory, and a decade later there were 1,357. By the turn of the century, there were 1,848.

According to historian Jay Wagoner, black pioneers, at first, worked jobs they had learned as slaves: cooks, barbers, laborers, drivers, maids, etc. But on the frontier, anyone could take advantage of opportunities. Soon blacks moved into other occupations—working as cowpunchers, merchants, prospectors, stagecoach drivers, restaurant owners and musicians.

In Tucson, another black pioneer was a barber by the name of John C. Clemons. He was an active member of the Colored Republican Party, which met at 31 N. Church St., and was the first black man empanelled on a Tucson jury. On May 4, 1907, the *Arizona Daily Star* reported, "The colored citizens having entered a protest some months ago, it appears that they will see one of their number in the jury — John C. Clemons, the bather. He is on the (jury) list. Now the women of Pima (County) are to be heard from."

In the 1930s, on the banks of the Santa Cruz River, Tucson celebrated Juneteeth, an African-American tradition that marks the emancipation of the slaves. Also in the '30s, many Tucson black men worked at the cotton press, extracting cottonseed oil for $3.75 a day. Others worked in the area of Davis-Monthan Field, clearing land. Any rattlesnakes they found were killed and the skins sold for $1.75 to the Tito Flores Pharmacy.

— *Jane Eppinga*

Originally published: February 7, 1997

Photo courtesy of the Arizona Historical Society, Tucson

Tucson's First Schoolteachers

In spite of their rowdy reputation, Arizona pioneers valued a public education and worked hard to provide it. In 1867, the Territorial Legislature passed the first county property tax to be used for education. The same year, Tucson formed School District One and hired Arizona's first public school teacher, Augustus Brichta — a New Yorker, graduate of Saint Louis University and a veteran of the Mexican-American War. Fifty-five boys attended the school, but no girls were allowed. Six months after the school opened, funds ran out and the school closed.

In 1871, the Legislature created the first Territorial school tax and increased the county tax. Tucsonans hired another teacher, Swiss immigrant John Spring. The one-room school he taught in had a packed dirt floor, no blackboard and splintery benches that fit three large boys or four to six toddlers. Parents supplied plenty of ash wood flogging switches, even though Spring believed in sparing the rod. Spring taught 138 boys ranging in age from six to 21. After about 18 months, rowdy behavior took its toll, and Spring asked Governor A.P.K. Safford to double his salary so he could hire an assistant. The Legislature felt they could hire two women teachers with Spring's salary, so they closed the school until they could find women teachers to hire.

Meanwhile, Estevan Ochoa, a Tucson businessman and political leader, and other townspeople began raising funds for the two-room Congress Street School. The school's Sonoran-style architecture offered no shade for the students and made it difficult to learn under the blazing afternoon sun. Ochoa and Sam Hughes, another prominent community leader, decided to hold a cakewalk to raise money for a shaded porch. After soliciting saloon patrons and other townspeople, they were able to raise enough money.

The townspeople's only job now was to convince single women to come to one of the wildest towns left in the West. *Tucson Citizen* editor John Wasson wrote an editorial asking for good schoolmarms, adding: "and when they get tired of teaching, we will find them good husbands."

Traveling east by train during the summer of 1872, Wasson met Maria Wakefield, a young school teacher from Stockton, California. He offered her the teaching job, and Governor Safford wrote her a travel warning in October 1873: "...you better start for Tucson after the 25th, as the Apaches are headed toward the eastern part of the Territory and cannot get to the western side before this time; also the moon is full. Bring the best lady teacher you can secure to take care of the girl's room."

Wakefield began her teaching career at age 15 in Rochester, New York. Most likely, her teacher got fed up and quit, making her (probably the oldest pupil) take over. At 5'2", Maria must have had a strong will to keep the students in line. After several successful years that included teaching the young Mayo brothers (William J. and Charles H. Mayo were founders of the famous Mayo Clinic), the 24-year-old adventuress took a teaching position in Stockton in 1869. There she met her future Tucson teaching partner, Harriet Bolton, age 40, from Maine.

The schoolmarms' trip to Tucson was rough — for five days and nights they were jostled around their stagecoach, barely able to wash their hands. The driver pointed out heaps of stones along the way, marking deaths due to Indian encounters. Prominent storekeeper Edward Nye Fish heard that the ladies were on their way and figured that if he wanted to marry a teacher he'd better get the jump on the other eligible bachelors. He and Dr. Charles Lord got a swift buckboard and set out to meet the stagecoach. After a 40-hour trip straight through to Yuma, they found the stage delayed there because of the threat of Apaches. For all his efforts, however, the would-be suitor was rejected. The ladies sent word to Fish that they were too travel-worn and in no shape to meet anyone.

Once in Tucson, the teachers didn't have to teach too long before good husbands were provided. Maria Wakefield married Edward Fish in March 1875, less than five months after she turned him away in Yuma. She was 18 years younger than her husband, but their marriage lasted 49 years. The following July, *Tucson Citizen* editor John Wasson made good his promise when he married Harriet Bolton. They were the same age and remained married for 30 years.

Both ladies continued to support public education throughout their lives. While legends endure regarding the places like "The Town Too Tough to Die," the Earp brothers and the Indian Wars, education pioneers settled for lesser glories: Ochoa, Safford, and Hughes have Tucson elementary schools named after them, while Wakefield, Spring, and Safford live on as middle school names.

— *Jim Turner*

Originally published: February 18, 2005

Maria Wakefield   *John Spring*

Congress St. School, c. 1907

Photos courtesy of the Arizona Historical Society, Tucson

The Pioneer Aguirres

The young man is Don Epifanio Aguirre; the woman is his bride, Mary Belle (Mamie) Bernard Aguirre. Their story typifies much about the early history of the Arizona Territory. He became active in civic affairs, and she was one of Tucson's first public school teachers.

Mamie Bernard was born in St. Louis in 1844. When she was 12, her family moved to Westport, Missouri, aptly named because it was a popular staging area for wagon trains to and from the West. Their mercantile business prospered.

Epifanio, born in 1834, was the scion of a Spanish family who had immigrated to Mexico at the time of Cortez. Epifanio's father, Pedro, settled in Las Cruces — then still part of Mexico — in 1852 and acquired large land holdings. After the Gadsden Purchase in 1853, Pedro and his family became naturalized citizens of the United States. By the late 1850s, Epifanio held the bulk of government freight contracts between the Southwest and Missouri along the Old Spanish Trail. He moved his base of operations to Tucson in about 1859 and was selected as a delegate to an 1860 convention that adopted a constitution for a provisional government of a separate Territory of Arizona.

While tending to his freight business, he often accompanied his wagon trains to Missouri. He made frequent stops at the Bernard store in Westport and fell in love with Mamie, despite the fact that neither spoke the other's language. He pleaded his case to her and her father through a bilingual friend, who served as interpreter. Apparently, he made the right kind of impression, and he and Mamie were married in August 1862.

Less than a year later, the couple set out for what Mamie called "the unknown lands" — Arizona Territory. They traveled with their young son, Pedro, by covered wagon through dangerous areas in Missouri and Kansas that were the scene of frequent Civil War skirmishes. They passed close by Lawrence, Kansas, which had been attacked and burned by a band of Confederate guerillas led by William Clarke Quantrill. More than 150 civilians were slaughtered in that raid.

The Aguirres settled in Las Cruces, but by August 1869 they had moved to Tucson.

Epifanio and his brother Conrado established a stagecoach line from Tucson to Altar, Sonora. The area was dangerous, with bands of Apaches attacking settlers. On January 20, 1870, Epifanio and four other men were killed by Apaches as their stagecoach crossed the border near Sasabe, Arizona.

Mamie was left a widow with three young children. She taught school in 1875 and 1876 at Tres Alamos, a settlement on the eastern end of Redington Pass on the San Pedro River north of Benson along what is now called the Pomerene Road. After an Apache attack that destroyed the school, she moved her family to the safety of Tucson.

In Tucson, she was hired as a teacher for the Tucson Public School for Girls at a salary of $100 a month. There were 20 girls in her class when she started. In Mamie's words, her students were "with few exceptions ... the most unruly set the Lord ever let live. They had an idea that they conferred a favor upon the school and teacher by even attending."

According to Mamie, the recess bell was a signal for the girls to climb out of windows into the street and to scream and misbehave. At the next recess Mamie refused to let the girls leave their desks and told them that the first to leave would be sent home. When one girl made an ugly face at her, Mamie slapped her and sent her home. By the end of the first week, five girls remained in class but Mamie had imposed discipline.

Governor A.P.K. Safford visited the school at the end of that first week. Mamie told him, "Governor, I have about broken up your girls' school trying to keep order." She also said if she could not have order, she would not teach even for $500 a month.

Gov. Safford laughed and told her, "Mrs. Aguirre, you just go on breaking up the school that way."

The next Monday all of the girls returned, and by the end of the year, there were 40 girls in attendance.

Later, Mamie became chair of the Spanish and English History departments at the University of Arizona. She also was an acknowledged expert on Indian artifacts and attended the St. Louis World's Fair in 1904 as a commissioner in charge of Indian relics. She died two years later in Los Angeles while visiting relatives.

— Jane Eppinga and W. Lane Rogers

Originally published: August 27, 1999

Photos courtesy of the Arizona Historical Society, Tucson

Tombstone's Chronicler

George Whitwell Parsons was born in Washington, D.C. on August 6, 1850. He initially studied to be a banker, but the allure of the mining boom in the Southwest led him to Tombstone in the 1880s, where he became well-known for his daily journal, detailing life during the town's heyday.

Parsons' father, Samuel Miller Parsons, was a lawyer who graduated from Yale Law School; his mother, Virginia Whitwell, attended Mrs. English's Boarding School in Washington, D.C. and was friends with former classmate Jessie Benton, who married Territorial Governor of Arizona John Charles Fremont.

After attending Brooklyn Polytechnic Institute with a major in accounting and bookkeeping, Parsons began his business career working as a clerk for several brokerage firms and importers. He also studied law in his father's law office on Wall Street, but was not particularly enthusiastic about a legal career and began to dread the cold northeastern winters.

In 1869, the year his mother died and a decade before he moved to Tombstone, Parsons began the journal that would make him famous. He kept at it for 60 years.

In 1874, Parsons moved to Key Biscayne, Florida. For a year, he worked in the salvage business, selling lumber from shipwrecked vessels that were destroyed during hurricanes. During his stay in Florida, Parsons became friends with William Temple Hornaday, who later became director of the New York Zoo. One night in 1875, Hornaday caught an alligator and trapped it inside the cabin he and Parsons shared. According to Parsons, that alligator ended up "in the Smithsonian."

After almost drowning in a hurricane off Cape Sable, Parsons decided to leave Florida and move to California. He sailed to Panama, crossed the isthmus on horseback and then took another boat to Los Angeles, arriving there on August 6, 1876. Not long after arriving, he decided to travel to San Francisco where he worked at the National Gold Bank and Trust Company for the next three years.

By 1879, Parsons was 30 years old, out of work and depressed. He heard of the Tombstone silver strike and wrote in his journal on January 5, 1880, "I think after all, that mines promise more for me and I wouldn't be surprised to find myself in them before many days. I am tough and strong and know how to get along with the working class."

On February 17, 1880, Parsons and his friend Milton Clapp arrived in Tombstone. He transitioned from banker to frontiersman by working in the mines, drinking in the Tombstone bars and courting a variety of women. During that time, he also became good friends with Wyatt Earp and John Clum, editor of *The Tombstone Epitaph*.

For the next seven years, he chronicled the daily happenings in Tombstone. One entry describes a night after an unsuccessful search in the rain for Apaches: "We dried as much as possible, cleaned guns and saw that they were in good working order, made some coffee into which one fellow's shoe fell, but coffee couldn't be wasted, and [we] laid all over one another to catch some sleep, an unsuccessful matter."

Parsons also wrote about the problems the sheriff was having with rowdy cowboys randomly shooting and sometimes killing the town's law-abiding citizens. In a journal entry, he wrote, "Bad mess this. Sheriff [Behan] is awake now that one of his friends [Frank Stillwell] is killed. Couldn't do anything before. Things are very rotten in that office. Fine reputation we're getting abroad."

Of the murders and assassinations in the Tombstone area, Parsons wrote, "Chalky times, very, 14 murders and assassinations in 10 days. More than one a day. A hanging be anticipated tonight, but not carried out. Cowboy raid on town expected tonight. Things quiet thus far. The two cowboys, Hunt and Grounds, were taken first to the undertakers and kept a while, but not dying quick enough were removed to the hospital."

When flooding destroyed the Tombstone mines in 1886, Parsons decided to return to California, where he felt a better future awaited him. In Los Angeles, he became active in many organizations and for three years served as the chairman of the Committee on Railroads and Transportation. While chairman, he came up with the idea that if a deep harbor were created at San Pedro, California, (just west of present day Long Beach) oranges could be shipped to New York in 12 days and to Liverpool and Le Havre in 14 days.

Parsons' proudest achievement was making the desert safe for travelers through proper mapping and marking of water sources. His sign post crusade resulted in the passage of a bill that helped to "discover, develop, protect and render more accessible" various landmarks and monuments. The bill was signed into law on August 21, 1916, by President Woodrow Wilson.

George Parsons stopped writing his diary entries in 1929, even though he lived until January 5, 1933. He left an estate of $250,000, including $1,000 for St. Paul's Church in Tombstone and $500 for a "fountain in the desert," which was built in front of the Andrus Canyon Club in Palm Springs.

Sources: Parsons's journal serialized in *The Tombstone Epitaph* from December 1967 to April 1968; *The Private Journal of George Whitwell Parsons*, Arizona State Archives Project; also Lynn Bailey and Don Chaput.

—*Jane Eppinga*

Originally published: March 19, 2004

Photo courtesy of Jane Eppinga

The Rev. Endicott Peabody

The portrait is of Boston brahmin Endicott Peabody, whose six-month sojourn in Tombstone was to have a lasting effect on the town.

During the spring of 1881, several months before the OK Corral incident, Julius Atwood, the bishop of the Arizona-New Mexico Episcopal Diocese, came to Tombstone to gauge whether the town was ready for the establishment of a permanent Episcopal church. Atwood found the townspeople very responsive and dispatched a Rev. Mr. Talbot to Tombstone to lead the congregation and raise funds for a building. Talbot lasted just three months, and the bishop replaced him with a 25-year old seminary student from Boston, Endicott Peabody, shown here in an undated photo.

Peabody was born in Salem, Massachusetts, in May 1857, but when his father accepted a position with a British bank, the family moved to England. After graduating from Trinity College, Cambridge, with an LL.B. degree in 1880, he returned to the U.S. and began working in a bank.

In 1881, Peabody decided to apply to the Episcopal Theological School in Cambridge, Massachusetts, even though his family was Unitarian. Only three months into his seminary education, he accepted the interim appointment to minister to Tombstone's Episcopalian congregation.

When Peabody arrived in Tombstone by stage, on Sunday, January 29, 1882, he later said he remembered that some of his fellow Bostonians had referred to it as "the rottenest place you ever saw." His first impressions did not offer much to contradict that assessment. He checked into the Grand Hotel where he described his room as "wretched" and "too well ventilated in the winter." A three-man committee from the church had been late meeting him because they had been engrossed in a card game. They apologized, and Milton Clapp, one of the committee members and cashier of the Safford, Hudson and Company Bank, invited Peabody to stay at his house.

At that time, the Episcopalians held their services in the courtroom of the Miners' Exchange Building with the minister occupying the judge's seat. There was some excitement about the new minister, and Peabody's first services were well attended. On February 12, 110 people attended Sunday service, and the church collected $25 in its offering plate.

Peabody loved baseball and immediately set about organizing the town's baseball team. He became the vice president of the Tombstone Baseball Association and served as the official umpire at all baseball games. He would agree to umpire a Sunday game only on the condition that the players first attend services.

Peabody also organized a Sunday school and an adult Bible class. Early on, Peabody complained that the only time he saw miners at a church function was when he conducted funeral services for one of their co-workers or family members. However, he eventually won many of them over, for on May 11, 1882, the *Tombstone Nugget* reported, "We overheard a miner yesterday say, 'Well if that lad's argument was a hammer and religion a drill, he'd knock a hole in the hanging wall of skepticism.'"

On May 25, 1882, a fire devastated the center of Tombstone. The fire broke all the windows in the courtroom, forcing Peabody to focus more of his efforts on finding a permanent place for Episcopalians to worship. His church's only assets were the rectory and a lot at the corner of Third and Safford.

Peabody spent the rest of his time in Tombstone fund-raising for a new church, collecting from gamblers and miners as well as business people. On one occasion, he interrupted E.R. Gage, the superintendent of the Grand Central and Contention Mines, who was playing poker in the back room of a hotel. To everyone's surprise, Gage counted out $150 from his pile of winnings and gave it to Peabody. The other players at the table quickly followed suit. Later, when asked why he was taking gambling money, Peabody replied, "The Lord's pot must be kept boiling, even if it takes the devil's kindling wood." Funds also came from the ladies' guild, the missionary district of Arizona and New Mexico, and a production of the Gilbert & Sullivan's "H.M.S. Pinafore."

Construction on a new church proceeded quickly, and the first service was held on June 18, 1882. That church, St. Paul's Episcopal, still stands in Tombstone today and is the oldest Protestant church building in Arizona. Its unbraced adobe walls rise to hand-hewn rafters cut from lumber hauled from the Chiricahua Mountains, some 50 miles away. The lighting fixtures in the nave were transported by boat around Cape Horn to San Francisco and then freighted to Tombstone. The photo of the interior of the church was taken around the turn of the century.

In July, Peabody ended his ministry in Tombstone. When he traveled back to Boston, he carried as a keepsake a bar of silver presented to him by the St. Paul's Women's Guild. He returned to the Episcopal Theological School, completed his seminary training in 1884 and was ordained in 1885. That same year he married his cousin, Francis Peabody.

With support by wealthy Bostonians, he organized and was appointed headmaster of the church-affiliated preparatory Groton School in Groton, Mass. He held that position until he retired in 1940.

Peabody visited Tombstone on Feb. 16, 1941, to deliver a final sermon on the 59th anniversary of his ministry. He died in 1944 at the age of 87.

— *Jane Eppinga and W. Lane Rogers*

Originally published: January 3, 2003

Peabody photo courtesy of Groton School; church photo courtesy of W. Lane Rogers

Percival Lowell: Stargazer

The man at the eyepiece of the telescope is Percival Lowell, early day astronomer and founder of Flagstaff's Lowell Observatory. He spent the better part of a lifetime probing the solar system — gazing into the lens of this Clark 24-inch refractor telescope (now a registered national historic landmark) from atop Mars Hill in Flagstaff.

Born of affluent parents (the city of Lowell, Massachusetts bears the family name) in the Boston suburb of Brookline in 1855, Lowell's upbringing mirrored his family's wealth and social position. Young Percival was sent to preparatory schools in France and graduated Phi Beta Kappa from Harvard.

Lowell later recalled that his interest in astronomy dated to his youth. He read books about astronomy and gazed at the stars through a telescope on the roof of the family home. With little formal training in the discipline, Lowell decided at age 39 to devote the remainder of his life to astronomy — particularly the study of Mars. During the next two decades, he amassed data, photographs, books, scientific papers and articles about the Red Planet.

He was convinced life existed on Mars. Using the rudimentary equipment available, he could see what appeared to be ice caps, oceans, lakes and even continents on the planet. Given the stimulus of such observations — incorrect as they would prove to be — it did not require a great leap of imagination to assume the existence of life on Mars.

In 1894, when the planet was close to Earth, Lowell dispatched A.E. Douglass to the Western U.S. to find a site for an observatory. Tucson was given serious consideration, but ultimately Flagstaff was chosen, and Lowell Observatory was built.

Lowell was not a man to hide his wealth and lived in Flagstaff in opulent grandeur. He was rarely seen except as he appears in this photo — in a starched white shirt and three-piece suit. Those fortunate enough to share his table dined lavishly.

Lowell set himself a grueling work schedule of regular observations of Mars. In 1897, the huge workload finally caught up with him and he suffered a breakdown from nervous exhaustion. Not until 1901 was he well enough to return to his work, which continued unabated until his death in 1916.

His mausoleum is on the grounds of Lowell Observatory on Mars Hill in Flagstaff. A 2005 photo of the now enclosed mausoleum appears at right.

In addition to his observations of Mars, Lowell contended there was a planet beyond Neptune, and he spent the last decade of his life looking for Planet X. On February 18, 1930, 14 years after Lowell's death, Clyde W. Tombaugh, a young astronomer recently hired by the Lowell Observatory, discovered Pluto.

Because of its small size — one-third the size of Earth's moon with one-fifth of its mass — and its highly inclined orbit, Pluto's status as a planet began to be questioned. In 2006, after many objects similar to Pluto had been discovered, the International Astronomical Union downgraded Pluto to dwarf planet or planetoid, restoring the solar system to a family of one sun and eight planets.

— *Joan Brundige Baker*

Originally published: September 2, 1994

Photos courtesy of Lowell Observatory, Flagstaff

Mayor's Award of Distinction

Prescott Mayor Sara Presler

Lowell has grown to be a major research observatory, while retaining its independence, characteristic welcoming stance towards interested people of all ages and backgrounds, and close mutually supportive relationship with the community of Flagstaff. Arizona is widely recognized as a national leader in astronomy and space science — endeavors that annually contribute more than a quarter billion dollars and 3,300 jobs to the state's economy. This contribution can either grow or wither, depending in large part on whether Arizona gets serious about controlling light pollution. As Mayor, I am excited to recognize the research and innovation at Lowell and encourage all of Arizona to celebrate our dark skies.

Sarah Herring Sorin

The woman pictured here is Arizona's first woman lawyer, Sarah Herring Sorin. She was born on January 15, 1861, in New York City, the first of Col. William and Mary Herring's five children. (Sarah's youngest sibling, Henrietta, later married Selim Franklin, see page 214).

The colonel — apparently an honorary title since no military records can be found — graduated from Columbia Law School and served as Deputy District Attorney for the City of New York. When his brother Marcus died in 1880, William inherited several mining claims in Bisbee. While in Bisbee settling the estate, he seems to have caught the mining bug, and shortly thereafter he and his wife moved to Bisbee with their two youngest children. Sarah stayed behind in New York and taught school while her younger brother, Howard, finished high school. Then she, Howard, and their sister Bertha joined the family in Bisbee.

After a time, William sold his Bisbee mining claims to the Copper Queen Consolidated Mining Company and moved his family to Tombstone in 1882, where he opened a law office in partnership with his son Howard. Daughter Bertha also worked for the firm as a stenographer, notary and administrator of probate cases. Meanwhile, Sarah taught at Tombstone School (the first woman schoolteacher in the town) and also served as principal and librarian. William defended Wyatt Earp at his murder trial, brought as a result of the shootout at the OK Corral the previous year, and won an acquittal for his client.

In 1891, Howard, after being given cocaine for a dental procedure, collapsed and died on the floor of the dentist's office. Sarah resigned as a teacher and stepped in to take her brother's place at the law office.

A year later, she applied for a license to practice law. Her examination was held in open court on Saturday, November 19, 1892, before a panel of two attorneys and a judge. It was reported that Sarah passed a rigid examination with distinguished honors. She was admitted to practice law in the First Judicial District Court in Tombstone on Monday, November 21. Some researchers have adduced additional factors which may have influenced her admission: her father's stature in local legal circles and her own as a respected teacher, sympathy because of the recent death of Howard, and the pro-women's suffrage views of two of the persons on the panel.

A month and a half later, on January 12, 1893, Sarah was admitted to practice before the Supreme Court of Arizona. In reporting her achievements, the *Arizona Weekly Star* described Sarah as a "genuine heroine" who blazed a path for women to higher fields for their talents.

Sarah decided that she needed a more formal legal education and enrolled in New York University's School of Law. NYU was one of the few schools that admitted women as law students and actively recruited them. Sarah received her LL.B. in 1894 with honors, graduating fourth in her class. She returned to Tombstone to work in the family law firm.

Although the firm handled a wide variety of cases including criminal defense for murder, burglary, robbery and forgery along with probate, guardianship and divorce, Sarah's area of specialty was mining law, and she was probably the first woman in the country to practice in this field.

Sarah made her first appearance before the Arizona Territorial Supreme Court in 1896, winning a ruling in her client's favor.

When Tombstone's economy began to decline in the late 1880s because of falling silver prices, labor strikes and mine flooding, the Herring family moved to Tucson and opened a law office at the corner of Pennington and Court streets.

On July 21, 1898, at the age of 37, Sarah married rancher and newspaperman Thomas Sorin, 15 years her senior. He had owned the *Tombstone Epitaph* with John Clum. He was also an expert on mineral resources and was in charge of Arizona's mineral exhibit at the 1893 Chicago World's Fair. Sorin's ranch was in Middlemarch Canyon in the Dragoon Mountains. Sarah divided her time between the law firm in Tucson during the week and the ranch on weekends.

Three months after her marriage, Sarah and her father were on opposite sides of the courtroom in *McElwee v. Tombstone Mill and Mining Company*. The colonel lost, as Sarah secured an $8,000 judgment for McElwee.

On April 16, 1906, William Herring successfully filed for Sarah's admission to practice before the U.S. Supreme Court. Six months later, Sarah and her father traveled to Washington, D.C. where they successfully argued the appellant's case in *Taylor v. Burns,* a dispute over title to a mining claim.

On November 6, 1913, Sarah made legal history when she appeared as sole counsel before the U.S. Supreme Court — "the first woman lawyer to argue a case unassisted and unaccompanied by a male lawyer" — winning on appeal on behalf of the defendant in *Work v. United Globe Mines.* UGM was a part of the Phelps Dodge copper empire.

After the death of her father in 1912, Sarah moved to Globe and served as counsel for the United Globe Mines and Old Dominion Copper Company. On April 30, 1914, she died of pneumonia in Globe. She is buried at Evergreen Cemetery in Tucson near Col. Herring and her mother. Tom Sorin died at his ranch in 1923 and is buried next to Sarah.

— *Jane Eppinga and Jacquelyn Kasper*

Originally published: July 28, 2000

Photos courtesy of the Arizona Historical Society, Tucson

Foote and Friends on the Road

In 1898, two men set out from Magdalena, New Mexico, on a grand adventure. Walter C. Johnson and Fred Clatworthy wanted to travel across the Arizona territory. Their plan was to explore the Grand Canyon, trek to Phoenix and points south, and then embark on a river journey down the Gila to Yuma. While in Flagstaff in preparation for the Grand Canyon leg of the journey, they met Sydney Foote, who was working as a time-keeper on the water-system crew. Unable to resist the thrill of the adventure, Foote quit his job and joined the expedition.

The three men, four pack animals — Nellie, Peter, Jackrabbit and Brute — and a wagon full of Flatworth's photographic supplies, began their odyssey in the winter of 1898. They skirted the San Francisco Peaks, passed through Cedar Ranch and arrived at the South Rim of the canyon near Hance Trail at Moran Point. They started down Hance Trail — a path that a Grand Canyon park superintendent would later describe as: "an improved Indian trail … mere scratches along the canyon walls." Foote, who documented the trip, wrote that the trail had not been improved since Hance's earliest prospecting days. He remarked that it took Hance 15 years to build it and it was a "wonder he made it at all."

Partway down the eight-mile trail, they happened upon Hance himself, who demanded they pay a $6.50 toll or they'd have to "file up the trail again." The group paid the toll.

At one point on the descent, Foote's burro, Brute, banged its load on a rock outcropping "so solidly that the poor animal was pushed off the trail…She caught with her forefeet (and hung there), Wallie pulling at her neck and Fred and I pulling all we could…. Luckily there was only an abrupt fall of 10 feet below her…. Finally, down she went, rolling completely over once. We thought she must have a broken neck for it was twisted awfully, or several broken legs; but imagine our surprise when after unpacking her, she scrambled to her feet and began to eat some grass! She wasn't even lame!"

The rest of the trip was uneventful, with a nice stay at the river's edge. "One can sit around until bedtime without a sweater or coat, while above, the ice is forming in the pail," Foote wrote. Clatworthy took the top photo on the climb back up the trail.

After retracing their steps to Flagstaff, the trio headed south. By 1899, they were near Catalina in Pinal County where the lower photograph was made. Foote wrote that the group lived quite comfortably and life on the road was rather lazy at times. The men rotated cooking chores and shooting wild game to supplement their supplies and provide fresh provisions.

They slept in the screened tent pictured, and carried chairs, chests, saddles, canteens, pipes, tobacco and a banjo. They must have picked up a human skull along the way — it is affixed to the tent peak.

As captured in the photo, the adventurers were equipped with some high-class firearms. They are, left to right: a lever-action Marlin 1887-1889, an 1881 Marlin shotgun, an 1873 model Winchester (probably, from the apparent diameter of the barrel, a .38 caliber and not a .44), and, most intriguing for collectors, a shotgun that appears to be either one of the Great American Parkers or an English piece, perhaps a Boss or a Westley Richards. The revolvers hanging from the tent are unidentified.

When the three men finally reached the end of their journey at Yuma, they sold the burros and split up. Foote continued his adventure by riding a bicycle from the Mexican border to San Francisco. He took a ship to Portland, Oregon, and again rode a bicycle to Walla Walla, Washington, and from there to Salt Lake City.

Little else is known of Foote or Johnson after they went their separate ways. Fred Clatworthy became a noted nature photographer and lived out his days in Estes Park, Colorado.

— Joan Brundige Baker; firearms identification by Scottsdale expert Gary Bausman.

Originally published: April 26, 1996

Photos courtesy of the Museum of Northern Arizona

Godfrey G. Sykes:
An Englishman Comes to Arizona

Godfrey G. Sykes, shown near the Carnegie Desert Botanical Laboratory on the outskirts of Tucson circa 1908, was an English engineer and a man of multiple talents and interests. Emigrating to the United States in 1879, he worked successively as a cowboy, a rancher, a builder, a scientific researcher and a writer. He had a virtually unquenchable thirst for adventure and travel. And he was lucky enough to live out his dreams, many of which had Arizona as the backdrop.

He came to America to become a cowboy in Texas, like the characters he had read about in Western novels. He worked at a series of odd jobs along the East Coast before saving enough money to travel to Abilene, Texas, where he became a cowhand on the Chisholm Trail to Dodge City.

In 1886, after convincing his brother Stanley to leave England and join him in the U.S., the two brothers set out on horseback, first to Albuquerque, New Mexico, and later to Flagstaff, where they established their own ranch.

They named their ranch Turkey Tanks and took the turkey track print as their cow brand. They also opened a small workshop in Flagstaff, where they fixed and mended nearly anything paying customers could provide. The workshop attracted a number of like-minded individuals with frontier inventive skills and scientific interests. The informal group became known as "the Busy Bees" and included the Sykes brothers, Dr. Andrew E. Douglass (an astronomer then employed with Percival Lowell at the Observatory), Balzer Hawk (Flagstaff's postmaster) and George Babbitt, Sr., one of five brothers who settled in Flagstaff in the mid-1880s and great uncle of former Arizona Governor and Secretary of the Interior Bruce Babbitt. Douglass was to originate the science of dendrochronology and founded Tree Ring Research Laboratory at the University of Arizona in 1937.

In the early 1890s, Godfrey interrupted his ranching

and tinkering to take off on a two-year trip to Japan and Australia. While on board various ships, he and his fellow adventurers swapped many tales; ironically, the ones that were to have the most effect on him dealt with the lower Colorado River back in his adopted home state. In 1894, Godfrey returned to Arizona and almost immediately set about preparing for a boat trip down the Colorado from Needles to the Gulf of Baja. It was during this excursion that he happened upon about the most bizarre-looking tree he or anyone else in the party had ever seen. Mature specimens ranged to 50 feet in height and looked to some like altar candles and to others like an upside-down carrot. He called it a *boojum*, referencing a "mythical thing … from far-off, desolate regions" from Lewis Carroll's *The Hunting of the Snark*.

After the trip, Godfrey returned to Flagstaff, and both he and his brother began working for Percival Lowell, who was building a 40-foot revolving dome for the new Lowell Observatory. Godfrey would later construct a dome for Lowell's tomb on Mars Hill and a dome for the Desert Sanatorium in Tucson.

In 1906, Sykes moved to Tucson to work with Dr. Daniel T. MacDougal at the Carnegie Desert Botanical Laboratory (now a part of the University of Arizona and called the Desert Laboratory) located on Tumamoc Hill, west of Tucson. The purpose of the laboratory, opened just three years earlier, was to study desert ecology. Sykes worked the Carnegie Lab until 1929, during which time he participated in numerous expeditions around the Southwest and Mexico.

Late in Sykes' life, he wrote *Westerly Trend* which was a lively account of his life and times in turn-of-the-century Arirzona. The subtitle to his autobiography was a great characterization of his life: "Being a Veracious Chronicle of More Than Sixty Years of Joyous Wanderings Mainly in Search of Space and Sunshine."

— *Dave Tackenberg, Joan Metzger and Anjanette Riley*

Originally published: September 30, 2005

Photo courtesy the Sykes Family Collection, Arizona Historical Society, Tucson

Margaret Adams: The Little Princess

The girl on horseback is Margaret Adams, daughter of Phoenix hotelier J.C. Adams and a figure in Arizona politics for many years. The photograph was taken in 1895 when she was five years old — two years before her father opened the Adams Hotel.

Margaret Adams was as close to being a princess as any little girl in Phoenix ever was. She was the only child of one of Arizona's most powerful and successful businessmen, and she lived in a hotel that was at the very center of political and business life in the Arizona Territory.

She arrived in Phoenix in 1894 with her mother, who had come to the desert from Rock Island, Illinois, to regain her health. At that time, Phoenix was a dusty backwater with a population of 4,000 people and little in the way of social or cultural amenities.

Mother and daughter first lived at the Luhrs Hotel and the next year stayed at the Ford Hotel. When J.C. Adams joined them, he saw a frontier town ripe for development.

Mr. Adams, the energetic and talented son of a Methodist minister, had earned enough money selling wallpaper as a traveling salesman to finance his way through Northwestern Law School.

Following law school, he joined a law firm and was elected to the Rock Island City Council at the age of 21. But after his wife's stay in Arizona, he saw opportunity in the West. He persuaded department store magnate Marshall Field of Chicago to visit Phoenix and convinced him to lend the money for a new hotel, despite the fact that he (Adams) had no experience in running one.

Within six months of groundbreaking, the Adams Hotel was completed. It opened on January 19, 1897, with a reception for members of the Territorial Legislature. Lobbyists and out-county legislators took rooms in the Adams during the legislative session, and soon more bills were being written there than at the Capitol seventeen blocks away. A photo of the Adams Hotel in the '20s appears opposite.

Mr. Adams set out single handedly to convince the nation that Arizona was more than a semi-civilized frontier. His hotel was the last word in elegance. It was built of pressed brick and fine lumber. The rooms were large and fitted with French windows, which opened onto verandas extending around the building. There was a spacious lobby, two restaurants, an elegant stairway, an Ealon and Prince electric elevator, plus furnishings and decorations chosen by J.C. himself from the best Chicago had to offer.

J.C. advertised his hotel to a national audience: "200 rooms, 66 with private porcelain baths, new and modern; passenger elevator, conducted from Nov. 1 to May 1 on American plan, rates from $3 per day and up; May 1 to Nov. 1 on European plan, rates $1 per day and up."

It was in that rarefied atmosphere that Margaret Adams spent her early years. At first, she attended Center School along with the other kids in town. But when two classmates were arrested in a theft and shooting spree, her parents decided the Territory was too rough for their daughter and sent her off to finishing school at Principia Academy in St. Louis, which she attended from 1901 to 1906. When she returned to Arizona, she never again lived outside the state.

She married Foster Rockwell in 1912. He was an All-American quarterback from Yale who was coach of the Phoenix Union High School football team. They had two children, Betty and John. Foster managed the Adams in later years, and son John took over in the 1940s.

The original Adams Hotel was destroyed by fire in 1910 and was re-built on the same site. The lower photo from the 1920s shows this second incarnation, which stood until 1973 when it was demolished to make way for what is now the Wyndham.

In 1944, Margaret ran for U.S. Congress on the Republican ticket. At the time, Democrats out-numbered Republicans four-to-one, and her loss in the election was hardly surprising. She served as GOP committeewoman from 1948 to 1952, and was instrumental in bringing national Republican figures to the state to rally support for the party.

Her daughter, the late Betty Adams Rockwell, served as a Republican member of the Arizona House of Representatives from 1965 to 1988.

— *Arizona Capitol Times*

Originally published: December 28, 2001

Photos courtesy of the Arizona Historical Society, Phoenix

Thomas Farish: State Historian

Unlike today, when the State Historian is an honorary position created by a governor's proclamation, in late Territorial and early statehood days this was an official, paid, government position. Concerned that many of the earliest settlers were dying and that knowledge of early Arizona history would be lost with them, the Twenty-fifth Territorial Legislature passed a bill in 1909 creating the Office of Arizona Historian. (This position later became State Historian.) According to the legislation, the task of the Historian was to collect Arizona's history so that an "accurate record may be preserved of those thrilling and heroic occurrences." The salary was $2,400 a year ($48,454 in today's money) with a travel and research budget of $1,800 ($36,340).

Mulford Winsor became the first Arizona Historian, and when he left office in late 1909, the Arizona Federation of Women's Clubs persuaded Governor Richard Sloan to appoint Sharlot Hall to the position. He did, and she became the first woman in the Territory to hold a territory-wide office.

Hall spent nearly 14 months traveling around the Territory collecting first hand accounts and materials from those who had participated in Arizona's development. However, it was not until statehood and Governor Hunt's appointment of Thomas Farish as Historian in 1913 that the state moved forward with the official publication of Arizona's history.

Like Sharlot Hall before him, Farish made a concerted effort to contact and interview many of the early pioneers. He was in a good position to do so, having known and worked with many of them himself. He arrived in Arizona in 1879, where he settled in Tombstone as the Superintendent of the Toughnut mine. Over the next 20 years, he was involved in other mining ventures, served as Governor Zulick's secretary, Territorial Treasurer, immigration commissioner and in the Territorial Legislature.

He researched newspapers, military reports, official federal and state documents and Congressional hearings seeking information about the Territory's early years. The materials he collected are filled with hand-written, first-hand accounts of pioneers, scribbled reminiscences, typescripts and even interviews he conducted in the historian's office at the state Capitol.

Some recollections are rich in detail; others sparse. Some are filled with a settler's own experiences, while others tell tales of their neighbor's misdeeds. His research reflects the prejudices of his time; he rarely interviewed women or pioneers of other races, and he viewed Native Americans as obstacles to progress.

In the end, he completed an eight-volume work of Arizona's history. On January 15, 1915, *The Arizona Gazette* said of his first two volumes, "The books fairly bristle with interest and are read with the same pleasure that one reads the most extraordinary novel ... the real, true history of the men and women who, selfishly or nor, pushed the vanguard of civilization into the fastness [sic] of the deserts and mountains and made possible the noble civilization we now enjoy."

One reviewer outside Arizona was not nearly so generous in his praise, claiming that it was obvious that Farish was not a trained historian, that he had included long, dull sections of hearings, quoted up to 20 pages of individual's accounts and included rumor and innuendo in his story.

While Farish certainly did not analyze the materials he collected in the same manner as a modern historian would, nevertheless, his work provided a foundation upon which others have built.

— *Melanie Sturgeon*

Originally published: February 11, 2005

Photo courtesy of the Arizona State Library, Archives and Public Records; History and Archives Division, Phoenix.

Award of Merit

GladysAnn Wells, Director of the Dept of Library, Archives and Pubic Records

Dr. Melanie Sturgeon's article about Thomas Farish was interesting and informative. I especially appreciated the explanation of how history was compiled and composed during the early part of the last century. Perhaps we all need to remember the human element when we read historical accounts of any time period or event. This reality, personal selection of material for an historical essay, should emphasize the essential need for permanent records that remain available for interpretation. State archives across the country seek to ensure that all will have access to the records of society's actions so that each may formulate his/her own conclusions.

On another professional note, Mulford Winsor, mentioned briefly in the article, played many leading roles in early Arizona. He arrived in 1892, was the first Territorial Historian, went on to establish the *Yuma Sun*, participated as a delegate to the 1910 Constitutional Convention, chaired the State Land Department and prepared the first State Land Code. Mr. Winsor served as a State Senator and concluded his public service as the Arizona State Librarian for nearly 20 years (1932-1956). What an amazing contribution to Arizona!

Politicans

Charles Poston, the Father of Arizona

The man at right in the top photo is Charles Debrille Poston, Arizona's first delegate to Congress and the Father of Arizona, so designated in 1899 by the 20th Territorial Legislature. The photograph was taken at the time of the 16th Territorial Legislature in 1891. With him are Maricopa County Representative Louis H. Chalmers (at left), a prominent Phoenix attorney and first president of the Phoenix Country Club, and James H. Tevis, Cochise County Representative, at various times a street car conductor, baker, river boat captain, farmer, rancher and miner.

Charles Debrille Poston, born in Hardin County, Kentucky, on June 24, 1825, orphaned at age twelve and with a limited education, became a lawyer, an elected official, a government employee, a writer, a businessman and a world traveler.

As a young man, he studied law for seven years as an apprentice to the Hardin County (Tenn) clerk's office. He then apprenticed at the Supreme Court of Tennessee, and at the age of 22 was admitted to the bar. He practiced law both in Tennessee and Washington D.C. In 1848, he married Margaret Haycraft. The couple had a daughter, Sarah Lee; a second child died shortly after birth.

Lured by gold fever in 1850, he moved to San Francisco where he clerked in the U.S. Customs House. He became friends with Mexico's powerful Iturbide family and became an agent for companies investing in Sonora. Three years later he led a party along the Gulf of California and into present-day Arizona exploring for minerals and investments in territory they expected would be soon sold to the United States. Towards the end of this trip, he traveled down the Gila River to Fort Yuma and made friends with the fort commander, Samuel Peter Heintzelman.

In 1856, just three years after the Gadsden Purchase and having secured $2 million in funding, he founded the Sonora Exploring and Mining Company with Heintzelman as president and himself as general manager. He used Tubac as his headquarters, taking over the Spanish mines at Cerro, Colorado and Arivaca. He was the only civil authority in Tubac, printing his own money and officiating at marriages and baptisms for the 800 or so residents. It was during this time that he became known as "Colonel" Poston.

His company discovered several rich silver deposits and at one point employed more than 250 men. But with the onset of the Civil War in 1861 and subsequent depredations by Apaches, Poston was forced to abandon the mining operations.

He accompanied Heintzelman to Washington, D.C. as a civilian aide and lobbied Congress and the President to create a separate Arizona Territory, even going so far as to have Tiffany cast a $1500 ink stand out of Arizona silver as a gift for President Lincoln.

In 1864, Poston was elected Arizona's first congressional delegate and secured the first congressional appropriation for promotion of irrigation. The next year he lost his re-election bid to John Goodwin, Arizona's first territorial governor. After that, Poston worked in Europe as a foreign correspondent for the *New York Tribune*, wrote a travel book, *Europe in the Summer-Time*, studied the pyramids in Egypt, and was commissioned by then-Secretary of State William Seward to deliver a copy of a treaty to the Emperor of China. He also visited India where he developed a fascination with the Parsi people and Zoroastrianism. In 1872, he wrote *The Parsees*, in which he described the followers of Zoroaster.

After a decade overseas, he returned to Arizona and worked in a variety of government jobs in Phoenix, Nogales, Florence and elsewhere. While serving at the U.S. Land Office in Florence, he wrote a book of poetry entitled *Apache Land*.

His wife died in 1885 after a long bout with cancer. He remarried the next year to a woman many years his junior, but the marriage soon failed, probably because Poston had begun to drink heavily. By 1897, he had become a virtual pauper. Whitelaw Reid, the publisher of the *New York Tribune* and a frequent winter visitor to Phoenix, sent a dispatch to the *Tribune* in 1897 describing Poston's condition. Under the headline "The Fate of the Noble Genius" he wrote, "Arizona's first delegate to Congress, Colonel Charles D. Poston, (is) ending his eventful and varied career in solitude, entirely in poverty and amid scenes of squalor, in a wretched adobe hut. That single tiny room is at once the kitchen and boudoir of Arizona's first congressman — a learned, cultured gentleman, lawyer, traveler, author, explorer, soldier… He came here when 50,000 wild Indians roamed at will over the Territory, and its white inhabitants were a handful of settlers scattered on the banks of the Gila."

In 1899, the Arizona Territorial Legislature named Poston the Father of Arizona and granted him a pension of $25 a month. Three years later on June 24, 1902, he died in Phoenix, having been run down by a stampeding horse on Second Street. He managed to drag himself back to his room on Melinda's Alley not far from where he had earlier in the month posed for the lower photo. He died later that afternoon, alone and unattended. Somewhere in the lobby of today's Hyatt Regency Hotel is the location of Poston's adobe. In 1925, Poston's remains were reinterred at the top of Poston's Butte near Florence.

— *Jane Eppinga*

Originally published: October 1, 1999

Photos courtesy Arizona Historical Society, Tucson

Charlie Shibell: Pima County Sheriff

Charles Alexander Shibell was elected sheriff of Pima County on November 7, 1876. He was expected to enforce the law in a county that covered more than 12 million acres and a city (Tucson) with more than 5,000 citizens at a time when the entire area was infested with outlaws.

A lifelong Democrat, the slender, gentle Shibell seemed an unlikely lawman. He had come to Arizona as a teamster, worked as a merchant, rancher and miner and had served as an undersheriff. Nonetheless, he had an early baptism into the job. Nine days after taking office, he made his first arrest in a murder case. Thomas P. Kerr had shot and killed Matt Bledsoe in Hovey and Brown's Saloon in an altercation over a poker bet. Shibell was able to take Kerr into custody without incident. Two days after being arrested, when the deceased Bledsoe was declared the aggressor, Kerr was released.

Shibell stood for re-election in 1880. His Republican opponent was Robert Paul. From the start, the election was controversial. Ike Clanton and Johnny Ringo, who had been named election officials in the San Simon precinct (now part of Cochise County), had such notorious reputations they were replaced by the Pima County Board of Supervisors before the election even was held.

On November 2, Pima County voters trooped to the polls. Robert Paul appeared to be well ahead until the returns arrived from San Simon. With only 10 or 12 registered voters, San Simon was reporting 100 votes for Shibell and only one vote for Paul.

J.C. Hancock, who observed the voting, wrote, "They gathered all the white people of the little place — men, women and children, probably eight or ten in all — and voted them.... (Then they) voted the Mexicans and Chinese aliens, and then descended to horses, cats and dogs. To make sure that no one had been neglected, they voted everyone over again."

The Republicans protested, and the election was overturned by the Territorial Supreme Court on April 12, 1881. Robert Paul became sheriff, and Shibell returned to the mercantile business. But six years later, he rejoined the sheriff's office as undersheriff.

On February 22, 1888, he joined a posse chasing train robbers near Stein's Pass, New Mexico. The posse followed the robbers into Mexico and arrived in Janos, Chihuahua on March 6. When they stated their mission to the Mexican police, they were arrested and jailed for illegally entering Mexican territory. It took two weeks for American authorities to negotiate their release, and when they were allowed to return to the U.S., it was without their firearms or horses.

In 1889, Charlie Shibell was elected Pima County Recorder. He held office for 20 years until his death on October 21, 1908, at the age of 57. He died of "writer's palsy" a term used to describe a neurological disorder characterized by trembling hand movements. Shibell also served as the secretary for the Arizona Historical Society from December 29, 1888 until December 28, 1892.

— *Jane Eppinga*

Originally published: June 9, 1995

Photo courtesy of the Arizona Historical Society, Tucson

Selim Franklin and the Thieving 13th

This is Selim Franklin, member of the 13th Territorial Legislature and the leader of the Tucson delegation that bargained and horse-traded to establish the University of Arizona.

When the 13th Legislature convened in 1885, Tucson citizens had one thing in mind — acquiring the state capital, then located in Prescott. To that end, they held a mass meeting and raised a fund, in those days it was called a sack, of $4,000 to smooth the way.

The group sent Frederick Maish to Prescott to inform the Tucson delegation.

Many years later, in a speech he gave in 1922 at the first celebration of Founders' Day at University of Arizona, Selim Franklin told the full story of what happened.

When Maish got to Prescott, the majority of lawmakers already had decided not to move the capital. According to Franklin, Maish said, "Boys, there is another sack where this one comes from, and another one after that if we need it. Tucson will get the capital all right. I will attend to that. Here are some bills," and he gave each of the legislators $20 in paper money.

Franklin said the cash did the trick. "We took the money. We entertained our friends of the lower house, according to the customs of the country.... We, and our associates, enjoyed ourselves immensely."

Indeed, the House voted to suspend the rules and pass a bill moving the capital to Tucson. But in the upper house — then called the Council — the bill died. Voting with the majority in that chamber was Tucsonan C.C. Stephens.

In an effort to make amends, Stephens pushed a bill out of the Council establishing a state university in Pima County. That left it up to Franklin to gain House approval, something he said would be difficult as there was nothing left to trade for votes.

Maricopa County had gotten what it wanted that session: the insane asylum in Phoenix, the normal school in Tempe and state aid in building a railroad from Phoenix south to the Southern Pacific line.

Elsewhere, Yuma County had hung on to the territorial prison, a bill to divide Cochise County had been defeated and other counties had received their share of pork.

With nothing to trade, Franklin said, all that was left was "force of argument or persuasion."

"I told my associates it was conceded that the 13th Legislature was the most energetic, the most contentious and most corrupt Legislature that Arizona had had. We were called the fighting 13th, the bloody 13th, the thieving 13th, and we deserved those names, and we all knew it.

"We had employed so many clerks for our committees that each member had one and a half clerks. We had subsidized the local press with extravagant appropriations so that our shortcomings should not be published in their columns. We had voted ourselves additional pay in violation of the Act of Congress."

He then told the legislators that by establishing a university, those sins would be forgotten.

"I pictured to my associates the commencement days of our future University of Arizona, when the graceful maidens in white gowns and the stalwart youth, seated amidst bowers of flowers facing great stretches of green lawn on which the people had assembled, would raise their voices in praise of the glorious 13th Legislature, which had given them the great opportunity of their lives. 'For your own salvation, gentlemen,' I told them, 'you must vote for this bill.'"

In the end, Franklin prevailed. The sole dissenting vote was cast by a disgruntled Cochise County legislator, still smarting from Pima County's opposition to his bill to divide Cochise County.

— *Howard Fischer*

Originally published: September 10, 1993

Photo courtesy of the Arizona Department of Library, Archives and Public Records

The Governor's Mansion

This two-story log cabin was the home of the territorial governor when the capital of the Arizona Territory was at Prescott. There is no evidence of electrical wiring, thus we assume the photograph was made sometime before the turn of the 20th century. There are two men in the photo, one on the porch sitting on what appears to be a barrel and another lounging beneath the pine tree at the left. Neither is identified.

On February 24, 1863, when President Abraham Lincoln signed into law legislation making Arizona a territory separate from New Mexico, it was assumed that Tucson, which was the only real town in the entire territory, would be named the capital. That assumption was incorrect. The citizens of Tucson had largely supported the Confederacy during the Civil War, and for that reason a site further north near Fort Whipple was chosen for the capital.

On May 30, 1864, a meeting of officials who had been dispatched to Arizona by the federal government was convened by newly appointed Territorial Governor John Goodwin. Among other details, the meeting chose a name for the capital: Prescott, in honor of historian William Hickling Prescott who had written *The Conquest of Mexico* in 1843.

When the first Territorial Legislature met on September 26, 1864, the Capitol was still under construction. The only building of any size was the Governor's Mansion—which had been built at a cost of $6,000 and was the only two-story building north of the Gila River; thus, the Legislature convened there.

In September 1865, Goodwin was elected Territorial Delegate to Congress, and Richard McCormick was appointed his successor as governor. Two years later, McCormick's 23-year-old wife Margaret died in childbirth. Rose bushes planted by her at the mansion are still in evidence.

By 1866, Tucson had enough political clout to take the capital away from Prescott. But a decade later, in 1877, Prescott was again made the territorial capital, and remained so until 1889, when upstart Phoenix was chosen as the permanent capital.

During the 1920s, poet and historian Sharlot Hall spearheaded a drive to restore the old Territorial Capitol and the Governor's Mansion. She lived in the mansion until her death in 1944. Today it is the Sharlot Hall Museum.

— *W. Lane Rogers*

Originally published: March 3, 1995

Photo courtesy Arizona Historical Society, Tucson

The 20th Territorial Council, 1899

Until Arizona became a state, the Legislature was called the Territorial Assembly and consisted of a 12-member Council and a 24-member House. These are the members of the 20th Territorial Council and their staff in front of the Phoenix City Hall where the Territorial Assembly was headquartered before the Capitol building was completed in 1901.

Arizona's capital had been moved a number of times before Phoenix was chosen as a permanent site. The first government was organized on December 29, 1863 at Navajo Springs in Apache County. Both Tucson and Prescott were home to the territorial government between 1864 and 1889. But on January 26, 1889, the 15th Territorial Assembly, meeting in Prescott, designated Phoenix as the new capital and scheduled the move to the city on February 7, giving themselves less than a fortnight to pack up and get there.

The citizens of Phoenix had kindly offered the upper floor of their city hall to the Legislature and provided space for the offices of the governor, his secretary and the Territorial Library on the main floor. In a burst of generosity, they also had subscribed all costs of moving the government, paying for food, drink and Pullman accommodations on the train from Prescott to Los Angeles and back to Phoenix. (Apparently, it was feared that the stage ride down the mountain from Prescott to the Salt River Valley might cause the legislators such mental and physical suffering they would be unfit to make law when they arrived.)

The Phoenix City Hall was the home of the territorial government until January 21, 1901, when the Territorial Assembly met at the newly completed Capitol building at Washington Street and 17th Avenue.

The members of the 20th Territorial Council are listed below.

Front row:

E.J. Trippel, Chief Clerk
J.B. Finley, Pima
Aaron Goldberg, Maricopa
Morris Goldwater (President), Yavapai
George A. Wolff, Navajo
George W.P. Hunt, Gila
Charles C. Warner, Cochise

Second row:

J.M. Murphy, Mohave
D.K. Udall, Apache
J.H. Carpenter, Yuma
T.S. Bunch, Coconino
A.C. Wright, Pinal
George A. Olney, Graham

Third row:

Maude Scarborough, Committee Clerk
F.J. Duffy, Asst. E. & E. Clerk
Joseph Morgan, Asst. Journal Clerk
W.B. Kelly, Sergeant-at-Arms
R.S. Macclay, Assistant Chief Clerk
Frank Luke, Enrolling and Engrossing Clerk
P.C. Merrill, 2nd Asst. E. & E. Clerk

Top row:

J.L. Byrnes, Committee Clerk
H.L. Fuller, Committee Clerk
R.H. Jones, Journal Clerk

The man in the light-colored suite at the right of the top row and the woman in the boater in the second row are not identified.

— *Arizona Capitol Times*

Originally published: January 6, 1988

Photo courtesy of the Arizona Department of Libraries, Archives and Public Records; History and Archives Division, Phoenix

The Governor's Race — for the Train

The bald pate and rotund body seen here on the Capitol veranda is that of George W.P. Hunt, photographed on Valentine's Day, 1912, delivering his inaugural address as the state's first governor.

Earlier that morning — 10:23 a.m. Washington time — President William Howard Taft, no lightweight himself, had affixed his signature to the proclamation of statehood for Arizona, ending a 20-year effort. As Taft signed his name, a camera whirred in the background, the first time moving pictures were made of a presidential function.

Shortly after 9:00 a.m. Arizona time, whistles, bells and yells went up announcing receipt at the telegraph office of the news that Arizona had at last emerged from its territorial womb. "I congratulate the people of this, our newest commonwealth, upon the realization of their long cherished ambition..." wired Taft to outgoing Governor Richard E. Sloan.

Hunt, headquartered at the Ford Hotel, then set out for the Capitol to take the oath of office from newly sworn-in Chief Justice Alfred Franklin. In a display intended to show the citizenry that his administration would be a frugal one, Hunt waved away automobiles and carriages and walked to his inaugural — a 45 minute jaunt punctuated by frequent stops to press the flesh.

He was late, but not nearly as late as he might have been had a sharp-eyed trainman not saved him the day before.

The previous morning, Hunt, his wife and his seven year-old daughter, Virginia, had boarded the train at Globe and taken a circuitous route to Phoenix via Safford, Benson and Tucson. Arriving at Tucson late in the afternoon, he was met by perennial presidential candidate William Jennings Bryan, a man the press was wont to call the "great commoner." Unbeknownst to Hunt, an informal reception had been put together on the station platform — not for him, but in Bryan's honor. The governor-elect found himself in the role of introducer, and the long-winded Bryan wanted to be introduced to everybody.

The clock ticked and the train began pulling out of the station, Hunt, forgoing dignity, abandoned Bryan and dashed from the platform, chasing after the train, his arms flailing, his voice rising in epitaphs. "A lively race followed," chronicled the *Tucson Citizen*. "Governor Hunt, though somewhat handicapped in the matter of weight, led easily. Even at that, the official party would have been stranded in Tucson had not the rear-end brakeman observed the race and signaled the train to halt. When it started again, the governor and his friends were safely aboard."

Thus, the governor's race (for the train) was won, and the inauguration of the people's choice proceeded in a timely fashion.

— *W. Lane Rogers*

Originally published: February 10, 1993

Photo courtesy of W. Lane Rogers

Admissions Day Parade, Feb. 14, 1912

This parade was held in Phoenix on the day Arizona was admitted into the union as the 48th state. For 20 years, Arizonans lobbied Congress for statehood, and when President Taft finally signed the statehood proclamation on the morning of Valentine's Day in 1912, the state had reason to celebrate. Phoenix Mayor Lloyd B. Christy ordered all business suspended, and the citizens devoted themselves to a day-long celebration. At noon, George W.P. Hunt was sworn in as the first Governor of the State of Arizona, at 2 p.m., the Admissions Day parade was kicked off with a 48-gun salute (one for each state in the union) and in the evening, an outdoor inaugural ball was held on Central Avenue in front of the Adams Hotel.

This photograph shows the parade heading east on Washington Street between 3rd Avenue and Central. Every organization in town was represented: the militia, fraternal orders, labor organizations, fire department, school children, horsemen, Spanish-American and Civil War veterans, as well as three marching bands. Leading the way (at least in this photograph) was Miss Arizona and her court of attendants in a large mule-drawn wagon. (Close inspection reveals that she is carrying a Miss Arizona sign and wearing a crown with a large letter A on it.)

As far as we know, the only sour note during the day was the Rev. Seaborn Crutchfield's lengthy invocation preceding Gov. Hunt's oath of office. Rev. Crutchfield, a devout Democrat, spent ten minutes or so thanking God for Gov. Hunt's election. That was more than the Republicans in the audience could swallow, and the next day an editorial appeared in one of the newspapers complaining "that a minister of the gospel should use an occasion of that sort to deliver a political speech is something new in the matter of inaugural experience." The editorial suggested that the Rev. Mr. Crutchfield be excluded from giving the invocation at inaugurals in the future.

— *Arizona Capitol Times*

Originally published: February 18, 1984

Photo from the Arizona News Service archives

The Baby Secretary, 1913

The man at the desk is Arizona Secretary of State Sidney Preston Osborn. When this photo was taken in 1913, Arizona was the newest of the 48 states and was known in some circles as the "Baby State." Sid Osborn was the "Baby Secretary of State," youngest in the nation at age 29. His sister, Kathryn, is beside him. The other men are Johnnie Shivvers Norton and Richard McGillen, Assistant Secretary of State. The other woman is unidentified.

Sid Osborn was the first-born son of Neri Osborn, a clerk in the State Treasurer's Office and an active Democrat. Even as a youth, he was interested in politics, going so far, according to one story, as to sign one of his textbooks "Governor Sidney P. Osborn."

In 1899, when he was 15, he got a job as a page at the Territorial Legislature, the same position his father had held many years before in Prescott, when that city was the territorial capital. After high school, he worked in Washington, D.C. for two years as secretary to Arizona's Congressional delegate J. F. Wilson, and then returned to his hometown to pursue a career in journalism and politics. He worked for a time on a local paper (possibly the *Arizona Sun* or *Arizona Democrat*) and, in 1911, ran successfully for Secretary of State. He was re-elected in 1914 and again in 1916, but in 1918 in a bid for the Democratic nomination for governor, his luck ran out. He lost in the primary.

For the next 20 years, he was out of elective office. He stayed active in Democrat politics and was editor of *Dunbar's Weekly*, a political opinion newspaper, during much of that time. When Roosevelt was elected in 1932, Osborn got a patronage job as director of the Arizona Internal Revenue Service. After that he felt confident enough of the political climate to run for office again. He made another unsuccessful bid for the nomination for governor in 1934, and then finally got the nomination and won the office in 1940, twenty-two years after his first try. He told a friend at the time, "All I ever wanted was to be governor." He was re-elected three times and won the 1944 election with the largest percentage of votes — 78.9% — in state history. He died in office in May of 1948.

— *Reba Wells*

Originally published: November 19, 1986

Photo courtesy of the Arizona Historical Society, Phoenix

Award of distinction

Secretary of State Jan Brewer

I found the "Baby Secretary, 1913" article with the photo of Sydney P. Osborn sitting in the original Secretary of State office in the old Capitol building to be an impressive story.

After his stint as Secretary of State, Osborn later went on to become the only person in Arizona history who was elected to four consecutive terms as Governor. It was an intriguing story of someone who fervently aspired and pursued a career in politics and after many attempts, found ultimate success.

Hunt on the Campaign Trail

These photos show George W. P. Hunt campaigning somewhere in Arizona. The date of the top photos could be anytime between 1912, when he became the first governor of Arizona after statehood, and 1930, when he ran his last successful campaign.

Hunt had a long and illustrious career in Arizona politics, but his start in the state was inauspicious. He arrived in Globe in October of 1881 at the age of 21, on foot, with a burro hauling all his possessions. He had left home three years earlier, after his father suffered financial reverses, and had spent several years drifting around the Southwest from Colorado to New Mexico to Texas, prospecting and working at whatever he could find when his funds ran low.

In Globe, he got a job at Pascoe's Restaurant. Later he worked at the Old Dominion Mine, tried his hand at ranching and finally got a job as a clerk in a store. There he found his niche, advancing in his career until by 1900 he was named president of the company.

Hunt got his start in politics as a member of the Territorial Legislature and was president of the state's constitutional convention in 1910. When Arizona finally became a state two years later, he ran for governor as a Democrat and was elected. He won again in 1914.

He ran again in 1916 and lost to Tom Campbell by 30 votes. He challenged the results, claiming fraud had occurred at several polling places. Initially, he refused to vacate his office, but a ruling by the Arizona Supreme Court in January 1917 forced him to leave. However, he continued his challenges in court, and in December 1917, the state Supreme Court declared him the winner over Campbell by 43 votes.

The bottom photo shows Hunt and a 23-year old Jesse Addison Udall in Holbrook during the 1916 campaign. (In 1960, almost 44 years after the picture was taken, Udall was named to the state Supreme Court and served until his retirement in 1972.)

Hunt sat out the 1918 election and took an appointment as ambassador to Siam (Thailand) in 1920, but was back in the state a year later in time to be elected governor again in 1922. He went on to win reelection in 1924, 1926 and 1930.

To his many supporters, he was honest, generous and a man of great personal warmth. He was a strong supporter of education, a better highway system, prison reform and better conditions for the workingman.

To his opponents, he was pompous, officious and much too powerful. They dubbed him George IV (after his fourth election), a name that stayed with him until his reign ended as George VII. After his 1930 win, he was defeated twice in primaries. He died just a few months after his last campaign, on Christmas Eve, 1934.

— *Stan Matthews*

Originally published: February 4, 1987

Top photos courtesy of the Arizona Historical Society, Phoenix

Bottom photo is courtesy of the Jesse A. Udall Collection, University of Arizona Library

First Republican-Controlled Senate, 1921

These are the members of the 1921-1922 Arizona Senate, the first chamber of the Arizona Legislature to be controlled by Republicans. The margin was just one-vote, but that was certainly better than the make-up of the 1919-20 Senate which was composed entirely of Democrats.

The unprecedented outcome in the Senate was the result of a nationwide Republican wave that carried Warren G. Harding into the White House in 1920. But one Democrat Party leader, Mr. G.L. Coffey of Greenlee, didn't see it that way. He blamed it on divine intervention. The House Chaplain, Rev. Seaborn Crutchfield of Phoenix, often prayed for the Republicans, whom he described as "wandering in the wilderness of error."

When it became evident after the 1920 election that the Republicans had gained control of the Senate, the *Arizona Republican* reported that Mr. Coffey accosted the venerable Crutchfield in the lobby of the Adams Hotel and told him, "You ought to take a lesson from experience and not pray for the Republicans. (In the past) you have done that against the advice of far-seeing Democrats, and you now see the disastrous result."

Democrats regained control of the Senate in 1923, capturing all but one of the 19 seats. Republicans would have to wait until 1967 when the effects of a U.S. Supreme Court decision mandating "one-man, one-vote" were imposed in Arizona. Since that time, the GOP has had a majority in the state Senate for all but three legislatures: the 32nd (1975-76), 33rd (1977-78), and 40th (1991-92). Meanwhile, since 1967, when they took control of the House for the first time, Republicans have never relinquished the majority.

(Standing, from left):
Senate Secretary Roy Davidson, and Sens. Celora Stoddard (R-Maricopa), W.A. Saunders (R-Apache), John P. Cull (D-Cochise), Charles E. Larson (R-Coconino), H.B. Wilkinson (R-Maricopa), Elias Hedrick (R-Pima), Charles Burton (R-Yavapai), W.P. Sims (D-Cochise), F.O. Goodell (R-Pima), H.A. Elliott (D-Greenlee) and A.J. Eddy (D- Yuma).

(Seated, from left):
Sens. W.D. Claypool (D-Gila), Joseph Lines (D-Graham), F.A. Woodward (R-Gila), James Curtin (D-Mohave), Charles MacMillin (D-Pinal), James Scott (R-Navajo), J.L. Schleimer (D-Santa Cruz) and David Morgan (R-Yavapai).

— *Arizona Capitol Times*

Originally published: January 12, 1983

Photo courtesy of the Arizona Department of Libraries, Archives and Public Records; History and Archives Division, Phoenix

Another Time, Another Babbitt

This is State Senator James E. Babbitt, member of the pioneer northern Arizona family and uncle of former Governor and former Secretary of the Interior, Bruce Babbitt.

Senator Babbitt, the youngest member of the Legislature when first elected in 1933, saw many of his bills become law during the decade before his death in 1944.

He was instrumental in establishing *Arizona Highways* magazine, helped pass several family relief bills, a bill to see that old age pensions were paid and a bill to install permanent air cooling at the state hospital for the insane.

He was an avid outdoorsman and sponsored many bills dealing with game and fish and with water and soil laws.

James Babbitt was born in Santa Monica, California, and received his law degree from the University of Southern California. He was called home to Flagstaff in 1929 to become corporate attorney for Babbitt Brothers Trading Company, the family firm.

During the Great Depression he had the unenviable task of having to collect outstanding bills from friends and neighbors who had fallen on hard times. Folks in Flagstaff still remember him fondly and with kindness, even though his name is on many a foreclosure document.

At the state House, he fought the old guard for leadership. He lost out as Speaker of the House by one vote in his first term, but was named Speaker pro tem by 1936, just before he moved on to the Senate. He was no pushover and rebelled against Governor Sidney P. Osborn's power, even though they both were Democrats. At a speech in Flagstaff, the governor said he was considering an old Mexican custom of putting rebellious legislators out in the mountains to think things over. Babbitt leaped to his feet and proclaimed that Arizona would not tolerate dictators, even in the form of a governor.

In 1944, when he was 42 years old, Babbitt went on a hunting trip with a group of friends. He had been fighting a cold but refused to cancel the trip which was to a remote area of Fossil Creek near Strawberry. The group bagged a bear early in the day, but as an unexpected cold rain turned to sleet, Babbitt grew so weak he could not manage the steep climb out of the canyon to the Rim and shelter.

His party hiked to Fossil Springs to get help. The next day a search party found James Babbitt's body 100 yards from the spot where his companions had left him. The coroner ruled he had died from exposure. He left a wife and two young daughters, Mary Phyllis and Dorothy, and a whole county of admirers.

Family members left their own endeavors to fill his place both in the Legislature and the trading company. Brother John G. Babbitt was appointed to the Senate seat, later winning his own terms and also serving on the Board of Regents. Bruce Babbitt's father, Paul, left a law practice in Los Angeles, moving with his family to Flagstaff to pick up the corporate attorney position in the company. And that is how it happened that ex-Governor Bruce Babbitt had an Arizona upbringing, despite his California birth.

— *Joan Brundige-Baker*

Originally published: June 25, 1993

Photo courtesy of the Arizona Department of Libraries, Archives and Public Records; History and Archives Division, Phoenix

Sports & Recreation

Mariner's Juvenile Band

The Best of All Games

Bisbee's Mighty Tug-of-War

Wild Hearts in Phoenix: Powderface Takes a Dive

Baseball in the Old Pueblo

Swimming Pool, Riverside Park, c. 1922

The Martin/Courtney Feud

Mariner's Juvenile Band

These are the members of Mariner's Juvenile Band, the pride of Tucson when this photograph was taken in 1898. The band was organized in 1897 by Barnett M. Mariner, who had organized bands in his home state of Maine before coming to Tucson. He got together some 30 boys, ages six (Scotty Gray, front row) to 15 (Jose Martin, top row) and rehearsed them in his own home during the first months they were together. Later, practice sessions were held in the new Tucson Opera House run by A.V. Grossetta, father of band member Warren Grossetta.

The band played every Sunday afternoon until sunset in the plaza park across from City Hall. It never missed a parade or civic celebration. Band members also traveled to Bisbee and Phoenix to perform.

At first the boys performed in street clothes, but by the end of 1898 they had acquired the fine uniforms they are wearing in the photograph. The uniforms were brilliant red with gold buttons, gold trim and matching caps — enough to make any boy proud.

Millie Mariner, Barnett's wife, was interviewed about this photograph in 1921. She said that "at one morning rehearsal we told the boys to wear their uniforms and we took a picture of the band. But the picture took all morning because no sooner would we get them straight than one of the boys would begin another scuffle."

In spite of this early example of fractiousness, many of the boys became prominent citizens in Tucson. Among them were Warren Grossetta, Hiram Corbett and George Martin. Their descendants still live in the Tucson area.

— *Joan Metzger*

Originally published: July 4, 1984

Left to right Top row: Allen Bernard, Jose Martin, Willis Roletti, Frank Crum, (?) Kennedy, Edgar Paul, Manuel Montijo. Second row: Leo Goldtree, George Martin, Willis Buehman, Tom Angus, unidentified, Andy Martin, Albert Roletti. Third row: Willie McFadden, Harvey Cake, Ed Bernard, Joe Clark, Emmett Ford, Alfred Trippel, Mortis Copple, Louis Pellon. Fourth row: Fritz Bernard, Hiram Corbett, Harry Burnett, Maurice Holliday, unidentified, Leslie Hardy. Front row: Charles Little Hardy, Warren Grossetta, Deb Anderson, Scotty Gray.

Photo courtesy of the Arizona Heritage Center

The Best of All Games

This is Willie Marshall, Warren Country Club's first golf pro, hitting a fairway shot in 1910. Over his right shoulder, in the distance, is the Warren/Bisbee Trolley. The trolley provided transportation to the golf course, which was located just south of Warren, within sight of the Mexican border.

Marshall arrived in Bisbee in November 1901 and joined a small contingent of professional golfers who wintered in the Southwest. They taught golf, repaired clubs and organized tournaments in the winter but returned to their home courses and greener links in the summer.

Groundbreaking for the Warren District Country Club began on January 30, 1908, and the first match was played February 18. The speed of construction undoubtedly meant that the course was rugged and crude. The putting greens consisted of oiled packed dirt, the fairways were carpeted with gravel and cactus, and hazards included ore cars, trains and mine settling ponds.

Marshall's first impression of the course is unrecorded, but for public consumption, he put it in the best light. The *Bisbee Daily Review* wrote: "Mr. Marshall speaks highly of the Bisbee course and says it well bears out the reputation, which has already traveled to the far east, of being one of the finest in the country."

He stated further: "In a general way, I may say that I was agreeably surprised at finding so good a golf course here. I think the topography of the course is excellent, and one would have to travel a long way to find anything that would equal it, outside of the fact that there is no turf. If it only had grass it would be a wonder, but it is possible to play very good golf on it, even without the turf."

Boosting the sport of golf, Marshall also said: "It is the best of all games because it is the only ballgame in which your opponent does not interfere with your ball…. If you cannot find anyone at hand to play with, why, play by yourself. You can play as fast or as slowly as you wish, and you are never too young or too old to enjoy the sport. It is an ideal game for women, and there is nothing better than mixed foursomes…."

The professionals often played each other during country club matches. The *Review* reported on one of the matches in January of 1910: "In the professional match played at Douglas Sunday, the El Paso professional won by two up. The match was very close between the El Paso man (David Levie of Scotland) and William Marshall, the golf expert of the Warren District Country Club. Marshall being right after him all the way. In a return match March 21 at El Paso, Marshall came in second to Levie, and Adams of Douglas finished last."

Marshall did not return after the summer of 1910, and the Warren Country Club contracted with John Adams, golf pro from Douglas, to be on hand Tuesday and Thursday of each week.

The Warren District Country Club was demolished in the 1930s and a new one built near Naco. Today it is called Turquoise Valley Golf Course.

— *Tom Vaughan*

Originally publsihed: July 28, 1995

Photo courtesy Bisbee Mining and Historical Museum, Fountain Collection

Bisbee's Mighty Tug of War

In December of 1903, handbills began appearing around Bisbee announcing a mighty tug-of-war competition. Tug-of-war was popular in the early 1900s, particularly in the rough and ready mining towns of the West, where a man's strength and brawn was a measure of his success.

A battle could last for hours. Teams lined up on either side of a center mark. A ladder-like device with cleats was placed on the ground, and the team members lay on their sides with their feet gripping the cleats as they pulled across the mark. The last man on each side sat at the back of the line as the anchor.

Four teams — Irish, Swedes, Bisbee miners and a group from Globe — signed on to compete in the contest. Later the Globe contingent dropped out and was replaced by a Slovenian team. Since ethnic rivalry ran high and legal gambling flourished in Bisbee; it is no surprise that a lot of cash was wagered.

The night before the contest, the *Bisbee Daily Review* reported "the Annex [Saloon] was jammed with the friends of the contestants, and a bet of $100 that the Irish would win was snapped up in a minute. Another bet of $50 was made that the Swedes [would] out-pull the Slavs. No event in Bisbee has caused so much betting and excitement as this tug-of-war."

The *Review* described the first match which pitted the Irish team against the Swedes: "For the first 30 minutes it was nip and tuck, with no advantage. During the next 30 minutes the boys with the light hair gained a little, and at the expiration of one hour and 20 minutes had 18 inches of rope belonging to the Irish on their side of the line, and Hanson, the big Swede anchor, announced that he would be in that position when the call came for breakfast. Then the tide began to turn. The Irish responded to every call by their captain, and with superhuman efforts, cleat by cleat, they pulled away from the Swedes. At the expiration of one hour and 45 minutes, with the last cleat gained, the Irish had won the first contest."

The next teams to compete were the Slovenians and the Bisbee miner's team. The Slovenians defeated the Bisbee team in just 20 minutes. All teams returned the next evening, but there was disagreement over the order of events. The *Review* said, "...for a time bedlam was turned loose, and all four nationalities seemed to be talking at once." No deal could be brokered, and the tournament was called off.

Later that week, two friends, one Irish and one Slovenian, met at a local saloon. The discussion fell upon the best tug-of-war team, and the Slovenian produced $1,000, "putting his money where his mouth was." The Irishman placed a few telephone calls, made rounds of other drinking establishments and returned with cash to cover the bet.

The men signed a written agreement detailing the terms of the match: the prize would be $2,000 plus gate receipts after expenses, and the winner would take all; the distance to be pulled would be 36 inches from center; expenses could not exceed $100 and all claims had to be turned in at the box office on the night of the match; a $250 forfeit would be posted with the promoter, and the remainder of the money would be deposited at the Bank of Bisbee.

On the night of the match, crowds filled the Opera House. Special officers kept people away from the cleats and a betting window opened with the *Review* estimating over $5,000 exchanging hands during the evening.

The *Review* described the fans as

> ... [a] good natured crowd that jostled against the ropes and hurled jests and cat calls.... [A] group of ladies were eager witnesses of all of the preliminaries ... and were more than once on their feet cheering.... All classes were represented. The merchant stood in line with the laborer for three hours, and the banker elbowed the knight of the green cloth....

> At 9:01, referee Jack Taylor fired the starting gun and, quick as a flash, the Slavs had taken up the slack and had four or five inches to their credit.

> At 9:20, the Slavs made their main effort and... gathered in about 10 more inches of the hemp.... At the expiration of the first hour, the Slavs had 20 inches... [but]... at the two hour mark, the Irish regained the first cleat they had lost ... and bedlam was turned loose. Slowly but surely those powerful backs, arms and legs were brought into action, and cleat by cleat the Slavs were dragged across the mark.... At exactly 11:54, the last cleat was gained, and the noise that broke loose was deafening!

Jubilant Irish fans and the team let loose a volley of yells, whistles, hugs and backslapping, but sportsmanship reigned and no disrespect was tossed on the losers. The *Review* reported, "It is doubtful if there ever was in the history of tug-of-war contests a more determined team of winners. It is certain there never were better losers... Be it said to their credit that not once did the losing team show the white feather. Sick at heart and sore in body, they never gave a cleat without a show of struggle...."

— *Tom Vaughan*   *Originally published: September 26, 2003*

Crowds surround tug-of-war contestants near Bisbee's Brewery Saloon in 1900.
A team can be seen pulling, with the anchor man at the back of the line.

Photo courtesy of the Bisbee Mining and Historical Museum

Wild Hearts in Phoenix: Powderface Takes a Dive

The larger photo shows Powderface, the wonder horse, at the Territorial Fair in Phoenix, probably in 1905, the year the fair re-opened after a disastrous fire in 1891. Powderface was one of the few horses in the world trained to dive off a platform into a tank of water.

Powderface belonged to William Frank "Doc" Carver, a trained dentist and carnival sharpshooter with an act like Annie Oakley's. Carver told the story of crossing a bridge during a storm in the 1880s when the bridge started to collapse. His horse dove into the water, giving him the idea for his horse diving act.

Carver and his horse sometimes wintered in Phoenix — the doctor at the Adams Hotel, and Powderface at what is now Eastlake Park (at 16th and Washington Streets). During the summer, the two traveled the carnival circuit performing feats of derring-do. Powderface was required to climb a ramp, braced by a wooden scaffold, to a platform some 30 feet above ground. To the amazement of spectators, he then jumped into a tank of water.

While on tour, Carver's son Al was usually in charge of building the ramp and tower; his daughter Lorena often rode the horse as it dived from the platform. In this photo, Powderface is riderless, although note the person behind the horse who may have encouraged the equine with a good solid shove.

This act at the Territorial Fair brought forth a storm of protest from local animal lovers. John Canning, Phoenix humane officer, closed the act, but not before a local photographer had preserved it for posterity. Carver continued performing the act at fairs around the country, and although he died in 1927, the act became a permanent attraction at Atlantic City's Steel Pier. Animal rights groups finally closed it down for good in the 1970s.

Doc Carver's exploits with horse diving are recounted in the 1991 film, "Wild Hearts Can't Be Broken," which is based on real life. The film recounts how Sonora Webster Carver, Al Carver's wife, is blinded in a horse-diving accident yet continues to ride and jump in the act.

The Arizona Territorial Fair, which had not been held for fourteen years after an 1891 flood destroyed the fairgrounds down by the river, was a huge success when it reopened in 1905 at its new location at 19th Avenue and McDowell Road. With the support of two prominent businessmen, J.C. Adams and M.H. Sherman, it became a permanent event. Now the Arizona State Fair, it has been held every fall except during the Great Depression, World War II and one year when the cotton crop failed.

— *Arizona Capitol Times*

Originally published: September 10, 1986

DR. W. F. CARVER.

Photos from the Arizona News Service archives

Baseball in the Old Pueblo, c. 1908

These are the members of Drachman's Elysian Grove baseball team in Tucson. Standing left to right are Frank "Pancho" Navarro, Emanuel "Manny" Drachman (team captain and catcher), Herb Drachman, William Armstrong and Julian Montano. In the foreground are Julian Vargas, Manuel R. Cota, Desidero "Chonte" Bustamonte, John "Huero" Johnson (pitcher) and Miguel "Mike" Franco.

Manny Drachman started playing baseball at the age of 13, when a Tucson team was organized to play the soldiers at Fort Lowell. He learned to throw a curve ball from a railroad man in the early 1880s, and he had quite a reputation as a pitcher until an injury forced him to move to the catcher's position. Over the years, he played with and managed many Tucson ball clubs, including the Excelsiors, True Blues, Tucson Grays and Groves.

In the early days, baseball was played in a vacant area known as Military Plaza, roughly where the Santa Rita Hotel now stands. But in 1903, Manny Drachman took over the 13 acres of Carillo Gardens located between the east bank of the Santa Cruz River and Main Street, south of Simpson. There were a number of ponds for swimming and a grove of shady cottonwoods on the property. Manny changed the name to Elysian Grove and added a baseball diamond, an outdoor theater and a saloon. Baseball games were played on Sunday afternoon and were a popular attraction. Drachman's teams played clubs from Bisbee, Tombstone, Benson, Florence and Phoenix, among others.

Manny Drachman was involved in baseball all his life, not only as a player and manager, but also as chairman of the local baseball commission, a position he held until he died in 1933. He lived long enough to see voters approve a $35,000 bond package in 1927 to build an official municipal baseball park. The ballpark was later renamed Hi Corbett Field after the man credited with bringing spring training to Tucson. Manny's son, Roy P. Drachman, started Drachman Realty, a force in Tucson economic development since 1946.

— *Joan Metzger*

Originally published: March 13, 1985

Photo courtesy of the Arizona Historical Society, Tucson

Swimming Pool, Riverside Park, c. 1922

The swimming pool at Riverside Park was the place to be in Phoenix on long hot summer afternoons in the days before air conditioning. The pool — and it was a monster in size — was in effect a very cold, slow running stream for it was fed from a deep well. The photograph fails to do justice to the daunting height of both the high-diving tower on the right or to the copper-sheathed slide on the left, challenges only the more daring accepted.

The pool featured two rafts chained to the bottom. (The smaller one is in the center of the photograph.) On the slope above the swimming pool was a low wooden building that housed the dressing rooms. There the unequipped could rent a dreadful, black, shoulder-to-knees bathing suit labeled "Stolen From Riverside Park."

As to the beginning of Riverside Park, there is a report that a fellow named Walter Kane or King built a swimming pool on the spot in 1900. Historian James Barney said that the very first swimming pool in Phoenix was built in the 1870s in the inner court of the Phoenix Hotel at Washington and Pima St. (3rd Street). It was a canvas covered, roughly scooped out affair with boarded sides and fed by running ditch water. In 1887, Dyer's "Birdseye View of Phoenix" (see page 56) showed the Phoenix Swimming Baths on the northeast corner of Van Buren and Central. Finally there was also the Natatorium at Eastlake Park on the corner of 16th Street and Washington.

—*Arizona News Service*

Originally published: December 8, 1982

Photo from the Arizona News Service archives

The Martin/Courtney Feud

This is the 1947 Bisbee Yankees baseball team. Clint Courtney, second from left on the bottom row, was Bisbee's catcher during the 1947 season and later played in the major leagues with the St. Louis Browns. He was runner-up to pitcher Harry Byrd of Philadelphia as American League Rookie of the Year in 1952.

The Yankees played in the Arizona Texas League, which included teams from Tucson, Globe-Miami, El Paso, Juarez and Phoenix. The second baseman on the Phoenix team in 1947 was none other than Alfred "Billy" Martin, who later played second base for and was the frequent manager of the New York Yankees. Both Courtney and Martin were cocky and scrappy young talents, and it was inevitable the two would clash. Their feud became one of the most famous in baseball history.

Arizona's minor league baseball had always been rough and tumble, with gambling, brawling, rioting and even gunfights. So when Martin and Courtney began to scrap, the fans were delighted and filled up the ballparks. Here are some personal recollections: Raymond Stout, who watched the games with his father, Slim Stout, reports, "The park would always be full when the Phoenix club was in town. If Martin and Courtney came together at second base or home, there would be trouble." Natalie Denny writes in the *Brewery Gulch Gazette*: "[Martin and Courtney] invariably would get into an argument. One time, the police had to break up a near riot caused by their quarreling."

Each time the Bisbee and Phoenix baseball clubs met during the 1947 season a fight erupted. The playing managers of both clubs encouraged physical contact. The mellower of the two, Bisbee manager Charlie Metro, set the example by bumping into infielders when he ran the bases. Phoenix manager Arky Biggs encouraged his team to play knock-em-down baseball and got tossed out of several games that season for fighting.

It is hard to identify how the feud began. In the book *Billy Martin* by Gene Schoor, Martin is quoted, "Down in Phoenix I missed one game, and a kid by the name of Eddie Lenne was playing second base and Courtney jumped into him and spiked his leg open ... I couldn't get Courtney that day ... but from that day on, every time I got a chance, I took a punch at him. Every time."

In September of that year, the two teams played a series at Phoenix, battling for second place. In one game, Courtney tried to stretch a single into a double by barreling through second baseman Biggs. From that point, the action got confusing and ended in a bench-clearing brawl. Courtney and Biggs were tossed out of the game, and Biggs ended up in the hospital with a broken finger.

Sports writer Lou Pavlovitch of the *Bisbee Daily Review* wrote: "In every contest of the three-game series at Phoenix there were fights, squabbling and all-around rowdiness as the rival Phoenix Senators and Bisbee Yankees engaged in a heated battle for second place .... There were pillows and bottles thrown at the umps ... booing, threats, and the situation was nightmarish to say the least."

The battle for second place continued when the two teams played at Bisbee later that month. Anticipation of fighting ran so high that the Cochise County sheriff announced plans to ring the field with armed deputies. The close proximity of peace officers must have helped; there were no fights or riots despite Bibee losing all three games.

Martin made it to the majors in 1950. Courtney followed at the end of the 1951 season. In the off season, he was obtained by the St. Louis Browns at the request of manager Rogers Hornsby. The stage was set for the next phase of the feud.

In July 1952, the Browns were playing a series at Yankee Stadium. Courtney, in contention for Rookie of the Year honors, caught for the Browns, and Martin played second base for the Yankees.

During one play, Courtney smashed into Yankee catcher Yogi Berra at home plate as he scored a run. The play infuriated the Yankees. A few innings later, Courtney occupied first base when a pitch got by Berra. Second baseman Billy Martin caught Yogi's throw well before the slow running, short-legged Courtney reached the bag. Courtney tried to run over Martin, but the scrappy second baseman sidestepped and tagged Courtney violently — right between the eyes. The inning ended with Martin trotting off the field and Courtney scrabbling around in the dirt groping for his glasses. Unable to find them, Courtney must have thought Martin had taken them and gave chase, catching up with him near the dugout. The two began whaling away on each other.

After being separated, Courtney was thrown out of the game, suspended for three days and fined.

The following year in a Browns' home game, a Yankee player bowled over Courtney at home to score the winning run. Both benches emptied, and the play turned into another free-for-all. Martin joined the melee, headed straight for Courtney, and both players suffered bloody faces. To add insult to injury, during the fracas someone stepped on Courtney's glasses.

— *Tom Vaughan*

Originally published: August 19, 1994

Photo courtesy Bisbee Mining & Historical Museum

*Courtney's 1953
Topps baseball card*

*Martin's 1952
Topps baseball card*

Baseball card images courtesy of the Topps Company

Transportation

Queen of the Colorado

This is the *Mohave*, the largest and most palatial of the paddlewheelers on the Colorado River 130 years ago. The photo was taken in 1876, when the *Mohave* was docked at Yuma taking on school children for a May Day excursion. The ship had been launched earlier that year, replacing a smaller boat (also called the *Mohave*) that had been dismantled and completely rebuilt.

Steam navigation on the Colorado was a matter of necessity in the early days. When Fort Yuma was founded in 1850, the only way to provide supplies was by overland wagon trains sent out from San Diego. The route was difficult, dangerous and unreliable. It was immediately obvious that a river route was needed. In 1852, the *Uncle Sam*, a 65-foot sidewheeler, successfully made the trip from the Gulf of California upriver to Yuma Crossing. After that, dozens of settlements along the Colorado clamored for goods from California. The demand led to a thriving riverboat trade that made the Colorado the major means of transportation in the Arizona Territory. Towns as far inland as Prescott, Wickenburg, Phoenix and Kingman were supplied by the river and owed much of their growth to the riverboats.

River traffic flourished from 1860 until 1877, when the Southern Pacific Railroad arrived in Arizona from the West Coast. Riverboaters apparently thought the rail line would stop at the California border and were surprised when the Southern Pacific decided to extend the line into Arizona. That would account for the rebuilding of the *Mohave* just one year before the Southern Pacific arrived.

Almost immediately river trade began to dwindle. For a while there was business transporting goods up-river from the rail line, but by 1900 only two or three of the paddlewheelers were left, and they were being used by the U.S. Reclamation Service. When Laguna Dam north of Yuma was completed in 1909, access to the Gulf of California was blocked and river trade ended altogether. The last paddlewheeler sank at dockside at Yuma in 1916 and was carted off in pieces by the citizenry.

— *Mark Santiago*

Originally published: December 3, 1986

Photo courtesy of the Arizona Historical Society, Yuma

Toll Gate, McDowell at Central

This photograph was taken when Central Avenue (then called Center Street) was a toll road north of McDowell. The original belonged to the late James Barney, who said the toll road was built in the 1890s. We guess the photograph was taken around that time.

The toll road was built by the Central Avenue Driving Association. It was a dirt road, eight miles long and 100 feet wide, with a row of olive and ash trees on either side. Property owners north of the gate paid $2.50 a month for sprinkling and improvements. Buggies and wagons paid a 25 cent toll. Bicycles were free.

The toll keeper was "Cap" Jefferies, a retired Civil War veteran who got his job through the Grand Army of the Republic, the veterans organization for soldiers who fought on the side of the Union. Mr. Jefferies had founded the Phoenix Bakery, but sold out to Ed Eisele in 1880. (The bakery became the Holsum Bakery in later years and is still in business today.)

In his retirement, Mr. Jefferies spent his days at the palm-thatched office at the left of the photograph telling war stories to all who would listen. He claimed to have fought with Meade at Chickamauga, a story that may have been an embellishment of the truth, but which regulars on the toll road soon learned by heart.

— *Arizona News Service*

Originally published: December 1, 1982

Photo from the Arizona News Service archives

Grand Canyon Railway

This is the Grand Canyon Railway's steam engine No. 282, photographed September 17, 1901, the day it made its inaugural run between Williams and the Grand Canyon with a tender, three water cars and one combination passenger/baggage car. Number 282 was a ten-wheeler (in a 4-6-0 configuration) — the standard engine type of its day.

Harry Slee — who may be the uniformed figure in the foreground of the photo — was the engineer on the inaugural run, which left Williams at 7 p.m. and arrived at the Grand Canyon at 10 p.m. It deported the canyon the next morning at 8:30 a.m. and steamed into Williams at 11:20 a.m.

William O. (Buckey) O'Neill — territorial journalist, lawman, politician and businessman — was captivated by the canyon, and in the late 1890s he began to promote the notion of a rail line from Williams to the South Rim. But before the line could be built, O'Neill became one of Teddy Roosevelt's Rough Riders in the Spanish-American War and was killed in Cuba in 1898.

The Atchison, Topeka and Santa Fe Railway Company saw merit in O'Neill's notion and, three years after his death, built the 64-mile rail line. In conjunction with Fred Harvey, the company also built the El Tovar (opened 1905) and Bright Angel lodges at the canyon and the Fray Marcos in Williams.

Tourists were the mainstay of the shortline spur, but ranchers soon discovered the value of the railroad. Cattle and sheep could be transported economically, thus eliminating the need to drive herds over long distances, and water could be hauled by rail during times of drought. To a lesser degree, the mining and logging industries took advantage of the rail line as well. However, eventually the mines closed and the trees ran out.

Over the years, numerous notables rode the Grand Canyon line. President Theodore Roosevelt made three trips. Presidents Franklin Roosevelt and Dwight Eisenhower, President Sukarno of Indonesia, as well as kings, queens, shahs and maharajahs all visited the Grand Canyon by way of the railroad.

In 1951, steam engines were replaced by diesels. Efficiency increased, but the pleasure of riding the rails diminished. Post-war prosperity put an automobile within reach of the everyday working man and provided a fine highway system for travel. On July 30, 1968, engine No. 703 carried three passengers to the Grand Canyon. It was the line's last day of service.

In the '70s and '80s, many attempts were made to revive the line as a tourist attraction, the premise being to unite a nostalgic public with steam locomotion. Most efforts, however, were more romantic than practical. Then in 1989, entrepreneur Max Biegert and his wife Thelma put together a financial package that worked. Five early-century steam locomotives were purchased and restored. The Fray Marcos and the depot at the Grand Canyon were restored and reopened.

On September 17, 1989, the reborn Grand Canyon Railway made its inaugural run, and passenger service to the Canyon was again available. In 2006, the line had a passenger load of approximately 240,000 persons, which translates to a reduction of approximately 40,000 vehicles entering and exiting Grand Canyon National Park.

— *W. Lane Rogers*

Originally published: November 28, 1990

Photo courtesy of W. Lane Rogers

Railroad Bridge Collapse, Salt River, 1905

This is what was left of the Phoenix & Eastern Railroad bridge after the Salt River flooded in March 1905. That's Tempe Butte in the background. The Phoenix & Eastern was a branch line that connected Tempe, Mesa, Florence and Winkelman with the Santa Fe terminal in Phoenix. It was the second rail line to cross the Salt, the first having been the Maricopa & Phoenix railroad, which in 1887 connected Phoenix with the Southern Pacific main line from Tucson.

The Maricopa & Phoenix had a history of troubles with its bridge across the Salt, periodically having to rebuild the approaches, or the bridge itself, at the whim of the river. When Frank Murphy, Phoenix's indefatigable empire builder, incorporated the Phoenix & Eastern in 1901, he was determined that his railroad would have a bridge that could withstand the worst the river could deliver. He built a five-span, steel structure on heavy concrete support piers, solidly anchored into the river bottom and cutting into the base of Tempe Butte just back of Hayden's Mill. In January 1904, with advertisements heralding "The Bridge of Steel, that's all," Murphy started rail service across the Salt.

All went well for over a year. But then, of course, came 1905. During the early winter months, the mountains were deluged with rain. By March, arroyos, creeks and rivers were breaking all previous waterflow records. The Salt was running 25 feet deep at the Phoenix & Eastern's river crossing and was pushing along a huge front of uprooted trees and other debris. At twilight on the evening of March 20, the Phoenix & Eastern's train to Phoenix safely crossed the bridge. Fifteen minutes later the north span collapsed, followed closely by a second span. Later that night, the river began to subside, and additional damage was averted. Amazingly, the bridge was repaired within a fortnight.

On April 8, with much publicity, the Phoenix & Eastern hosted an excursion across the just-repaired bridge by the student body of the Phoenix Methodist Episcopal Sunday School. Apparently, in deference to this wholesome activity, the Salt waited three days before letting loose again. On April 11, the river rose once more and another section of the bridge was swept into the river, leaving the rails suspended in the air.

Ironically, the Maricopa & Phoenix bridge, which ran parallel to Murphy's Bridge of Steel, just a little downstream, withstood both of the 1905 floods even though it was older and built of wood.

Between 1912 and 1913, shortly after Murphy's Phoenix & Eastern had become the Arizona Eastern Railroad, they built a new bridge across the Salt, and it is that bridge which is still in use today, having survived floods in 1980 and 1993. The Arizona Eastern was purchased by the Southern Pacific in 1925. The Union Pacific acquired the Southern Pacific in 1996. Meanwhile, the Maricopa and Phoenix Railroad eventually was absorbed into the Atchison, Topeka & Santa Fe Railway system, which as a result of a 1996 merger became the Burlington Northern Santa Fe.

— Arizona News Service with additional research by James Burns

Originally published: January 18, 1984

Photo from the Arizona News Service Archives

Nathaniel Plumer and Tucson's Speedway Boulevard

The man in the inset photo is Nathaniel E. Plumer, for whom a Tucson street is named. Born on February 24, 1866, in Detroit, Michigan, he came from a long line of New Englanders and was a distant relative of Daniel Webster.

After a few years in Michigan, his parents moved back to their Boston home, and young Nat was educated in the Boston public schools. His first employment was with the George H. Hammond Meat Packing Company. He subsequently worked for Cudahy Meat Packing as their eastern representative. During that time, he developed an interest in land and purchased a considerable amount of real estate.

He arrived in Tucson in 1899, making the long trip, like so many others, to seek a cure for tuberculosis in the dry desert air. As his health improved and he was able to work, he formed a real estate and insurance business with Fred Steward. Their offices were on North Stone Avenue.

In 1903, Plumer and Steward founded the Southern Arizona Bank & Trust Co. Plumer served as president, a position he held until his death.

He actively sought depositors. He became fluent in Spanish and Tohono O'Odham and encouraged Hispanics and Native Americans to participate in the banking business. Before he acquired an automobile, he frequently was seen riding around Tucson on his favorite horse, talking up banking to prospective clientele.

In 1910, Plumer and Steward decided Pima County ought to have a roadway for motoring enthusiasts. By then both men had purchased automobiles, and they wanted to drive some place where they could get up a little speed. A third friend, Tenney Davis Williams joined them. The larger photo opposite, taken about this time, shows (l-r) Williams, Steward and Plumer in their automobiles, a Stoddard-Dayton, a Cadillac and a Maxwell, respectively. The boy in the photo is not identified.

Plumer asked Pima County to supply road scrapers to open up a desert trail east of town. Williams solicited funds for the project from Tucson merchants. The new road was called Speedway; the cost to build it was just $750.

On New Year's Day in 1910, Speedway was opened officially with a celebration and an auto race with entries both from Tucson and Phoenix.

Plumer and Steward developed other projects. The partners opened a Tucson subdivision near East Fifth Street and Tyndall Avenue. As part of their promotion, they gave away a home. The subdivision included a golf course — two acres of cleared desert with an unusual hazard: snake holes. Whenever a ball went down a snake hole, the golfers left it there, with no score tallied.

Plumer organized the Railway Holding Company, which secured the right-of-way and depot sites for a railroad. The holdings then were used as an inducement for the Southern Pacific to build in Tucson.

The Railway Holding Company returned its investment with a profit, and then specified that the profit be used to build a YMCA building. Plumer became a trustee of the YMCA and president of the board, which raised the balance of the funds necessary for construction. Plumer also directed the construction of the building and the procurement of equipment for the new Y.

Plumer became a force in the movement to abolish gambling in Tucson and to prohibit liquor sales. Generally, he voted Republican and insisted that he was on the side of good government. He was a trustee of the Congregational Church and arranged for the sale of the church property to the City of Tucson for a new city hall and for the construction of a new church.

After years fighting his illness, Plumer succumbed to tuberculosis in May 1917. He left a wife and an eight-year-old daughter. Tucson mourned the loss of an important civic leader.

— *Jane Eppinga*

Originally published: September 8, 2000

Photos courtesy of the Arizona Historical Society, Tucson

Kaibab Bridge, 1921

These men are working on the Kaibab suspension bridge over the Colorado River in the Grand Canyon. The bridge was to link Bright Angel Trail on the South Rim with the Kaibab Trail on the North Rim. At the time, the only means of crossing the river between the two trails was by small canvas boat. (The closest ferry crossings were at Lee's Ferry, upstream near the Utah border and downstream at Needles on the California border.) Construction began in January 1921.

The bridge was 11 miles by trail from the South Rim of the canyon and about 4,500 feet below the rim's edge. Pack trains carried all the lumber, cement and cables brought in by train from the railroad yard at Grand Canyon village to the construction site.

Transporting the cables was probably the greatest challenge for the packers. Each cable weighed 1,200 pounds. Rope was used in a trial trip so that engineers could estimate the proper spacing between the pack mules. The cable was stiff and relatively inflexible, and there had to be enough stretched between the mules to allow them to negotiate the switchbacks in the trail. When the cable was finally packed down the trail, each mule had a man walking at its head.

The bridge was built with two main steel cables strung about 10 feet apart and anchored in the rock 80 feet above the canyon floor. The crew used a pulley attached to one of the cables to get across the river, allowing gravity to carry them to the midpoint, then pulling themselves by hand to the other side.

Once the main cables were in place, the vertical cables visible at the left of the photo were attached. (Two workers are suspended from the main cables apparently working on the vertical cables.) Wooden crosspieces and a wood floor were added as the construction progressed. (The man in the lower area of the photograph appears to be working on the bridge floor.) Later a seven-foot wire-mesh siding was added for safety.

The bridge was suspended 60 feet above the normal flow level of the river and 13 feet above the highest known flood level.

Working on the construction crew was not for the fainthearted or those who feared heights. The crew consisted of a lumberjack from Alaska, a miner, a cowboy, an amateur astronomer and several amateur photographers, one of whom undoubtedly took this photograph.

Surprisingly, there was only one serious accident during the bridge construction. On a supply trip to the construction site, a horse slipped and went over the edge of the trail dragging two other horses with it. A quick thinking young handler cut the lead rope and saved the rest of the pack train.

— *Bonnie Greer*

Originally published: November 30, 1988

Photo courtesy Arizona Historical Society Pioneer Museum

Phoenix Streetcars

The top photo shows Phoenix Streetcar #100, pride of the fleet, pictured with various dignitaries circa 1929.

In the late 19th century, just about every city of any size had a streetcar or trolley line. In Phoenix, there was the Phoenix Street Railway System, which operated from 1887 to 1948. It was owned and operated by the great promoter and subdivision mogul, Moses H. Sherman, until 1925, when the City of Phoenix took over operations.

Sherman was a prominent member of the community and had his hand in numerous business developments. He was a co-founder of the Valley National Bank, a supporter of developing irrigation canals for the city and proprietor of the first city water works. In January 1889, Phoenix boosters, including Sherman and fellow developer M.E. Collins, convinced legislators to move the state capital from Prescott to Phoenix. Among the inducements Sherman provided were a donation of 10 acres of land for a new Capitol building and a streetcar line from the downtown area to the new seat of government.

He developed other streetcar lines to promote his subdivisions, which were expanding the boundaries of the city. For a nickel (at least in the beginning) you could ride Sherman's streetcars anywhere there were tracks. The streetcar company was never a financial success. It was reorganized many times through the years, each time acquiring a new name.

It was called variously: Phoenix Railway Company, Valley Street Railroad Company, Arizona Improvement Company, Phoenix City Railway Company and finally Phoenix Railway Company of Arizona.

The first streetcar line, consisting of one car, operated along Washington Street between Seventh Avenue and Seventh Street in 1887. The car was pulled by a mule and there was little effort at maintaining a standard schedule. Passengers got on and off wherever they wanted to.

A second line was introduced in 1889, running along Center Street (now Central Avenue), and additional cars and mules were purchased. By 1892, the system consisted of five cars, eight miles of track and 25 mules and horses. In 1893, electricity started to replace the mules. By 1909, the system was completely electrified and a double track had been laid throughout the downtown.

That was the high point for the company. The next year saw the beginning of a series of disasters. A fire destroyed the storage barn and much of the company's rolling stock. In 1913, a strike against the company proved long and bitter. Management brought in strikebreakers, and many citizens boycotted the streetcar line. A competing company opened in Glendale, and although unprofitable, it was said to have hurt Sherman's company in Phoenix.

Maintenance and general upkeep of the system was costly and a continuing problem. In 1912, the Arizona Corporation Commission conducted safety hearings and ordered changes in the way maintenance was handled. Controversies and disagreements with authorities continued until 1925, when the city of Phoenix finally took over management of the system.

By then the automobile was on the way to replacing the streetcar. In Maricopa County the number of registered automobiles rose from 646 in 1913 to more than 53,000 in 1929, when it was estimated there was one car for every three people in the metropolitan area.

With the increasing number of autos came a corresponding number of paved streets. Phoenix was rapidly on its way to becoming the automobile-centered city of the future.

Despite improved maintenance and better management under city ownership, the streetcar system was no match for the personal automobile. Eventually the streetcars were replaced with transit buses. In 1941, the city operated 17 streetcars and 23 buses. The last four streetcar lines were replaced with diesel buses in 1947 and 1948.

On February 17, 1948, the city gathered together 150 pioneers, city officials and employees for a ceremonial final ride on the last three cars remaining from the street railway system. The dignitaries made a round trip on the Washington line from the courthouse to the state Capitol. That event closed the book on rail mass transit in Phoenix for more than 60 years.

In December 2008, the new METRO light rail system is scheduled to begin transporting passengers. The lower photo shows one of the system's 50 trains during a demonstration run in August 2008. The initial 20-mile route will connect Tempe to Phoenix Christown Spectrum Mall at Bethany Home Road and 19th Avenue. Trains will run every 10 minutes during peak times and 20 minutes off-peak. Total price tag for the project is approximately $1.4 billion with 41% coming from the federal government. Six future extensions are currently planned

— *Dave Tackenberg*

Originally published: May 24, 2002

Phoenix streetcar 100 with dignitaries, c. 1929.

Historical photo courtesy of the Arizona Historical Society, Central Arizona Division

Modern photo courtesy of the Downtown Phoenix Partnership

INDEX